memorial
fund
in memory
of

Max Enderlin

from a gift
to utsa
By

the donors
of the
UTSA Memorial Fund

A.G. SPALDING AND
THE RISE OF BASEBALL

A.G. SPALDING AND
THE RISE OF BASEBALL

The Promise of American Sport

Peter Levine

New York   Oxford
OXFORD UNIVERSITY PRESS
1985

Oxford University Press
Oxford   London   New York   Toronto
Delhi   Bombay   Calcutta   Madras   Karachi
Kuala Lumpur   Singapore   Hong Kong   Tokyo
Nairobi   Dar es Salaam   Cape Town
Melbourne   Auckland

and associated companies in
Beirut   Berlin   Ibadan   Mexico City   Nicosia

Published by Oxford University Press, Inc.,
200 Madison Avenue, New York, New York 10016

Library of Congress Cataloging in Publication Data

Levine, Peter.
    A.G. Spalding and the rise of baseball.

    Includes index.
    1. Spalding, A. G. (Albert Goodwill)   2. Baseball
players—United States—Biography.   3. Entrepreneur—
Biography.   I. Title.
GV865.S7L48   1985   796.357′092′4 [B]   84-20679
ISBN 0-19-503552-6

Printing (last digit):   9 8 7 6 5 4 3 2 1

Printed in the United States of America

For Gale

Acknowledgments

When I first began talking about Albert Goodwill Spalding in my sport history class at Michigan State University, mention of the name conjured up memories of a Brooklyn childhood full of street games—stickball, off the wall, stoopball, the junior high school punchball championship of P.S. 234—all played with a small, pink, hollow, rubber ball with the name Spalding on it (we called them Spaldeens), which I either bought at any number of local candy stores (along with the usual egg cream, charlotte russe, and baseball bubble gum pack) or which my father "borrowed" for me from his afternoon job as a playground supervisor for the board of education. I also remember driving down a neighborhood street some years later with my brother and my cousin when a Spaldeen bounced off the sidewalk with two little boys in hot pursuit. My brother slammed on the brakes of our parents' blue Pontiac, rolled down the window, and fell into a chorus of "Let the Ball Roll," as we all broke into laughter and shared a moment together shaped by a childhood rich with our own memories of family, street games, and Spaldeens.

My parents and brother are gone now, but working on this book about the man whose name was emblazoned on those balls, in more ways than are obvious here, has kept them alive and important for me. More tangibly, my work has been equally enriched by a range of associations, both large and small, that deserve mention here.

Peter Vinten-Johansen, my friend, running partner, and holistic medical adviser, read my manuscript in its entirety and offered important suggestions about content and style. He also suffered through mile after mile of musings about Spalding and life that, if nothing else, quickened our pace. Richard White shared many of those same miles and pages. His critical comments, moral support, and friendship played no less a part in my work. Steve Botein also read much of my work and provided good counsel. Bob Lipsyte encouraged me in this project from the outset, offered many useful suggestions, and came up with a wonderfully unusable title that deliciously captured Spalding's style. Larry Gerlach, Jeffrey Goldberg, and Don Mrozek (who first suggested sport history to me as a viable subject) also read various versions of my work and made useful suggestions along the way. Max Bruck read not a word of this manuscript, but his friendship and understanding were more important to me than anything else he might have offered.

The Spalding family gave constant encouragement, provided important photographs and other material. I especially want to thank Mrs. Suzanne Winston who became my friend in the course of writing this book.

The library staffs of the New York Public Library, the Newberry Library, the San Diego Historical Society, and the Point Loma Theosophical Society opened their collections to me. Archie Motley of the Chicago Historical Society and both Cliff Kachline and later Tom Heitz of the Baseball Library at Cooperstown, were especially helpful in facilitating my use of important collections. Larry Finfer went out of his way to help me obtain photographs. Grants from the American Philosophical Society and from Michigan State University helped defray the expenses involved in travel and research.

Closer to home, Michael Bennett and Annie Pitts of the Michigan State University Library cheerfully filled my frequent requests for material borrowed on interlibrary loan. Darlene Evitts, Sandy Cuthbertson, and Judy Skae typed through several drafts of my scrawl and, by their skill, fortified my resistance to word processors and computers. Peter Berg's work as a research assistant made my life with nineteenth-century newspapers bearable.

My family—Gale, Ruth, and Cleo—in different ways shared the experience of my work and enriched both it and my life. Cleo could no longer chase Spaldeens, but still, after seventeen years, loyally curled up near me while I chased after them in my own way. My daughter, Ruth, and I shared the closeness and joy of cheering for the Detroit Tigers—no mean feat for a boy who spent his weekends at Ebbets Field while secretly worshiping at the altar of Mickey Mantle and Yogi Berra. My wife, Gale, never goes to baseball games and can't quite understand my fantasies of becoming a forty-year-old point guard for the New York Knickerbockers. Still, she is still my best friend and closest companion, without whom this book would mean very little to me. I dedicate it lovingly to her.

April 1984   Peter Levine
East Lansing, Michigan

Contents

Introduction

On June 1, 1895, the *Sporting News*, a weekly newspaper devoted to sports and amusements, carried alongside each other two quarter-page advertisements complete with extravagant claims. One was for Barnum and Bailey's Greatest Show on Earth, "the World's Largest, Grandest, Best Amusement Institution." The other was for A. G. Spalding and Brothers' Base Ball Goods, "The Standard of Comparison the World Over." In a special way the paper's layout was appropriate. Although their careers overlapped for only a short time, Barnum and Spalding were essential figures in satisfying the entertainment and leisure-time needs of late-nineteenth-century America. Although Barnum is available to us today through Broadway and biography, Spalding has not received the popular attention his rich life deserves.[1] This book corrects the balance by focusing on Albert Goodwill Spalding, by his own account, and by those of his contemporaries, "the father of American baseball."

A flamboyant personality possessed of insatiable ego, A.G., as he was most often called, was professional baseball's first recorded 200-game winner, compiling most of his record in Boston between 1871 and 1875. In that year he jumped to Chicago, was befriended by William Hulbert, the president of the club, and with him helped form the National League. First as captain and manager, later as president and principal owner, Spalding molded the Chicago White Stockings into the most successful professional baseball team in the 1880s. Wheeling and dealing with the likes of Cap Anson or Mike ("King") Kelly, resisting attempts by discontented players to form their own clubs, or shaping the structure of the National League, he was the key figure in the establishment of the white world of professional baseball as a viable commercial enterprise and as an acceptable pastime for Victorian America.

Spalding's colorful career as baseball man paralleled his success in business. In 1876, along with his brother, $800, and his reputation as a ballplayer, he opened a sporting-goods store in Chicago that eventually made him a millionaire and that still bears his name. It is not surprising that, in an age that transformed robber barons into cultural heroes, A.G. emerged as the most recognizable man in American sports.

Although he understood the possibilities for personal fortune inherent in sport, historical context, not individual genius, best explains Spalding's accomplishments. Indeed, it is precisely the manner in which his personal story intersected with the larger culture that makes him so attractive.

Spalding's life—from his decision to make baseball a career, in 1871, until his death, in 1915—coincided with dramatic economic, demographic, and social changes that transformed America into a modern state. Middle- and upper-class Americans, taking their cues from an array of secular and religious spokesmen of American success, found much to applaud in this transformation. Embracing values that celebrated self-reliance, the work ethic, and aggressive individualism, all buttressed by a Social Darwinist framework that emphasized both the survival of the fittest and civilization's inexorable forward march, they looked back with pride on their ancestors' ability to carve a nation out of a seemingly boundless frontier. They took equal satisfaction in acknowledging their own contributions to national progress—the large corporations they developed in order to maximize profits, and especially the increase in their material comfort, opulently displayed in their homes and new urban surroundings and made possible by the technology and industrial growth that they designed and engineered.

At the same time, the very circumstances of American development— the closing of the frontier, the growth of large cities, European immigration, industrial expansion, and violent struggles between workers and capitalists—also raised doubts about America's future. What would take the place of the violent testing ground of the frontier to shape American character? What would keep sedentary urban life from softening the basic tissue of America's dominant middle class? What might prevent the influx of East European immigrants from diluting the purity of American stock while making them effective industrial workers? What could be done to reduce the uncertainty and the risks of rapid economic expansion?

Responses to these fears, as we know, were wide-ranging. They included an aggressive foreign policy; a variety of efforts, some of them tinged with violence, to control workers and to acculturate immigrants; a search for new ways to counter the pace and banality of urban-middle-class culture; new forms of business organization; and a reliance on efficient, rational procedures devised by experts to bring order and control to every area of American life. Whether he was expressing pride in America's progress, concern about its future, or actively engaged in his own affairs, Spalding's life illuminates these major tendencies of his age.[2]

Although Spalding's claim to being a representative figure rests on his exploits off the diamond, it was his early interest and skill in the game that provided the opportunity for them. The first two chapters trace this beginning, the impulses and environment that shaped his future, and the sense of confidence and order that sport gave him and that he was to offer to a whole class of people for similar purposes.

A.G. broke into the ranks of professional baseball when the distinction between amateur and professional was quite novel and when the game itself was haphazard and unstable. But he came of age in a society fascinated with notions of career and with the importance of efficient organization and the leadership of trained experts. Spalding was hardly a progressive reformer in the sense that Jane Addams was, nor was he an engineer of "scientific management" like Frederick Taylor. Yet, as Chapter 3 demonstrates, his climb from the role of player to that of club owner and ultimately to that of the creative force behind the success of the National League depended on similar calculation about his own future and on the need for stable organization and the strong leadership of a new class of professional baseball magnates with which he identified.

Between 1876, when he established the National League, and 1901, when he became its president, Spalding figured in every major event in the early history of professional baseball. Chapter 4 emphasizes this significant role in ways consistent with the portrayal of a provocative personality whose actions shed light on broader patterns and themes. For instance, in shaping a policy that established baseball as a stable business enterprise and a national form of entertainment, A.G. was not above crushing potential business competitors and controlling the marketplace in a manner that a John D. Rockefeller or an Andrew Carnegie would have admired. And while the so-called Brotherhood War that Spalding put down in 1891 hardly matched in intensity Chicago's bloody Haymarket affair of 1886 or any number of violent confrontations between labor and capital that marked the late nineteenth century, he clearly identified himself as a "captain of industry" and relished opportunities to make baseball a successful business enterprise, no matter what the consequences to individual ballplayers. Through it all, his firm belief in the need for competent leadership by professionals and for efficient organization to solve baseball's problems reverberated in the larger culture, very concerned with bringing order to every aspect of society.

Spalding's career as a baseball magnate was merely one facet of his larger success as a businessman. Reflecting the transition from individual entreprenurial enterprise to corporate capitalism that occurred in the late nineteenth century, A.G. and his brother creatively shaped a new industry in sporting goods. Proud of his achievements as an entrepreneur, Spalding approached the business of baseball and the selling of sporting goods similarly. His personal motto was "Everything is possible to him who dares," a sentiment that fit nicely into the value system of a society that defined success and individual worth in materialistic, acquisitive terms. Whether expanding and rationalizing their operations, introducing new products, advertising their wares or absorbing their competition. A. G. Spalding and Brothers, as Chapter 5 makes clear, was at the cutting edge of business development at the turn of the century.

Spalding was quick to see that the realization of sport's potential as a profitable commercial venture depended on promoting it as an activity that served a significant social purpose. Chapter 6 shows that A.G. joined moralists, recreationists, and reformers in espousing the value of sport—whether as an antidote to the supposed debilitating effects of urban life, a reminder of a rural past and an incubator of American character, a cure for the nervous anxiety observed by contemporaries to be engulfing middle-class America, or even as a means of controlling potentially subversive immigrants. Gallivanting around the world with baseball players in 1889, falsely establishing baseball's American origins in 1907, and on other occasions, he consistently encouraged participation in sport as a critical means for developing what he considered to be uniquely American values and character traits that in his mind had secured both his fortune and his nation's.

Spalding's desire to justify sport was clearly self-serving: it nurtured his material interests and his considerable demand for public attention. There is no doubt, however, that like many of his generation he was concerned about America's future, the need for strong character and social order to secure it, and the role that sport, especially baseball, might play in the process. Even retirement to San Diego, California, as Chapter 7 points out, failed to diminish such interests. Quite at home in the "booster" atmosphere of a burgeoning tourist and commercial city that doubtless reminded him of his earlier days in Chicago, Spalding became involved in the curious world of Katherine Tingley and her version of theosophy, which offered its own plans for shaping character and society. Although intrigued by, if not committed to, the philosophy of the religious community in which he resided, Spalding did not forget the debt he owed to baseball, both for the man it had developed and the personal success it had allowed. Indeed, A.G.'s unsuccessful bid to capture a U.S. Senate seat in California in 1910 hinged on a campaign that credited the game with having made him fit to hold such office.

The fact that an uneducated ballplayer and businessman could competitively engage in national politics on the basis of credentials garnered from a career in baseball suggests something about the powerful appeal that sport was beginning to have in American society and about the intensity with which people sought new means of dealing with a whole range of problems that accompanied the inception of "America's Century." As the last chapter suggests, Spalding—much like P. T. Barnum and Henry Ward Beecher, nineteenth-century popularizers of diverse attractions, from circuses to romantic Christianity—did not so much create such circumstances as take advantage of them in appealing to an audience looking for more than a pleasant way to spend a Sunday afternoon. Able to recognize the possibilities for personal gain and social purpose inherent in the promotion of sport, Spalding acted on them in a manner that encouraged the commercialization of sport and its transformation into a significant social institution in America. For better or worse, the place of sport in contemporary American society owes a good deal to a man who creatively shaped the culture of his own time.

A.G. SPALDING AND
THE RISE OF BASEBALL

1

Rising in the World

Albert Goodwill Spalding was born and raised in country towns in the shadow of Chicago—sheltered by the amenities of wealth and by his mother. As an adult, he relished stories that glorified his rags-to-riches rise to financial success. As a young man, his eye was early on the main chance. Yet neither impulse came out of a background of poverty or want.

Albert was born to Harriet and James Spalding on September 9, 1850, in the small farming village of Byron, Illinois. The Spaldings, although married only two years before the birth of their first son, were well-established members of their community. James had turned 320 acres of land purchased from the government into a respectable estate that allowed him to rent out two large farms and several houses in town. Managing his investments and buying and training his horses seem to have occupied his working hours. According to his wife, "he was a man of sufficient means to enable us to have every comfort," who "took life leisurely, and was prosperous in every way." Harriet contributed to the family's position by bringing to her marriage a large inheritance garnered on the death of her first husband—money that allowed her to fill her spacious village home with fine mahogany furniture and "tea service of gold-banded china."[1]

Only brief glimpses of Albert's childhood years in Byron emerge from his mother's reminiscences and from the historical record. A sister, Mary, was born in 1854 and a brother, James Walter, two years later. As their mother tells it, all three enjoyed a happy existence as obedient, proper children of respectable parents who enjoyed the "solid comfort of... home life."[2]

The apparent security of a sheltered world as children of one of the town's leading families was shattered in 1858, when, after a year-long illness, Albert's father died at the age of forty-six. According to the family genealogy, however, the young boy "never realized the extent of this loss, for the widowed mother with constant devotion, wonderful strength of character, and inspiring heroism filled the place of both father and mother to the little children left to her care."[3] Certainly this is how Harriet Spalding saw her life. Taking heed of her husband's dying injunction "to bring your boys to industrious habits," she resolved "to live entirely for [her] children" with "all [her] heart and all [her] thoughts centered on them."[4]

Consistent with this impulse, in 1862 she sent Albert to live in the neighboring town of Rockford, where he was to board with an aunt and attend public school. Although this decision, followed a year later by the entire family's move there, forced Harriet to give up "comparative ease for a life that might be more difficult," her "ambition" to provide her "children ... as good opportunities as I could give them," determined her course. "Straws in the wind," as she called them—stories of her children ridiculed because of their fine shoes or because they wore fine silk clothes—motivated her. The bad examples set by Byron's menfolk who idled away rainy days in the town's stores "with their trousers tucked into their boots, sitting on kegs, cracking jokes and talking" only encouraged her to take action. In her mind, such behavior, not part of "the way...to bring up ... boys," would be replaced by the "wholesome influence" afforded by "the simple life at Rockford."[5] Much to her surprise, part of that influence was to include Spalding's discovery of baseball and the choice of a future she never would have anticipated for her son.

Harriet's selection of Rockford as the town in which to fulfill her husband's mandate was certainly appropriate. Already populated by 7,000 industrious souls in 1860 and located some one hundred miles west of Chicago on the Rock River, it enjoyed a reputation, carefully nurtured by its newspaper editors and business leaders, as a place of economic promise for any young man bent on securing his fortune. Regular columns on Rockford's progress noted its prime location at "the center of the richest and most productive farming region on the globe," the advantages provided by the Rock River for generating steam power, and the city's situation on the lines of the Chicago and Northwestern Railroad as factors destined to transform the city into a major manufacturing center. Locals could also boast that their city, already an important transfer point for flour and wheat from Minnesota and Iowa, was the home of the Manny reaper, a farm implement popularly used throughout the Midwest and turned out in a factory that contained a 7,200-

pound iron-cutting machine—the "largest machine built in the United States."[6]

Such statistical expressions of material progress were the common fare of Rockford's booster mentality, as was the concern for the type of citizen the town's environment produced. Someone with Harriet Spalding's concern for raising her children to be industrious and successful could only have been pleased by descriptions of her new home as "one vast workshop of honest, ingenious and loyal workingmen," a place where "energy, enterprise, business capacity, skill, [and] industry all find employment."[7] For her, at least, an 1868 sketch of the city's promise served as a good summary of her own reasons for deciding to settle there. "Whether a man wishes to invest capital in manufacturing ... or in commercial pursuits, whether he has children to educate, or he desires the advantages of religious instruction and worship, or whether...he desires in one of the most charming cities of the Northwest, a local habitation and a name, he will find his wishes met in Rockford."[8]

Perhaps for Harriet, but hardly in the beginning for her son. Spalding's first year there as a twelve-year-old boarder left him so lonesome and homesick that fifty years later his memories of it still haunted him "like a nightmare." Remembering himself as "an overgrown, unbaked country boy, as green as the verdant prairies," he recalled that he was so bashful that he "was almost afraid to go out of doors, lest I should meet and be spoken to by someone not a member of my family."[9]

Baseball alone provided Spalding with relief from such anxiety and despair. As he remembered it, going to the commons and watching other boys play ball offered "the only bright skies for me in those dark days of utter loneliness." Separated from his family, he felt a powerful urge to participate in these games: "no mother, parted from her young, ever had a stronger yearning to see her beloved offspring than I had to break into those crude games of ball."

Young Spalding's desires were apparently not strong enough to overcome his shyness, for though he yearned to "get in," he recalled that he would "rather have died than suggest such a thing." Fortunately, however, as in other success tales of late-nineteenth-century America with which he consistently identified, "the unexpected happened."[10] One day, while he was alone in his usual place beyond center field, a ball was hit mightily in his direction. This act of "special Providence," according to Spalding, changed his life. "That ball came for me straight as an arrow. Impulsively I sprang to my feet, reached out for it with my right hand, held it a moment and then threw it home on an air line to the catcher." After the game one of the boys offered congratulations and invited Albert to play the next day. Spalding blushed but "managed to stammer" that he would. Concluding his account, he added that he did play and "from that day, when sides were chosen, I was usually among the first to have a place. And this was my real introduction to the game."[11]

As a successful baseball magnate and businessman, Spalding would offer to a whole generation of Americans participation in sport and particularly in baseball as a means of alleviating anxiety and of promoting proper character. In part, his early experience with the game in countering feelings of loneliness and in providing him with self-confidence paralleled these later social concerns. It also marked the beginning of an association with the sport that was to define his life.

By all accounts Spalding was a natural. Within a few years the informal games on the commons resulted in the formation of a local schoolboy club known as the Pioneers. Spalding briefly played first base but soon became the pitcher for the team whose members played mostly among themselves and occasionally against several men's clubs organized in Rockford. According to Spalding, his very first experience on the mound convinced him that "pitching was [his] vocation," a talent that came to him "very naturally," so much so that he pitched "as swiftly and nearly as accurately in my first effort as I was ever able to do afterward."[12] Rockford's leading businessmen apparently agreed with this self-appraisal, for in 1865 they asked Albert to join their newly formed baseball club, known as the Forest City's.[13]

Spalding's new status as pitcher for Rockford's most prominent baseball team at the early age of fifteen underlines the changing nature of organized baseball in these years. As any standard history of baseball recounts, the organized teams and competition that originated in the 1840s with clubs like the New York Knickerbockers and became formalized in the National Association of Baseball Players in 1858 intended the game to be recreational amusement for urban, upper-class gentlemen. Club rules stipulated membership on the basis of class, insisted that players receive no payment for play or travel, and required that all expenses be covered out of membership dues rather than paid admissions. Matches scheduled on midweek afternoons and followed by gala banquets and balls were social occasions rather than intense competitions.

Almost from the outset, however, this amateur "gentlemen's game" was transformed. Baseball's popularity among soldiers during the Civil War helped stimulate interest in it among all classes of people. Most significantly, in cities as small as Rockford and as large as Chicago, the recognition that winning baseball teams might be profitable investments while also serving as significant symbols of a city's prominence and potential propelled important changes in the game. Those clubs that openly claimed high membership standards, for instance, found the desire to win so overwhelming that they increasingly admitted as members anyone whose qualifications consisted of baseball talent rather than of requisite social status. Other aggregations made no pretense about their desire to secure young, good ballplayers as members. Indeed, by 1865, although still openly committed to the standards of amateurism associated with organized baseball's origins, such clubs were not above charging admission, paying ballplayers, or providing them with full-time jobs off the diamond because of their performance on it.[14]

The Forest City's fit this mold. Organized in August 1865 by Rockford's businessmen, the club boasted over 150 members in its first year. Included among its officials were the editor of the local newspaper, a banker, a lawyer, and, as president, Hiram Waldo, a bookstore owner and county school commissioner.[15] Intent on promoting their city through baseball, club members provided business employment for a ballplayer who needed it or—as in the case of young Spalding, despite his mother's concern—arranged for the high school principal to excuse him from classes on days when his presence was required on the mound.[16] By the time Spalding became their pitcher, the Forest City's, like other clubs, were also staging regional baseball tournaments, charging twenty-five cents admission, and offering cash prizes to winning teams in the hopes of turning a profit and attracting popular attention to their community. Just such a tournament held in Chicago during the summer of 1867 gave Spalding his first real taste of public attention and encouraged him to pursue a career in baseball.

Sponsored by the Forest City's closest rival, the Chicago Excelsiors, the three-day affair, held in late July at the Dexter Park racetrack, included the Rockford nine and featured the Washington Nationals. Composed of government clerks and college students from the nation's capital who conveniently left work and classes early whenever baseball duty called, the Nationals were the pride of Washington, D.C., reputed to be the best team in the United States, and on a summer tour of midwestern cities determined to establish their claim. Playing in Columbus, Cincinnati, Indianapolis, Louisville, and St. Louis, the Nationals embarrassed all comers: their victories included a 90–10 rout of Columbus, stopped mercifully after seven innings, and a 106–21 shellacking of Indianapolis.[17]

Although the Excelsiors suffered a similar experience, by a 49–4 score, the Forest City club, with Spalding on the mound, defeated the Nationals. As Spalding recalled it, "the nine from the pretty little city of Rockford" left the Nationals "utterly crushed and humiliated by the unexpected drubbing by the schoolboys."[18]

In fact, the score was 29–23, something less than a "drubbing." Moreover, the twenty-three runs that Spalding let in do not conjure up images of a Sandy Koufax or a Christy Mathewson. Nevertheless, at a time when games were played on unkempt fields unbounded by walls or grandstands; when pitchers stood forty-five feet from home plate and tossed the ball underhanded and straight-armed to a bare-handed catcher located some thirty feet behind the batter; when batters were permitted to ask for the ball to be pitched high or low as many as nine times before a single umpire awarded them first base; when infielders rarely moved from their bases; and when balls caught on the fly by gloveless fielders were rarities, Spalding received much credit for the victory. Henry Chadwick, already known as the most knowledgeable baseball writer in America, put it succinctly when he noted that because of the young man's "very effective pitching . . . the Nationals sustained their first and only defeat of their tour."[19]

The city of Rockford celebrated for a week, rewarding its players with watches and gifts, while the Rockford *Register* touted Spalding as "undoubtedly the best pitcher in the West." Not surprisingly, although the *Register* did not "claim . . . the superiority or the equality of the Forest City with the Nationals," in typical booster style, the paper asserted the club's ranking as one of "the best . . . in the Union" and "its superiority over the Excelsiors."[20] Remembering the event years later, Spalding recalled that he was never more proud of an accomplishment in baseball, especially of his determination as a "kid pitcher" to overcome his fears and pitch so well against so formidable opponent.[21]

Spalding's victory over the Nationals marked a significant moment in his young life. Eager to reestablish themselves as the premier team of the Midwest, the Excelsiors offered Rockford's local hero the chance to move to Chicago and pitch for their team. Although Spalding would not be paid directly for his services, a Chicago wholesale grocer assured him a job as a clerk in his firm at a salary of $40 a week, with hours that would not conflict with his baseball commitment.[22]

The Excelsior offer forced Spalding to consider "for the first time . . . the business end of the game" and his place in it. Writing in his autobiographical history of baseball, *America's National Game*, he recalled pondering whether acceptance of the offer violated the spirit of the National Association of Baseball Players' rule that prohibited player salaries. Already able to see "the day soon coming when professional Base Ball playing would be recognized as legitimate everywhere," Spalding questioned both the smallness of the offer and the hypocrisy of being paid as a grocery clerk for his baseball ability. As he put it, "I was not able to understand how it could be right to pay an actor, or a singer, or an instrumentalist for entertaining the public, and wrong to pay a ball player for doing exactly the same thing in his way."

Complicating his decision were practical calculations and family loyalties. "From a mere business standpoint," Spalding wondered, would it be "be wise for me at my age to sever the relations that had been established at the home of my youth? Did not they constitute an asset with which I might not lightly part?" And what of his mother? "Ought I, just as I was becoming a man, to leave her whose tender care and fond affection had been so lavishly bestowed upon me through the years of my boyhood life? Would she approve of my going to a large city, with its dangers in the busy whirl, and its greater dangers in the temptations that so thickly abound?"

Counseled by his mother and by Hiram Waldo, whom Spalding referred to as "Rockford's grand old Man" and who remained a lifelong friend, the young pitcher accepted the Excelsiors' terms and moved to Chicago in September 1867.[23] After only one appearance in a Chicago uniform, however, his employer's business failed, and Spalding returned to Rockford. Although still uncomfortable with existing conventions that denied open professionalism, he quit high school and went to work as a clerk for a local insurance company and for the Rockford *Register*, a local newspaper conveniently owned by I. S. Hyatt, vice-president of the Forest City's and a man, in Mrs. Spalding's words, "as much interested in the ball club of the town as he was in his own business."[24]

Calculations about his own future and about baseball's, included in Spalding's recollections, may well have benefited from the hindsight of a man whose personal success was tied to an acceptance of professional baseball as legitimate fare for late-nineteenth-century America. Yet they are also consistent with how young men in Rockford and elsewhere were encouraged to think about their lives. Spalding grew up in a town preoccupied with self-promotion and in a society that offered constant hints on how to achieve material success. An invariable accompaniment to the newspaper stories about Rockford's promise were advice columns that provided young men and their parents practical information on "rising in the world." Attention to hard work, honesty, sobriety, calculation, order, and other virtues highlighted stories on Commodore Vanderbilt's notions on how to succeed in business, as well as those offered by lesser-known authorities who sought to help parents prepare their children "for the steep climb to success," that appeared regularly in the Rockford *Register*.[25] There was even the opportunity, in December 1866, to hear P. T. Barnum, "the Prince of Humbugs," give a talk entitled "Success in Life, or The Art of Money-Getting." According to one newspaper account of the event, Barnum's entertaining lecture "set forth with a force and clearness ... the various principles that lead to prosperity," including "the choice of suitable vocations, wise plans," and "persevering effort."[26]

Whether or not Spalding heard the man whose role in shaping Victorian popular culture was to parallel his own, he clearly was open to Barnum's message. In 1867 Spalding began keeping a scrapbook of clippings from Rockford and Chicago newspapers. Devoted primarily to baseball, the collection also included stories on subjects as diverse as Shakespeare and the history of banking and currency in the United States. Appropriately, for a young man already considering a career in baseball and concerned about the propriety of play for pay, the baseball coverage focused on the Cincinnati Red Stockings.

Managed by Harry Wright, the son of an English professional cricketer and already acknowledged as the best in his trade, the Red Stockings actively recruited salaried ballplayers and invested money in facilities and advertising in the hopes of establishing the team's prominence and winning recognition for the city it represented. Crucial to these efforts was the leadership of a young lawyer named Aaron Champion, who organized the club in 1867 and served as its president. In 1868 Champion spent $11,000 refurbishing the team's playing field while entrusting Wright with $15,000 to lure the best ballplayers in the country to Cincinnati. Although the Red Stockings belonged to the National Association of Baseball Players, which still openly deplored professionalism, they had by 1869 become the first organized team on which all players received salaries for a season's play.[27]

It was no accident, then, that Spalding cut and bordered in black ink a column on Cincinnati that attributed the club's promise to Harry Wright, noting that his players had confidence in him because they knew "that not a move is made anywhere in the game without his noticing it and calling the proper plan to meet it." Also marked off by Spalding in the same article was a brief notice that Wright and his brother had opened a "store in New York for the sale of bats, balls, bases and all the paraphernalia needed for outdoor games." "We hope they make a fortune," the author of the story concluded, "because they are eminently deserving of it."[28]

Spalding's obvious curiosity about baseball's possibilities coincided with the efforts of men like Wright and Champion to promote the move toward professionalization. His own performance as a pitcher for the Forest City's did nothing to deter his interest. Between 1867 and 1870 Spalding led the club to forty-five victories in fifty-eight games. Touting themselves as "the champions of the West," the club's backers raised over $7,000 in 1870 to send the team on a seventeen-game eastern swing that included stops in Canada, New York, Massachusetts, Pennsylvania, Cleveland, and Washington, D.C. The Rockford nine won thirteen and tied one, while losing only three games. In October 1870 the Forest City's even defeated Harry Wright's Red Stockings by a 12–5 score.[29]

Spalding's performance on the trip firmly established his reputation as a pitcher. One New York reporter, no doubt aiming at his audience's funny bone, nevertheless indicated the kind of national attention and acclaim the young pitcher received. Describing his pitching style, he noted:

> On receiving the ball he raises it in both hands until it is on a level with his left eye. Striking an attitude he gazes at it two or three minutes in a contemplative way, and then turns it around once or twice to be sure that it is not an orange or coconut. Assured that he has the genuine article . . . and after a scowl at the shortstop, and a glance at homeplate, [he] finally delivers the ball with the precision and rapidity of a cannon shot.[30]

Accomplishments and renown of this order heightened Spalding's confidence in his ability as a ballplayer and his desire to make baseball a career. Baseball had shattered early feelings of loneliness and self-doubt and had prepared him to "get on in the world." Articles clipped for his scrapbook in the fall of 1870 that described the rapid transformation of the game "from a simple pastime" to a "systematic business" only supported his own calculations about the sport's potential as a business and his place in it.[31] By 1871 he was ready to leave the confines of Rockford in pursuit of his version of the American dream.

2

Boston's Hero

In early January 1871, at a meeting of the Forest City baseball club, Rockford's "leading businessmen" unanimously resolved to reorganize the club and place it on a "war footing." Recognizing, as one observer noted, that the club had done much "to spread the fame of Rockford far and wide," its members agreed "that it would be to our pecuniary advantage to put our hands deep down in our pockets ... to maintain a first class club."[1] The cause of such concern was easy enough to identify. No longer could the Forest City's count on the strong arm of Albert Spalding to carry the day. Indeed, by 1871 the Rockford nine could be certain of seeing their favorite son only when, as a paid professional in the red and white of the Boston Red- Stockings, he bore down on his former teammates in pursuit of fame and fortune.

Almost prophetically, the call to turn professional came from Harry Wright, a man whose exploits Spalding had charted as he calculated his own future. Wright's success in Cincinnati only encouraged his desire to make baseball a professional sport by establishing a new league, distinct from the National Association of Baseball Players. Having been lured to Boston as player and manager at the close of the 1870 season at an annual salary of $2,500 and having already appropriated half a lineup and a name from his old Cincinnati club, he spent the fall of that year building the rest of his team and his league.[2] Spalding figured in both plans.

Spalding's performance against Cincinnati and Henry Chadwick's enthusiastic endorsement of him as a "thorough representative of the spirited young men of the Western states" encouraged Wright to travel to Rockford and buy himself a pitcher.[3] As it turned out, he not only signed Spalding to a contract at an annual salary of $1,500 but also acquired the services of two other Forest City players, the second baseman Ross Barnes and the outfielder Fred Cone.[4]

Older and confident now, sporting a handsome mustache and carrying his 170 pounds on a six-foot, one-inch frame that earned him the so-briquet of "Big Al," Spalding expressed none of the anxiety about leaving home that had colored his earlier move to Chicago. His mother recalled that she decided to "let him go . . . for [she] knew Albert could never stand it to be confined to an office."[5] Spalding's own recollection, however, focused only on the significance of the decision as it related to his role in the development of professional baseball. As he remembered it, it was only after Wright agreed to present the Red Stockings as a professional team that he signed. "I had determined to enter Baseball as a profession," he noted. "I was neither ashamed of the game nor of my attachment to it. Mr. Wright was there offering us . . . cash . . . to play on the Boston team . . . Why, then, go before the public under the false pretense of being amateurs? The assumption of non-professionalism would not deceive anybody. It was not possible that any could be found so simple as to believe that . . . Harry Wright . . . and the rest were in the game merely for healthful or philanthropic reasons, then why engage in duplicity?"[6]

Spalding may well have presented such views to Wright, but they could hardly have impressed a man who had been working for over a year to establish a professional league and whose own move to Boston hinged on that accomplishment. Indeed, only weeks before the opening of the 1871 season, "Harry Wright's league" took shape. Meeting in New York City on St. Patrick's Day, representatives of ten clubs, including Boston's Red Stockings and Rockford's Forest City's, organized the National Association of Professional Base Ball Players (NAPBBP) and announced their intention to operate openly as professionals. A steering committee headed by Wright drew up the league's constitution. It included provisions concerning player contracts, vague recommendations about admission prices, and regulations that offered franchises to any clubs able to come up with $10 registration fees. League clubs agreed to arrange their own schedules and to play each other the best three out of five games in a season ending by November 1. The team winning the most games during the season or, in the case of a tie, the club with the highest winning percentage would take home the pennant.[7]

Baseball's first professional league lasted only five seasons, buffeted by unstable financial support, uneven competition, and haphazard organization. Through it all, Spalding flourished. His years in Boston established him as the premier pitcher in baseball, while his association with Harry Wright provided both experience and direction for his base-ball career.

In days when no substitutes were allowed and a club's pitcher hurled every game, Spalding scarcely missed a turn in leading the Red Stockings to a second-place finish in 1871 and to four consecutive league cham-pionships between 1872 and 1875. Under Wright's tutelage, A.G. im-proved every year, winning twenty-one, thirty-six, forty-one, fifty-two, and fifty-six games in his five years with Boston. In 1875, on the way to his highest single-season victory total, "the best perpendicular pitcher in the country" produced twenty-four consecutive wins while pitching in sixty-three games.[8] According to a writer for the Boston *Journal*, his "peculiar manner of delivering the ball to the batsman suddenly," in a way "calculated to bother and decieve [sic] him," accounted for his success.[9]

Spalding's achievements coincided with significant changes in base-ball that underlined the professional game's emphasis on profit and victory. Eastern rowing regattas easily drew larger crowds and more extensive newspaper coverage than Boston's clashes with the Philadel-phia Athletics or the New York Mutuals, but baseball fans in numbers as high as 3,000 who watched the Red Stockings sweep to victory wit-nessed a brand of ball noticeably different from that of the gentlemanly days of the New York Knickerbockers.[10] One umpire still called the game, and batters still requested high or low balls while they waited out nine pitches for a base on balls. Now, however, if in the umpire's judgment three of those pitches were strikes, the batter was out. Catch-ers like Cal McVey, who handled Spalding, and shortstops like George Wright, Harry's brother, who filled the hole for Boston, garnered rep-utations for their abilities at their positions. Infielders now played off the bag and backed each other up, while catchers, still unprotected except for mouthpieces and the skin-tight, tipless gloves worn by most players, moved closer to the plate in order to deal with the new phe-nomenon of bunts or to throw out runners who now led off bases and attempted to steal their way home.[11]

Although these changes encouraged better defense and lower-scoring games, box scores often read like football totals, and errors were fre-quently as common as base hits. The fact that a full nine innings were played even if the team batting in the bottom of the ninth already had the game won contributed to the high totals. Indeed, on July 4, 1873, Boston celebrated Independence Day by blasting the Providence Reso-lutes by a score of 32–3, scoring twenty-one runs in the bottom of the ninth. Still, observers closest to the game agreed that the quality and style of baseball played by its first professionals marked a significant improvement over the amateur version.[12]

More sophisticated play, encouraged by the emergence of the professional game, also prompted ballplayers to stretch the rules in pursuit of victory. Spalding's own contribution came in response to the "cap catch" rule, adopted in 1873. Aimed at eliminating the clumsy exploits of players who tried to catch balls in their hats in order to avoid bruising their hands, the league prohibited such play and provided that the batter be awarded first base as a penalty for a fielder's catching a ball in that fashion. The rule also stated that a cap-caught ball was immediately "dead" and could not be put back into play until returned to the pitcher on the mound.

Not long after the new rule was on the books, as A.G. recalled it, he and his teammates put it to the test. Playing the Athletics in Philadelphia, he loaded the bases in the bottom of the ninth with no men out. After conferring with George Wright, Spalding threw a change of pace that resulted in an easy pop-up to the Red Stockings' shortstop. Wright caught the ball in his hat and threw it to Spalding, who tossed it to McVey. The catcher proceeded to start the ball around the horn, and the end result was an apparent triple play. At a time when spectators often lined the playing field and occasionally expressed their hostility toward umpires and visiting clubs in personal, physical ways, the umpire in charge of the contest found himself in a difficult situation. Faced with an angry, threatening crowd and a vague rule, which, if strictly adhered to, would lead to the Athletics' defeat and a potential riot, he sent the runners back to their bases and replayed the pitch.[13]

Although A.G.'s gambit proved unsuccessful, his enthusiasm for victory that it demonstrated and his talent as a pitcher earned him the club's top salary of $2000 by 1874. Boston's faithful reveled in his achievements and made him a local hero. The young pitcher also found himself the subject of supporters of professional baseball who were concerned with distingushing it as a wholesome spectator sport. Henry Chadwick, for example, purposively described Spalding as "intelligent and gentlemanly," a man who "both on and off the baseball field conducts himself in a manner well calculated to remove the public's bad impression as to professional ball tossers, created by swearing, gambling, specimens who form the black sheep of the flock." In fact, Chadwick concluded, Spalding "has sense enough to know that fair and manly play, and honorable and faithful service are at least as much the essential of a professional ballplayer as skill in the field and at the bat."[14]

Spalding learned more than pitching and deportment while at Boston.

Although he would eventually surpass his more modest tutor, A.G.'s opportunity to witness Wright's leadership of the Red Stockings served as education and inspiration for his own future career as club manager and baseball entrepreneur.

Both on and off the field, concern for detail and planning defined Wright's approach to the game. Just as Spalding's Cincinnati newspaper clippings suggested, his mentor emphasized discipline, teamwork, and practice as the keys to winning teams. As he told Chadwick, his role as a skilled teacher even included the aptitude to recognize the "special handling" required to bring out the best in all of his players. Wright showed equal ability in overseeing an annual club budget that had approached $35,000 by 1875 and in managing every aspect of the team's affairs, from scheduling and advertising games to negotiating player salaries.[15] Occasional opportunities to assist Wright in these efforts, particularly in connection with Boston's 1874 tour of England, further confirmed Spalding's sense that baseball's rewards were not limited to those of the player.

In 1874, with Boston established as America's best baseball team, Wright decided to fulfill a long-cherished desire to introduce the game to his homeland. Writing to James Ferguson, the president of the Philadelphia Athletics, he revealed plans for his venture and invited the Red Stockings' most formidable rivals along. Aware of the poor attendance figures at league contests and of the tenuous nature of club accounts, Wright assured him that the trip would pay for itself and that the "notoriety" gained by the two teams would encourage large crowds on their return to the United States.[16]

Although Spalding was incorrect when he recalled that his "intense yearning to cross the Atlantic" provided the impetus for the tour, he did have a significant role in shaping its itinerary.[17] While Wright stayed in Boston to prepare his team for the tour and for the upcoming season, he sent Spalding to England to make arrangements for the Americans' visit. He wrote to Ferguson that Spalding "as a man and a gentleman would be likely to create a very favorable impression . . . as an American Baseball Player and a professional." Wright added that "he also has the necessary business qualifications," to which he could "readily testify."[18]

As Spalding remembered it, his mission to England focused on efforts to convince the "Dooks" and "nobility" of the Marylebone Cricket Club to invite the American baseballers over in order to "exhibit to the old nation the new nation's adopted game." As it turned out, with the help of C. W. Alcock, a noted British cricket authority, A.G. successfully arranged invitations at Marylebone and at other clubs on the mainland

and in Ireland. The only catch was the promise he made that, along with the baseball exhibitions, the Americans would also participate in cricket matches at each stop.

Spalding's entrepreneurial talents caused minor consternation for Wright, who had little faith in the ability of American baseball players to play England's "national game." He nevertheless made plans to demonstrate the fine points of cricket to his charges while expressing real pleasure in Spalding's efforts and in the prospects the tour held.[19] After the receipt of a letter from Spalding informing him of plans to visit Dublin, Wright dropped a quick note to Ferguson applauding the idea. "We *must* take *Dublin* in," he exclaimed, "for with all our Mc's and O'R's, a game there would surely prove attractive and pay handsomely." Writing to Alcock in late May to thank him for his work, Wright could even hope that while baseball would "never supplant cricket . . . it will make a good change at certain seasons of the year" and become popular with British youth.[20]

Wright's entourage set out for Liverpool aboard the steamship *Ohio* on July 17 to bring baseball to England. From July 31 to August 25, the Red Stockings and the Athletics traversed the British countryside in railroad cars provided by George Pullman, playing fourteen games in London, Manchester, Sheffield, and Dublin. Boston won eight of the contests, but more attention seems to have been given to the cricket contests that were part of each stop the Americans made. Thanks to the hospitality of their British hosts, the various club teams fielded the customary eleven while allowing the Americans to play eighteen and sometimes twenty-two men against them. Showing no finesse and having numbers on their side, the Americans "won" every cricket match they played. But even Spalding, who felt "immortalized" by his success at bat against the Marylebone club, admitted that the odds were heavily stacked in the visitors' favor.[21]

From all accounts, baseball's British hosts were polite and at times even complimentary, but they were generally unswayed by the idea that America's game had any lasting future in England. Curiosity brought out reasonable crowds. Indeed, the London *Standard* commented on the large number of people, "greatly in excess of anything known on the Liverpool ground," who came out to witness the first baseball contest played by the American clubs on July 27. Dressed in their club uniforms—the Bostons clothed in red stockings, white flannel knickerbockers, white caps with red trim, and white shirts with the word *Boston* emblazoned on the fronts, and the Athletics clad in similar garb, highlighted by blue contrasts—the two teams received enthusiastic applause, "well deserved," as one reporter noted, "for a smarter collection of athletes or a finer-looking body of men it would be impossible to find, all of them being lithe, active, and wonderfully agile in the field."[22] Yet, although British commentators reported favorably on the "scientific" nature of baseball, its "incessant movement and variety," and the alertness of its players, they remained convinced that "few of the youth of Great Britain will desert cricket with its dignity, manliness, and system for a rushing, helter-skelter game."[23] The fact that the tour lost money led to a somewhat different assessment of the venture from Adrian ("Cap") Anson, then an infielder for the Athletics and the man who was to become Spalding's field manager of his Chicago team in the 1880s. Commenting on the pay cut he and other players suffered so that Wright could recoup money spent on steamer fares home, Anson noted that they had left for England as "argonauts" but "brought back but little of the golden fleece."[24]

Not that this mattered to American baseball fans, who warmly greeted their returning heroes. For Henry Chadwick, the visit "set to rest forever the much-debated question as to whether we ha[ve] a national game or not" while demonstrating "the character and habits of our American base ball professionals." On a more personal note, William Hulbert, president of the Chicago White Stockings, suggested that Wright's efforts in behalf of baseball would earn him the title of the "father of the game." Wright demurred. Having just become the father of his seventh "basebawler," he preferred only to be remembered as "the father of this little game."[25]

Spalding was to take a different course when similar claims became available to him. For the moment, however, he enjoyed the attention the tour afforded. The Rockford *Register*, for instance, praised the baseball tourists for behaving like "good boys when three to four thousand miles away from their mothers." "We wonder," the editorial continued, "if loves and prayers bridged the distance as ocean cables and electricity do, and shaped the conduct of those wild boys of the new world. 'Appy, proud H'America! Such glorious mothers; such noble sons."[26] Noble son Albert dutifully clipped the column for his scrapbooks along with others that marked him as a nationally known figure. Returning home to Rockford in November at the close of the 1874 season, he stopped in Towanda, Pennsylvania, his father's birthplace, and picked up another for his collection. Noting his visit, the local newspaper editor gushed that Spalding is "probably the most scientific player in the country . . . a gentleman of education . . . a fine looking and gentlemanly appearing young man . . . [who] has done much towards popularizing the national game" and who is "eminently fit to enjoy the enviable reputation which the achievements won in our National Game has given him."[27]

Spalding's visit to England and his role as Harry Wright's "business agent" clearly did nothing to diminish his enthusiasm for baseball or his self-confidence. In fact, as he recalled it, the experience "had much to do in arousing within me an ambition to raise my position from that of a professional player to that of a manager of a club team." "The desire to manage a professional team became so powerful an influence on my actions," he continued, that "I soon began to lay plans for a successful accomplishment of my ambitious views...."[28]

It was with false expectations, then, that the Rockford *Register* welcomed Spalding home for Thanksgiving 1874. Although the young hero had been to Europe, the editor noted, "he is not vain, but is the same unassuming, capable and good boy of yore. He will ever blush when he reads this, for manliness and modesty enter largely into his composition." The story concluded with the hope that "some good and sensible girl will capture him this winter, retire him from his base[ball] profession, and compel him to lead a matrimonial life in Rockford."[29] To be sure, married life was just around the corner, but it was to be in Chicago, not Rockford, and it was to take a backseat to Spalding's desire to turn his "base ... profession" into one of respectability and social purpose in Victorian America.

3

Spalding's Chicago White Stockings

On July 24, 1875, the Worcester *Spy* announced that Albert Spalding and three other players had forsaken the Boston Red Stockings for the Chicago White Stockings. "Boston is in mourning," the paper noted. "Like Rachel weeping for her children, she refuses to be comforted because the famous baseball nine, the perennial champion, the city's most cherished possession, has been captured by Chicago."[1] Sixteen years later, on April 18, 1891, the *Sporting News* reported on Spalding's retirement from baseball. "It is plain Mr. A. G. Spalding now....The man who has presided over the destinies of ... Chicago ... and to whom more than anybody the national game owes its prominence ... has refused re-election as president of the Chicago club."[2]

Even the most casual observer of late-nineteenth-century American baseball would find the *News*'s assessment accurate. Between 1876 and 1891, first as manager and then as president, A.G. established the White Stockings as professional baseball's most successful team, and baseball as a respectable leisure-time activity for middle-class Americans. His guidance of Chicago's fortunes proved at times inseparable from his involvement in the National League, an organization that he helped create and perpetuate and that he saw as the critical factor in the game's success as a commercial venture. In both pursuits, Spalding's style and actions reverberated strongly with how others in his society sought to manage their affairs.

A.G.'s calculations about "raising" his position from "professional player" to "manager," which the move to Chicago made possible, should not have surprised Boston's fans, who, like Spalding, lived in a society that defined individual success in material terms and instructed its youth to plan careers carefully, acquire skills, and take advantage of opportunities to "rise in the world." At least in Spalding's mind, much like the chance fly ball that had introduced him to baseball on Rockford's commons, fortuitous circumstances, this time in the person of William Hulbert, provided the chance to fulfill his ambition.

In 1871 Chicago was devastated by the great fire. Hulbert, a successful Chicago coal merchant, member of the board of trade, and president of the Chicago White Stockings, hoped to contribute to the city's rebirth and turn a profit by making his club a consistent winner.[3] Undaunted by NAPBBP prohibitions against engaging players already under contract, Hulbert made it his business to lure established talent to the Windy City. Spalding was his prime target.

Hulbert's style and solicitations made a good impression on A.G. As he remembered it, in terms that he liked to have applied to himself, Hulbert was "strong, forceful and self-reliant . . . a man of tremendous energy—and courage," who did things in a "business-like way." The Chicago entrepreneur reminded the Rockford man, "You've no business playing in Boston; you're a Western boy, and you belong right here." When Hulbert coupled this appeal to midwestern origins with the promise of the positions of field manager and captaincy in 1875, Spalding could not resist.[4] In early July A.G. wrote to Chicago's stockholders and offered his services as pitcher, captain, and manager for the 1876 season. Without hesitation they sent Hulbert to Boston to close the deal. They also directed him "to engage such players for the season of 1876 as [he] and Mr. Spalding should decide upon."[5]

Hulbert signed Spalding to a one-year contract at a salary of $2,000 and the promise of 25 percent of the club's gate receipts for the coming season.[6] With A.G.'s help, the two men also bought a team that would come to dominate professional baseball well into the 1880s. Determined to "bring a team of pennant winners" to Chicago, Spalding persuaded his Boston teammates Ross Barnes, Cal McVey, and Jim White to join him. Similar cajoling in Philadelphia secured the services of Adrian ("Cap") Anson.[7]

Boston's faithful expressed anguish and outrage at the secession of the "Big Four." Branding Spalding the "prime mover in the affair," they questioned the legality of the move and doubted the players' ability to perform in "the Hub" when their pocketbooks were destined for "Lake City."[8] On the last point there was little cause for concern, as the Red Stockings swept their fourth straight pennant, compiling a 71–8 record along the way. Although the other charge was accurate, there was no formal authority to squash the deal and, as Jim White put it, no attempt by Boston's management to meet the "fancy western prices."[9]

Other evaluations of the move, consistent with the advice that Spalding's generation read every day in their newspapers, accepted the defections as a predictable outcome of the development of professional baseball and expressed grudging pride in Spalding's ability to capitalize on his talents. As one subscriber to the Boston *Globe* observed, the only way to view it was as "any other business matter . . . between employer and employed." Referring to Spalding and his compatriots, he noted that "the fact is undeniable that on their part, baseball playing is simply a business. . . . They have worked for money and they never professed to work for anything else. If they have played so skillfully as to gain great éclat and become pets of an appreciative public, so much the better for them, and so much the higher salaries they can command."[10]

For those concerned with the larger issue of establishing professional baseball as a successful and stable business, the move had other implications. Uneven competition, collapsing franchises, numerous instances of gambling and game throwing, and rowdy, drunken behavior by ballplayers had rapidly diminished baseball's status as "a gentleman's game" and marked the professional version as a poor investment and as questionable fare for reputable people to enjoy. Henry Chadwick hoped that competition between a rebuilt Boston team and "Captain Spalding's Western White Stockings," although unlikely to counter all of these tendencies, would at least reverse poor attendance. Ample demonstration of such possibilities occurred in Boston on October 22, when, as the New York *Clipper* reported, the participation of "the quartet of seceders" on the side of the White Stockings in an exhibition with Boston "attracted one of the largest crowds of the season." The final score was Chicago 14, Boston 0.[11] Later, at a farewell gathering, Spalding, his eye characteristically on the future, toasted his former teammates and employers: "To the Boston club, its officers, members and stockholders—may they fly the pennant in 'seventy-six—if the Chicagos don't."[12]

There was other business at hand, however, before the pursuit of pennants. Although Chadwick hoped that increased competition might prove beneficial to professional baseball's future, he and other knowledgeable baseball men recognized the need to deal with the whole range of abuses associated with it if the game was ever to enjoy financial stability and popularity. In fact, led by Hulbert, efforts were well under way to organize a new approach to the game when Spalding arrived in Chicago with his new, Boston bride, Josie Keith, in late fall 1875. As it turned out, A.G.'s first responsibilities as Hulbert's employee were to help his new mentor draft a constitution and marshal support for a new professional league, the National League of Professional Baseball Clubs.

In very specific ways, Hulbert's conception sought to bring order to professional baseball by "reducing the game," as Spalding put it, "to a business system such as had never heretofore obtained."[13] Decisive here was the establishment of a league bureaucracy composed of club owners and including a president, a secretary-treasurer, and a board of directors, with authority to enforce rules and supervise league operations. Aimed at overcoming the shortcomings of past organizations, which were attributed to player involvement in the affairs of management, these provisions complemented others in the National League's constitution that were meant to bring stability and uniformity to the game. Rules more tightly binding players to their contracts, mandating franchises only in cities of at least 75,000 people, calling for a predetermined playing schedule with automatic expulsion for teams that failed to meet their obligations, adopting uniform ticket prices, and hiring paid umpires all focused on correcting abuses associated with the NAPBBP. In addition, regulations that forbade Sunday games, the selling of alcohol on club grounds, betting and pool selling—all with severe penalties for players who personally engaged in such activities—aimed to fulfill the league's objective "to encourage, foster, and elevate the game of Base Ball" and to "make Base Ball playing respectable and honorable."[14]

Although Hulbert took the lead in winning other clubs over to the National League, Spalding attended meetings and wrote letters hoping to persuade club owners to abandon the old association. For instance, after a January meeting in Louisville at which that city's club and Charles Fowle's St. Louis nine joined the new order, Spalding reported enthusiastically on its progress to an associate on his old Rockford team. Emphasizing that the new league "put the life of the player in the hands of the organization that employs him," Spalding noted that he and Hulbert were now ready to convince the eastern clubs of the necessity of the change. Confidently he concluded, "I assure you everything is now *right* in the West—I am very certain we shall carry the affair in the East."[15]

Spalding even found time to appease Henry Chadwick, who had referred to the announcement of the National League as "a startling coup d'état," a move that upset him primarily because he had been left out of its planning.[16] In a letter to Chadwick, Spalding admitted that "some of the rules and regulations may be too drastic and . . . prove unfeasible." He nevertheless underlined his commitment to "the principles of the League" and pledged to "do all I can to make it a success, for in my judgment on the success of this movement depends the future of baseball." A.G. characteristically intertwined his public and professional roles with personal needs and goals: his efforts at conciliation included informing the chief sportswriter for the New York *Clipper* of his plans to open a sporting-goods store in Chicago. Hopeful that the paper would accept his advertisements, the budding entrepreneur signed off, "yours in haste, Albert G. Spalding."[17]

Spalding clearly played an important though secondary role in the establishment of the National League. In later years, however, as with his remembrance of other events, he often exaggerated his part in the process. In 1910, for example, although he acknowledged Hulbert's importance, he suggested that the idea for the league originated only because of his own expressed concern that the "Big Four" and Cap Anson might be expelled from the NAPBBP for signing with Chicago. Visibly outraged at the notion, Hulbert, after a few moments of "deep thought," according to A.G., jumped from his chair and figuratively gave birth to the National League. "Spalding," he said, "I have a scheme. Let us anticipate the Eastern cusses and organize a new association. . . and then see who will do the expelling." Thus, Spalding concluded, "was a new association conceived."

To be sure, the description of this meeting was more modest than the one he offered a *Sporting News* reporter in 1895. On that occasion he recalled having asked Hulbert, "What is the reason . . . that we cannot draw off and form a new league?" Hulbert, according to A.G., had responded by saying "it was a capital idea." And in 1901, in defending his right to speak at the National League's annual meeting at a time when the organization appeared on the verge of dissolving, Spalding declared himself, along with Hulbert, to be one of its two founding fathers.[18]

Why should Spalding, a man constantly in the public eye from adolescence until death and consistently perceived in positive terms by a society that admired aggressive, strong, and determined men who successfully met every challenge, rely on such exaggeration to insure public attention? Certainly suggestive are his early experiences as a fatherless child who developed and maintained a close relationship with a mother who outlived him—experiences that perhaps created a compensatory need for public, overstated expressions of achievement and independence as a means of self-assertion. Less speculative, however, and more meaningful in terms of the connections between Spalding and the larger culture is the fact that self-confidence and self-promotion, even the acceptance of exaggeration as part of the art of success, were deemed essential for survival in an increasingly competitive and unstable world. People heard the message huckstered by a P. T. Barnum, preached by a Henry Ward Beecher, and extolled in the booster literature of cities like Rockford and Chicago.[19] As William Mathews, a University of Chicago professor put it, in an 1871 series of newspaper articles later collected into a book titled *Getting On in the World*, an essential ingredient for success, along with careful planning, aggressiveness, energy, and talent, was self-confidence. "Put yourself forward ... if you would be known. Blow some kind of a trumpet, or at least a penny whistle to draw the world's eye to you; but be sure that you *are* what you pretend to be before you blow...."[20]

Spalding clearly favored trumpets over penny whistles and, after 1890, when his recollections of past events appeared most often, certainly believed he knew who he was. In simplest terms, A.G. saw himself as a trained expert in his chosen field who had applied certain skills to guarantee his own success as well as that of the enterprise of professional baseball.

This perception was hardly unique to Spalding. Particularly for middle-class Americans, the last quarter of the nineteenth century fostered a growing sense that the increasingly complex nature of American life required careful organization of every sphere of human activity, be it sport, industry, or religion. Within each area, professionals trained to their calling would set the standards, solve problems, and instruct others. According to one historian, no area of American life escaped these tendencies; for better or worse, and whether in the doctor's office, in the home, in school, or on ball field, the notion of the professional as a "magician," a charismatic figure deserving of trust and capable of providing guidance, came to dominate the everyday world of Americans.[21]

Such broad cultural patterns dovetailed nicely with Spalding's own proclivities. They were also consistent with the tendency for "experts" in every field to emphasize the need for efficient management, specialization of roles, enforcement of discipline, rationalization of procedure, and new organizational structures in order to insure the stability and success of any enterprise whatever. Indeed, this approach, which some have labeled "progressive," marked developments as diverse as the growth of corporate capitalism, the rise of organized labor, efforts at social and political reform, and, in Spalding's mind, the development of professional baseball.[22]

For Spalding and others, the transformation of baseball from a playful pastime to a business enterprise required an organizational structure manned, as Henry Chadwick put it, by "professional experts," and able to insure standards of excellence, provide stability, and maximize opportunities for profit. He firmly believed and consistently made clear, particularly after 1900, when his own identification as a progressive was most obvious, that the National League served this function. Baseball's success as a stable, respectable business, A.G. asserted in 1915, depends on the National League, "that pre-eminent organization that has perpetuated Base Ball for forty years and made possible the existence of all clubs and leagues and ensured high salaries and continual employment to worthy players."[23]

Spalding's later view of baseball's progress and his role in the process, was the fruit, then, of mature reflections on a life in baseball encouraged by an insatiable ego and shaped by intellectual currents that emphasized self-promotion, the importance of professional experts, and the need for organization. Hindsight didn't hurt either. In many respects, his years with the White Stockings proved crucial in shaping his conception of the game and his place in it.

In keeping with the terms of his contract, Spalding's roles as captain, manager, and player found him juggling a variety of tasks not totally consistent with the new league's emphasis on the separate responsibilities of players and management. Hulbert's preoccupation with winning clubs over to the National League left it up to A.G. to find housing for his players, to place advertisements about the upcoming campaign, and to correspond with a barely established league office about baseballs and umpires. Even while home for Christmas in Rockford in 1875, A.G. was in touch with the secretary of the Riverside baseball club of Memphis, Tennessee, trying to arrange some games during a two-week southern trip that he hoped to take the White Stockings on, as "preliminary practice before commencing our regular professional season."[24]

Negotiations for this first effort at spring training did not interfere with the pressing matter of fixing Chicago's schedule for the 1876 season. League rules did not prohibit its clubs from playing nonleague games as a way of supplementing their revenues. Sifting through letters and sending off responses, A.G. negotiated terms with amateur teams with an eye toward guaranteed profit. For instance, when on the road, he always demanded a firm $150 with the promise that if 50 percent of the gate receipts exceeded that amount, the White Stockings would be entitled to half of the take. Invariably, he offered to send in advance "some fine lithographic pictures of our nine" to help promote the planned contests.[25]

Activities off the field did not diminish his effectiveness on the diamond. The National League's inaugural season marked Spalding's first as field manager and last as full-time pitcher. Appearing in sixty-one

games, finishing fifty-three and winning forty-six, "the best perpendicular pitcher in the country" led Chicago to the pennant with a record
of 52-14. According to one reporter, his "rapid" delivery, "frequent
change of pace," and "cool" manner accounted for his success. As the
Chicago *Tribune* commented after A.G. baffled Boston in July by an 11–
3 score, "clubs come to Chicago and spit on their hands with ferocity
and explain that they are going to 'knock the stuffing out of Spalding'
because 'anybody can hit him; he is the easiest man in the business.'
And they they don't do it all the same."[26]

Spalding's ability as manager received as much credit for Chicago's
success as his prowess on the mound did. Observers did not forget the
contributions of Anson, Barnes, and McVey, who finished among the
top five batters in the league. With justifiable pride and in ways that
doubtless pleased Spalding and Hulbert as much as the material rewards
that pennant winners brought, the Chicago *Evening Journal* congratulated
the White Stockings on their triumph by noting that "every man on the
club has shown himself to be a gentleman as well as a ball player, and
there never has been a breath of suspicion against them. They have
made friends in and out of the profession, and are a credit to the city
of their adoption. . . ."[27]

Not so kind were baseball scribes or Spalding's fortunes in 1877 when
Chicago finished in fifth place. Although injuries limited Spalding to
four starts, the real cause of the White Stockings' problems, according
to Henry Chadwick, was "bad management." Writing in the New York
Clipper, Chadwick noted that "professional club management ha[d] become as much a regular business as that of theatrical management" and
required the full-time attention of experienced people in order to work
properly. Although Spalding's success in 1876 demonstrated his talent,
his problems in 1877 resulted from a failure to apply it diligently. A.G.
simply "had too many irons in the fire," Chadwick concluded, "and in
his attempt to captain the nine, to run the general business of the club,
and at the same time to manage his own baseball business and store,
he undertook more than any one man could properly attend to, and the
results was [sic] a measureable failure."[28]

Chadwick's analysis did not go unheeded. Spalding, after all, had
helped create a new league, based on the assumption that baseball's
commercial success depended on the control of club affairs by businessmen rather than by players. Eager to take that role himself, A.G.
relinquished his duties as field manager to Cap Anson and retired from
active play after the 1877 season. For the next four years he served as
the White Stockings' secretary and, along with Hulbert, who simulta-

neously occupied the presidencies of both Chicago and the National League, continued to direct the club's front office.

An apprenticeship begun under Harry Wright and continued under William Hulbert ended abruptly in 1882, when Hulbert's death catapulted Spalding into Chicago's presidency. The founder of the National League succumbed to heart problems on April 10. On April 12 the club's stockholders held a memorial meeting in his honor. Two days later Spalding helped lower his coffin into the ground, and on April 26, at another stockholders' meeting, he was elected president along with a new board of directors that included the Chicago Board of Trade members John Lyon, Charles T. Trego, and John L. Walsh, also an influential Chicago banker. After buying out Hulbert's holdings in the club from his widow, Spalding and Walsh emerged as the White Stockings' principal owners.[29]

Under Spalding, Chicago flourished. Capitalizing on the talents of a team that he and Hulbert had shaped and that already had captured National League pennants in 1880 and 1881, A.G.'s White Stockings continued to dominate play for the rest of the decade. Altogether, between 1880 and 1890, Chicago never finished worse than fourth and won additional titles in 1882, 1885, and 1886. Over ten seasons, the club's winning percentage was .636, including the astounding and never surpassed major league mark of .798 in 1880. In that year "Anson's Athletes" won sixty-seven of eighty-four games, including a consecutive-game winning streak of twenty-two that broke the mark of the famed 1869 Cincinnati Red Stockings, a team, the Chicago *Tribune* noted in reporting the news, "held up to the emulations of ball players in much the same way that small boys are exhorted to imitate George Washington."[30] Even the mighty 1927 New York Yankees could muster a winning percentage of only .714, in the year that Babe Ruth smashed sixty home runs and Lou Gehrig forty-seven.

Although Chicago's prominence came at a time when league-leading home-run hitters rarely hit even ten, the team had its own array of stars that accounted for its success. Most popular was Cap Anson, who came with Spalding to Chicago in 1876 and remained with the White Stockings for twenty-two years. Born in Marshalltown, Iowa, Anson broke into professional baseball with Rockford's Forest City's, one year after Spalding had left for Boston. An inch taller than "Big Al," Anson not only managed Chicago for twenty years but also was one of the game's most competent and most heralded ballplayers. A right-handed-hitting first baseman not known for his speed, he was the first major leaguer to amass over 3,000 base hits. Cap also led the National League in hitting four times; his titles included a .399 mark in 1881 and a .421 pace in 1887, a year in which walks counted as hits. Only three times in twenty-two years did his batting average fall below .300. His lifetime average was .329.

Anson anchored an infield that by the mid-1880s was known as Chicago's "stone wall." At third base was Ned Williamson, an Indianapolis native whom Anson called "the greatest all-around ball player the country ever saw."[31] Williamson batted .259 in his eleven years with Chicago. In 1884 he led the National League with a phenomenal twenty-seven home runs—a feat attributable less to prodigious power than to a change in the ground rules at Chicago's Lake Front Park that, for one season, resulted in the counting as home runs of hits that in the past had been ground rule doubles.[32] Rounding out the infield were Tommy Burns at shortstop, Fred Pfeffer at second base, and Frank ("Old Silver") Flint at catcher.

Complementing the "stone wall" was a collection of outfielders who together batted .309 during their seven seasons with Chicago from 1880 to 1886. George Gore, a left-handed-hitting center fielder from Saccarappa, Maine, led the National League with a .360 average in 1880 and retired with a lifetime batting average of .301 over fourteen seasons. During that same, pennant-winning year of 1880, Abner Dalrymple, the club's left fielder, posted a league-leading 126 hits. On three different occasions, he led the league in at bats, and he recorded a career batting average of .288.

Even more impressive were the statistics and reputation of the right fielder Mike ("King") Kelly, who came to Chicago in 1880. During his tenure with the club, the King established himself as one of the best-known players in the game, famous for his flamboyance off the field as much as on it. Kelly led the league in batting in 1884 and 1886 and in runs scored in 1884, 1885, and 1886. Although statistics on stolen bases were not kept until 1887, his exploits on the base paths, eventually immortalized in the song "Slide, Kelly, Slide," brought him no less attention than did his reputation as a horseplayer, carouser, spendthrift, and drinker. Once observed downing a few by a Pinkerton detective hired by Spalding to keep tabs on his players, Kelly denied only a report that he had been drinking lemonade at 3 A.M. in Chicago's tenderloin district. "It was straight whiskey," he told Spalding. "I never drank a lemonade at that hour in my life."[33]

In a game in which pitching predominated, particularly after 1884, when pitchers were allowed to throw overhand, Chicago's success also depended on a corps of moundsmen cleverly rotated by Anson for maximum efficiency. Between 1880 and 1885, Cap relied on Larry Corcoran and Fred ("Goldy") Goldsmith to carry the load. Reputed to be the first player to use signals with his catcher, Corcoran, a Brooklyn boy, signed with Chicago as a twenty-one-year-old righthander in 1880. Over the next five seasons, he compiled a dazzling record of 190–83, including three no-hitters, a league-leading 268 strikeouts in 1880, and a cumulative earned-run average of 2.22. Complementing the hard-throwing Corcoran was the slow-ball pitcher Goldsmith. Traded by Spalding midway through the 1885 season, Goldy won ninety-eight games while losing fifty-two during his four full seasons with the White Stockings, establishing a creditable e.r.a. of 2.48 along the way.

During Chicago's last two pennant-winning years in the 1880s, mound duties were primarily shared by a different duo—John Clarkson and Jim McCormick. McCormick won forty-nine games and lost only fifteen during his two seasons with the club. Clarkson, a compact five foot, ten-inch, 150-pound righthander from Cambridge, Massachusetts, who had come to Chicago in 1884, led the league with fifty-three victories and 308 strikeouts in 1885. One of his triumphs was a no-hitter pitched against Providence on July 27, 1885. During his Chicago years, Clarkson compiled a record of 137–57, striking out an average of 268 batters in three full seasons with the White Stockings. Traded to Boston in 1887, he went on to establish a lifetime e.r.a. over twelve seasons of 2.81, with a won-lost record of 327–177. These credentials were good enough to gain him posthumous admission into Baseball's Hall of Fame in 1963.

Clarkson's confirmation as a baseball immortal followed similar honors bestowed on Cap Anson in 1939 and King Kelly in 1945. No less renowned than this trio was Chicago's utility outfielder between 1884 and 1887, William A. ("Billy") Sunday. Discovered by Anson at a baseball tournament in Marshalltown, Iowa, Sunday came to Chicago in 1883. A spot player whose best year in Chicago was his last, when he appeared in fifty games and batted .291, Billy was, according to Cap, the fastest man in baseball, who ran "like a scared deer."[34]

By the early 1900s, Sunday's national fame as an evangelical minister far exceeded any reputation he had made on the diamond. Baseball, however, still served him well. As he told his audiences, his first experience in the power of Christ came at the end of the 1886 season, in a tight game with Detroit in which the pennant was at stake. With Chicago ahead, Detroit put two men on base in the bottom of the ninth. Charlie Bennett, the Tigers' catcher, waited out a full count and then unloaded a drive to deep center field. Sunday took off after it, his glove in the air and his mouth full of prayer. Leaping over spectator benches in the outfield "as though wings were carrying [him] up," Sunday caught the ball and secured the victory. "Though the deduction is hardly orthodox," Billy informed his parishioners, "I am sure the Lord helped me catch that ball, and it was my first experience in prayer."[35]

Although Chicago's dominance relied less on prayer than on the skills of its players, the club hardly had a monopoly on talent. Within the National League, its most consistent competition in the early 1880s came from the Providence Grays, a team that won the pennant in 1879 and 1884 and finished in second place every year in between. Managed by Harry Wright, Spalding's mentor at Boston, the Grays featured three players all destined for the Hall of Fame—George Wright, John Montgomery Ward, and Charles ("Old Hoss") Radbourn. George had been a star both with the 1869 Cincinnati Red Stockings and with Boston and was at the end of his distinguished career when he played for his brother in 1879 and 1882. In contrast, Monte Ward's first years in professional baseball were with Providence, as a pitcher and right fielder. In 1879 Ward won forty-four games. One year later he earned forty more victories, including a perfect game pitched against Buffalo. Later famous for his exploits at shortstop and as captain for the New York Giants, Ward batted .275 during his seventeen-year career and led the National League in stolen bases in 1887 and 1892.

During the 1881 and 1882 seasons, Ward alternated on the mound with Charlie Radbourn, a right-handed hurler who had come to the Grays from Buffalo and who went on to become one of the most famous pitchers in the game. Over his eleven-year career, Old Hoss completed 489 games, won 309, and compiled an e.r.a. of 2.67. In 1883 he led the National League in victories with 48. Most astonishing, however, was his 1884 performance, which helped Providence to the pennant. Starting and completing 73 of the club's 112 games and pitching in 75, Radbourn won a league-leading 60 games while losing only 12. He also led the league in strikeouts (441), e.r.a. (1.38) and innings pitched (629 and 2/3).

Typical of the excitement that the Grays and White Stockings generated were their head-to-head struggles at the close of the 1882 season for league supremacy. After a slow start, perhaps complicated by Hulbert's death and Spalding's rise to the club presidency, Chicago found itself five games behind Providence in late June and given little chance, by the Chicago *Tribune*, to repeat as league champions. Although Chicago took two in a row at home against the Grays in that month, before large crowds of 4,000 fans, in early September the *Tribune* was still predicting a Providence pennant. Commenting on two losses to Boston, the paper described Chicago's performance as the "sorri[est] case of fall-down" ever seen. Sarcastically, it chastised some unruly fans for threatening an umpire over a call in Chicago's 7–2 loss to the Grays on September 2. "There was a million times more reason to mob the Chicago team than to mob the umpire," the paper noted, "but it never occurred to the rowdy element to lie in wait for the nine men who insulted an assemblage of 3,500 people and disgraced the city and humiliated their friends by their abominable play."[36]

As it turned out, the *Tribune's* obituary proved premature. At a time when the White Stockings alternated a variety of red-and-white uniforms, often at A.G.'s whim, they abandoned their red caps after the Boston series and returned, "for luck," to the old-time tricolored hats that they had worn in 1880 and 1881. Buoyed by sweeping three games from Troy, Chicago entertained Providence on September 12, 13, and 14 and had a chance to move into first place. Playing before crowds of between 5,000 and 7,000 that overflowed onto the outfield grass, Corcoran and Goldsmith turned back Ward and Radbourn by scores of 6–4, 6–5, and 6–2, and Chicago went on to take the flag by a three-game margin over the Grays.[37]

No less a problem for the White Stockings were the New York Giants, who battled Anson's charges unsuccessfully for the pennant in 1885 and 1886 and won the flag outright from them in 1888. Managed by Jim Mutrie, New York's lineup contained six players who became Hall of Famers, including Monte Ward, who came to the Giants from Providence in 1883. Ward played in an infield that featured William ("Buck") Ewing, a right-handed-hitting jack-of-all-trades fielder from Hoaglands, Ohio. Ewing batted over .300 in each of his seven years with the Giants, hitting .327 in the year New York won the pennant. Also in the lineup was James ("Orator Jim") O'Rourke. O'Rourke, like Ward, attended law school in the off-season, an avocation that no doubt earned him his nickname. Coming to New York from Buffalo, he played the outfield and occasionally caught during his four seasons with the Giants. Over a nineteen-year career in the majors, he batted .310.

When Orator Jim did go behind the plate, he often handled the Giants' top pitcher, Tim Keefe. A righthander from Cambridge, Massachusetts, Keefe won 336 games during his fourteen years in the major leagues. In his five years with the Giants, from 1885 to 1889, Sir Timothy, as he was called, led the league with an e.r.a. of 1.58 in 1885 and 1.74 in 1888, while compiling a 169–76 record along the way.

Also contributing to the Giants' success were Roger Connor and Michael ("Smiling Mickey") Welch. A huge, left-handed hitter at six feet three inches and 220 pounds, Connor played eighteen years, with a

lifetime batting average of .317. In seven years with the Giants between
1883 and 1890, Connors played first base and batted .328. Welch alternated on the mound with Keefe. During a thirteen-year career, the last
ten seasons of which he played with New York, the righthander from
Brooklyn won 309 games. His best year was 1885, when he won forty-
four games and compiled a winning percentage of .800, which topped
the National League.

In that year, when Welch and Keefe combined for sixty-six wins and
when Connor led the league with a .371 batting average, the Giants
battled Chicago for the pennant from opening day until the close of the
season. Over the Fourth of July holidays, New York climbed to within
one and one-half games of the White Stockings by taking three of four
from them, before crowds ranging between 4,000 and 11,000 people.
Three months later the Giants returned to Chicago for a four-game series,
with the pennant at stake. Before four consecutive capacity crowds of
10,000 people, which included Carter Harrison, Chicago's mayor, and
Nick Young, then president of the National League, Chicago took three
games and clinched the flag. As the Chicago *Tribune* reported it, the
difference between the two teams was neither speed nor brawn but
rather "strategy. . . . The White Stockings play a more brainy game." In
its own paean to Chicago, a local business firm recognized Anson's boys
in a piece of entreprenurial poetry that Spalding would have appreciated:

> The hearts of our boys are buoyant as cork
> They have grandly and signally beaten New York. . . .
> We cannot name all, but can't forget Kelly,
> Who caught New York's hopes and crushed them to jelly!. . .
> While Chicago's brave boys shall keep the ball "buzzin"
> Hartley's Cabinets remain TWO DOLLARS PER DOZEN.[38]

National League clubs hardly offered the only competition to Chicago's claim as baseball's best team in the 1880s. Owned by "boss president" Chris Von der Ahe, who made his money in beer and suffered
ridicule by sportswriters for his German accent, bulbous nose, and outrageous clothes, the St. Louis Browns dominated the American Association in much the same fashion that Spalding's club did the rival National
League.[39] Led by Charlie Comiskey, Arlie Latham, Dave Foutz, and Bob
Caruthers, the Browns won four consecutive pennants between 1885
and 1888 and finished in second place in 1883 and 1889.

Eager for recognition as baseball's best, Von der Ahe challenged Spalding to postseason play in 1885 and 1886, a practice unofficially inaugurated between the champions of the two leagues in 1884. Unlike those
governing the modern World Series, arrangements about the number

of games, sites, prize money, and even umpires were decided upon each year by the two clubs involved. In 1885 Spalding and Von der Ahe agreed on a twelve-game series, one game to be played in Chicago, three in St. Louis, and the rest in Pittsburgh, Cincinnati, Baltimore, Philadelphia, and Brooklyn. Each owner also offered to put up one-half of a $1,000 prize that would go to the team winning a majority of the games.[40]

After tying their first game, called because of darkness after eight innings, the two clubs played a controversial match before 3,000 boisterous St. Louis fans that ended in riot and forfeit. Enraged by a call in the sixth inning that kept alive a Chicago rally when the club was down two runs, spectators ran onto the field, disrupted the game, and sent the umpire, named Sullivan, packing. Later, from the safety of his hotel room, Sullivan awarded the game to Chicago by forfeit, despite the protests of Comiskey, St. Louis's captain, who demanded that the game be discounted.[41]

After splitting their next four games, the Browns beat Chicago by a 13–4 score in Cincinnati and claimed the world championship. As the Chicago *Tribune* reported it, the clubs had agreed to shorten the series and to forget about the forfeit, thus giving the series to St. Louis, three games to two. For his part, Spalding denied having made any agreement to discount the forfeit. In his mind, the series stood at three games each. Besides, he noted, any claim that the series was "for the championship of the world" was "nonsense." "Does any one suppose," he remarked, "that if there had been so much as that at stake that I should have consented to the games being played in American Association cities, upon their grounds and under the authority of their umpires?"[42]

One year later the two pennant winners met again. This time the clubs agreed on a home-and-home series, the total gate receipts to go to the winner of the seven-game event. Excited about his team's second consecutive pennant and the prospects of beating the Browns, Spalding wired Anson his congratulations and offered "as a token of my appreciation of your work ... each man a suit of clothes ... and the team collectively one-half of the receipts in the coming series with St. Louis."[43]

A.G. never had a chance to make good on his promise. After taking two out of three games at home, Chicago dropped three in a row to St. Louis at Sportsman's Park, losing the decisive contest by a 4–3 score in ten innings. According to the St. Louis *Republican*, the last game was "the greatest contest ever known to the history of baseball." Aided by John Clarkson's strong pitching, Chicago eked out a 3–0 lead after seven innings. In the top of the eighth, however, St. Louis rallied. With one run already in, Comiskey knocked a single through the hole at second.

Curt Welch, the Brown's center fielder, followed with a bunt down the third base line that cracked the "stone wall" when Tommy Burns threw the ball in the dirt to Anson at first. The next two batters flied out, and then Clarkson walked the catcher Doc Bushong to load the bases. With "the crowd ... nearly frantic" and "the noise ... deafening," Arlie Latham, the Browns' third baseman, known as much for his ability as a heckler as for his talent as a ballplayer, drove a ball into left field that Abner Dalrymple misjudged. Two runs scored. St. Louis added one more in the tenth, and the game and the series were over.[44]

Commenting on the Browns' triumph, the St. Louis *Republican* suggested that "Chicago should confine itself to the slaughter of hogs as a popular amusement," because "baseball seems to require more head-work" than that city can muster. In a more combative spirit, Cap Anson demanded another series in April for $5,000 a side.[45] According to one newspaper, Spalding was so disgusted with the performance of his athletes that he refused to pay his team's train fare home from St. Louis.[46]

Although Chicago did play a series of exhibitions with the Browns in April 1887, the White Stockings never again were champions under Anson and Spalding.[47] Not until 1906, long after both men had ended their relations with Chicago baseball, did the then Chicago Cubs of Tinker-to-Evers-to-Chance fame win another National League pennant. Working with a new team after A.G. traded Kelly, Dalrymple, Gore, and McCormick at the close of the 1886 season, Anson did manage a series of second- and third-place finishes, to Detroit and New York, between 1887 and 1890. But Cap's "chicks," "colts," or "black stockings," as they became known—references to the new young talent secured by Spalding and to the new uniform color schemes designed by Mrs. Anson in 1888—faltered throughout the 1890s.[48] Except for 1891, when Chicago finished in second place, three and a half games behind Boston, the club never did better than fourth with Anson as manager.

Chicago's success on the ball field yielded profits at the gate. Incomplete records from the 1878, 1879, and 1881 seasons suggest that gate receipts alone in these years ranged between $23,000 and $32,000.[49] During Spalding's years as president, business improved. Although A.G. viewed club finances "as a private matter" and consistently refused to open Chicago's books, scattered references suggest that a victorious baseball team could be good investment.[50] During the 1884 season, for instance, Jonathan Brown, Spalding's secretary, reported to the league office that the club had collected almost $24,000 in gate receipts for home games during June, July, and August. In October 1887 the New York *Clipper* took note that the club's stockholders had each received a dividend of 20 percent, a return made possible by a surplus of $100,000 accumulated by the team over the past few years. One year later the San Francisco *Examiner* told its readers that the White Stockings had netted a $60,000 profit during the 1888 season. Moreover, the paper noted, the club had invested a large portion of its capital in its Congress Street Park, leasing land worth at least $750,000, according to "real estate experts," with an option to buy at $400,000. Whether or not all could agree that "baseball" was "an esthetic and soul-elevating pursuit," clearly, the *Examiner* continued, it was "a tremendous source of revenue" and Chicago its "richest corporation." Somewhat disparagingly, it concluded that "the Chicago club is purely a money-making concern....It is organized as any other corporation, by people of wealth ... who ... haul in such profits yearly as would ... make even bonanza kings envious."[51]

However upset some people might have been about the transformation of sport into a business, for Spalding and others who committed themselves to promoting baseball as acceptable and profitable entertainment, a recognition of their achievements read as tribute rather than criticism. Indeed, so successful was Chicago that in December 1892 Spalding, Walsh, and Trego, its chief stockholders, reorganized the club by making the original corporation responsible solely for handling investments in real estate. Its properties included acreage in Hot Springs, Arkansas, where the club went for spring training, and also land in Chicago, where it planned to build a new ballpark. The ball team itself was incorporated as a separate entity with a capital of $100,000. As the new president of the White Stockings, James Hart, put it, "the old corporation [will] look after the land end of the business, while the new corporation will do nothing but hunt the pennant."[52]

Whether or not, as Spalding believed, "ownership of a great ball club ... involved man-killing experiences" and required going at "a pace that kills," there is no question that his personal handling of a variety of tasks had much to do with Chicago's success.[53] Consistent with his belief that "the man whose soul is absorbed in the business of playing ball has no soul left for the other business ... of conducting the details of managing men, administering discipline, arranging schedules, and finding ways and means of financing a team," A.G. throughout his tenure as president kept Anson as captain and field manager, leaving the other responsibilities to himself.[54] Deciding on spring training sites, trades, the need to discipline ballplayers, or even changes in league rules, the two men worked well together and yet maintained distinct roles. "Neither man interferes in the other's business," one writer noted. "Al Spalding holds Anson personally responsible for the general management of the team," another observed, "and Anson holds the players individually responsible to him." As Spalding told his players, "Mr. Anson is captain and manager . . . and has full charge of all players both on and off the field."[55]

Occasionally, however, Spalding overstepped the boundaries he set for himself. At a time when no substitutions were permitted unless a player became sick or injured, A.G. grew quite upset at an umpire's ruling in a game against Philadelphia in August 1886 that allowed the Athletics to replace their catcher, James McGuire, because of an alleged injury. Spalding ran onto the field to support Anson's protest that McGuire had only said his hands were "sore" rather than "hurt."[56] Several years later, Chicago's president stormed onto the field again— this time to get to the clubhouse after a loss to the Giants that he blamed on his manager. Surrounded by half-naked ballplayers, Spalding chastised Anson for twice popping up with the bases loaded. "That was all he said," the Chicago *News* reported, as "a certain red-faced gentleman hung his head and proceeded to dress himself."[57]

Fortunately for Anson, A.G.'s own chores as club president kept his forays onto the field to a minimum. Spalding handled all arrangements and correspondence concerning the day-to-day operation of the club, among them the scheduling of non-league contests, the hiring of mascots, the making of arrangements for umpires, the printing of tickets, and the advertising of games.[58] As he became more involved in National League affairs and in his sporting-goods business, he turned frequently to Jonathan Brown to handle such transactions. Yet, as late as 1884, A.G. personally contracted groups as diverse as the Calumet Lacrosse Club and Barnum and Bailey's circus to rent his ballpark, the latter paying $2,500 for the privilege.[59]

Renting grounds to lacrosse players or elephants, however, was less important to the club's success than securing talented athletes for Anson to manage. In what he came to describe as "the irrepressible conflict between Labor and Capital," A.G. quickly discarded his identity as a player as he pursued, controlled, and traded ballplayers in line with his own determination of what was best for the club.[60]

Even before he took over Chicago's presidency, Spalding exhibited both the style and the concerns that were to govern his relations with players, whether on the club or the league level. Cap Anson, who as manager benefited from A.G.'s wheeling and dealing, learned firsthand what others came to experience, when he tried to back out of the 1875 arrangement that first brought him to Chicago.

Hulbert's preoccupation with league business left Spalding to deal with Anson's request to remain in Philadelphia, the home of his new bride. Despite two trips to Chicago by Anson and an offer to pay $1,000 for release from his contract, Spalding held firm.[61] Writing to Anson in January 1876, he explained his position and in the process displayed an array of tactics—ranging from personal indignation, appeals to gentlemanly behavior, and veiled threats—that characterized later dealings with players. Spalding began by noting his personal hurt and "surprise" at Anson's change of heart. "I feel this letter of yours more keenly perhaps than anyone else," he wailed, because "of the several conversations you and I have had about this Chicago project...in which...you...expressed...a great desire to join the Western men in such a movement." At stake, according to A.G., was not only Cap's personal integrity and honor but also the future of professional baseball itself. "Now Anson," Spalding intoned, "by...insisting on *your* fulfillment [*sic*] of contract, can it be said that [Chicago] is demanding anything but what is *right* and *just*? You now have a good reputation for honor and integrity and an honorable man can make but one answer to the above question. If players continue to break contracts...they will certainly kill the hen that lays our golden eggs and thus make the majority of the fraternity suffer at the hands of the dishonorable few." Just in case Anson was not moved by appeals to his honor, Spalding closed by threatening "expulsion and...*no* reinstatement" with any National League club if he failed to meet his obligations to Chicago.[62] As was often the case when A.G. played hardball, he won. Anson was in uniform for the White Stockings' first National League game.

Even players less talented than Anson confronted similar experiences if Spalding was interested in them. In 1887, for instance, A.G. closed a complicated deal that sent a Chicago player to Pittsburgh in exchange for George Van Haltren, then pitching in California. Van Haltren, however, had no immediate interest in coming east. Quick to respond, Spalding accused "California baseball people" of complicity in keeping Van Haltren there. Threatening to blacklist the player from the National League, an action that A.G. said would effectively prohibit any league player from playing winter ball in California, he encouraged the recalcitrant to come to his senses, for "if he continues in ignorance...not he alone but some of his friends may be the losers." Two months later Van Haltren found himself in Chicago for the 1887 season.[63]

Indeed, despite occasional gibes that he was too cheap to hire the best talent available—in 1887, for instance, the *Sporting News* noted that A.G.

had purchased an extra-large milk pitcher as a center fielder on the assumption that milk was the world's best "fly catcher"—Chicago's well-earned reputation as baseball's most consistent winner provides the strongest evidence of Spalding's ability to obtain quality athletes. As one reporter put it, "when Spalding wants a man, money is no object."[64]

Spalding knew from his own experience as a player that holding on to good talent was just as important as finding it in the first place. National League club owners found this task of controlling ballplayers made easier after 1882 when the league adopted the reserve clause, which bound a limited number of players to their club of original contract and prohibited them from negotiating with any others unless granted their release. As the chief spokesman of league policy in the 1880s, Spalding consistently upheld the sanctity of the rule and others of similar intent in his quest to make professional baseball a stable and sound business. The agonies of Fred Pfeffer, Chicago's brilliant second base-man, demonstrates that A.G. had no qualms in applying it to serve the interests of his club.

A Chicago regular since 1883, Pfeffer had a good year in 1887, playing in 123 games, batting .278, and driving in eighty-nine runs. Unwilling to accept club terms, Fred coupled his demand for more cash with threats to take his wares elsewhere. Spalding would have none of it. Reminding both Pfeffer and the public of his power under league rules, A.G. told one reporter for the *Sporting News* in November 1887, "[T]his thing of a player growling and grumbling, and saying he is dissatisfied, and will refuse to play with a club is simply bash. . . . There has been much talk concerning Pfeffer's desire to leave the Chicago Club, but he will play here or no where."[65] By early February no progress had been made, so Spalding placed the blame squarely on Pfeffer's greed. "We have done nothing and affairs stand just as they did. . .last fall," he told the *News*. "Pfeffer wants more money than I am willing to pay. . . . He must decide whether to accept or reject." Fred apparently realized that Spalding meant business, for within a week he capitulated to the terms A.G. had originally offered.[66]

The most publicized example of Spalding's ability in, as he put it, "the subtle science of handling men by strategy rather than by force" was his sale of Mike ("King") Kelly to Boston in 1887 for the then unheard-of sum of $10,000.[67] Kelly's value as a player was indisputable. By 1887, however, Spalding was ready to deal. In December 1886, still incensed over having dropped the championship series to St. Louis, A.G. blamed the loss on the long-standing drinking habits of his ballplayers, which had left them "in no condition to play the Browns." Reneging on bonus clauses in the contracts of several players, including Kelly's, that promised extra cash for good behavior and temperance, Spalding justified his actions on the basis of reports from Pinkerton detectives hired to scrutinize their actions. Within a few months, A.G. decided to go a bit further, trading away his pitcher Jim McCormick and his entire outfield, including the infamous King.[68]

As Spalding told it, Kelly was a bad influence on the club's younger players and often undermined Anson's authority as manager. Spalding also believed that Chicago's patrons tired "of seeing the same faces year after year" and demanded "new blood" to maintain their interest. Ever the calculator, A.G. also reasoned that parting with so notorious a character for an extravagant price would attract useful publicity to himself and the club. Promising Kelly that he would help him obtain a $5,000 salary from Boston while selling him for twice the amount, Spalding orchestrated matters while the King played "the poor Baseball slave" act to the limit.[69] In the end, both men got what they wanted. One Chicago poet, published in the *Sporting News*, summed it up this way:

> Of his presence he's bereft us,
> Kelly of the diamond bold.
> He's deserted us for Boston,
> Although Albert laid the cost on,
> Ten Thousand clear in Puritanic gold.
> We surely have the pity of every sister city,
> In our loss of Kelly, the tricky and the bold.
> But we've entered for the pennant,
> And we'll win   depend upon it,
> Notwithstanding Mike has left us in the cold.
> Just hear those bank notes rustle,
> Ten thousand crisp and clean.
> True Boston's got Mike Kelly,
> But Spalding's got the lengthy green.[70]

A.G.'s decision to sell Kelly illustrates a major issue for baseball men involved in establishing their sport as a profitable and legitimate form of middle-class entertainment—the quest for respectability. First involved in the game as a player before its reputation as a gentleman's game became tarnished, eager for recognition as a successful entrepreneur, and armed with a clear sense that baseball initially provided him access to self-confidence and notoriety, Spalding enthusiastically endorsed the National League's pitch to make professional baseball respectable fare for America's middle class. Critical here was the public image of ballplayers. As King Kelly's exploits proved, however, they could not always be trusted to behave appropriately. Whenever the White Stockings stepped out of line, Spalding was there to enforce discipline, morality, and good behavior, whether they liked it or not.

A.G. stated his intentions most clearly in a letter written in 1883 to Henry Graham, a young Milwaukee player who wished to be released from his Chicago contract. Graham's reluctance to remain in the Chicago fold apparently stemmed from the club's reputation as a "loose" team— a reputation no doubt enhanced by the presence of Mike Kelly. Assuring him that the image was unwarranted, Spalding emphasized that the team's "audiences are composed of the best class of people in Chicago, and no theater, church, or place of amusement contains a finer class of people than can be found in our grandstands." To keep them there, Spalding noted, "we allow no gambling or open betting on the grounds." Moreover, "for the purpose of keeping the game pure and respectable, we do not allow the sale of liquor on the grounds," although "it would yield us a large revenue to do so." Concluding his defense of the Chicago organization, Spalding pointed out that the club's policies had the best interests of the players in mind. "It is certainly not the intention or the desire of the organization to entice young men into a business that will demoralize them." Rather, "we are trying to elevate them and with it [*sic*] the game."[71]

The process of "elevation" invariably dovetailed with A.G.'s desire to present a favorable public image of the game and its players and, if necessary, to keep the opposite from occurring. In November 1883, for instance, Spalding received a letter from a Florida man, Charles Jeffreys, who threatened public exposure in Chicago newspapers of the alleged untrustworthy behavior of two White Stockings, Frank Flint and Ed Williamson. According to Jeffreys, both men had failed to repay money he had lent them during a March Florida vacation. Barely questioning the accuracy of Jeffreys's complaint, Spalding fired off an angry letter to Flint warning him that if the debts weren't paid immediately both players might be fired. In a letter to Jeffreys, A.G. urged him not to contact the press and agreed to assist him personally in the collection of his money if he had not been repaid by April 1. Noting how unpleasant it was to have men in his employ "who treat friends that way," Spalding cautioned that "as you be[come] more acquainted with ball players as a class, you will not be quite so liberal in your loans to them."[72]

More pressing than the monetary misadventures of Chicago's nine, however, was the matter of alcohol consumption. It is not surprising that in a society that enjoined temperance as a middle-class virtue as early as the 1840s, Spalding's efforts at respectability often focused on taming the drinking habits of his players. Throughout his years as pres-

ident of the White Stockings, he employed censure, fines, and even
dismissal to enforce his standard of behavior on his players. In May
1884, for instance, during the club's worst season in the 1880s, Spalding
personally fined Frank Flint and George Gore $50 each on the basis of
a report from Anson that "dissipation" had lessened "their skill." Warning the players that a second offense would bring double the fine, A.G.
urged Anson "to be more strict in your discipline" and to enforce an
eleven o'clock curfew, even if it meant hiring detectives "to keep them
in their rooms. I will accept no excuse for *any* infraction of any rule."[73]

By 1887 the rules included a temperance pledge enforced on his players, with bonuses for total abstinence. In a public announcement of club
policy, Spalding proudly noted that "our men this year do not drink,
and they take pride in keeping up the reputation of the club. . . . We shall
no longer endure the criticism of respectable people because of drun-
kenness in the Chicago nine." Cultivating the middle-class audience he
was so concerned with, A.G. went on to say that the aim "of the Chicago
management is to secure the highest standard of baseball efficiency
obtainable. In fighting the encroachment of drink . . . we are simply striv-
ing to give our patrons the full measure of entertainment and satisfaction
to which they are entitled. . . . We don't intend to again insult ladies and
gentlemen in this city or any other by allowing men who are full of beer
and whiskey to go upon the diamond in the uniform of the Chicago
club."[74]

At times Spalding's efforts to curb drink looked like a comical obses-
sion. One writer for the Chicago *News,* in a column headed "The Chicago
Team in Hot Water," fabricated an interview with A.G. prior to the
club's annual spring trip to Hot Springs, Arkansas, in 1886. In it, A.G.
revealed his new scheme to cleanse his team of alcohol. "I am writing
a professor down there," Spalding told the reporter, "and he is making
arrangements to build a vat in which he can boil the whole nine at once."
"You see," A.G. continued, "the beauty of this scheme is that I get a
brand-new nine on April 1. I boil out all the alcoholic microbes which
may have impregnated the system of these men during the winter while
they have been away from me and Anson. Once get the microbes out
and the danger of a relapse is slight." "If this don't work," he concluded,
"I'll send them over to Paris next year and have 'em inoculated by
Pasteur."[75] Responding to similar humorous efforts at his expense on
the same issue a year later, Spalding remained firm in his resolve. "The
papers can poke all the fun they want to at my 'temperance aggregation,'
but I mean business and I'll stick to it in the end. I will not have a man
in the club who will not sign a temperance pledge for the season," he
warned, "and stick to it too."[76]

Consistent with his effort to appeal primarily to a respectable middle class, Spalding also abided by the National League prohibition against Sunday baseball. When Henry Lucas, owner of the league's short-lived St. Louis franchise, complained that this ban made it impossible to compete with Von der Ahe's Browns, who played on Sundays, A.G. offered little sympathy. "Strong sentiment among the better class against Sunday ball-playing," he told Lucas, made it imperative that the league stick with its policy.[77]

For Spalding, such practice was not only morally correct but also good business. Although Sunday games might attract Chicago's large lower-class population, middle-class fans might express their disapproval of violations of the Sabbath by boycotting weekday contests. Only after 1891, when the American Association merged with the National League and each club in the new organization retained the option to play on Sunday, did the White Stockings engage in Sunday contests.[78]

Winning teams and appeals to respectability aided Spalding in his efforts to attract Chicago's middle class to ball games. Exciting popular curiosity, cultivating political connections, negotiating streetcar schedules, and building ballparks were also part of his repertoire, plied in pursuit of his audience.

Quite compatible with his desire for public attention were A.G.'s conscious efforts to make the White Stockings a highly visible product. Newspaper coverage was essential here. The fact that John R. Walsh, one of the club's principal investors, owned the Chicago *Herald* certainly helped. As Spalding told A. G. Mills, president of the National League in 1884, after putting him on the paper's complimentary mailing list, "I am desirous that you get this paper regularly for it is disposed to make a specialty of baseball and is friendly to us."[79]

Controversy and criticism were also effective in generating popular interest. As Spalding put it, "good, liberal roasts in newspapers of wide circulation are much more effective than fulsome praise." To this end, he claimed to provide at least one writer, Harmony White of the Chicago *News*, with "ammunition" about the club by courier weekly. Spalding explained the arrangement "simply as a business proposition." "I could not afford to be neglected in his paper," he noted, "for since he had let up in his attacks our attendance was dropping off."[80]

Whether White understood things so precisely is uncertain. Nevertheless, a column that described A.G.'s transformation from "a well-fed middle-aged gentleman" to a raging, cursing bear stalking his inept players across the field after a loss to the New York Giants in June 1889 touched on his ability to draw attention to Chicago and its leader in ways that Spalding appreciated. So, too, did his September 1887 story, complete with a cartoon that depicted A.G. as George Washington confronting a fallen "pennant" tree and that described "President" Spalding's alleged offer of "a cool $5,000" to his ballplayers if they could win the flag. According to White, "this noble act," offered "after all hope of winning the pennant [was] gone," was fully appreciated by the White Stockings, who proceeded to lose their next three games as an expression of "gratitude."[81]

The object of both ridicule and praise, Spalding often occupied center stage whenever the exploits of his team received the coverage he so desired. During the 1886 season, for instance, A.G. accompanied the club on a road trip to Detroit. Although Anson maintained responsibility for managing his charges, on this occasion Spalding could not resist a personal exhortation that made good copy. Reporting on his pep talk, the *Sporting News* revealed that Spalding "told his lads" that if they lost, he would "trade the whole team off." Fortunately, the boys took "the old man at his word," and won. "Had they lost," the reporter concluded, "it's dollars to cents they would have walked home, as Spalding's blood was up and he meant just what he said."[82]

A.G.'s quest for notoriety in behalf of his business complemented other attempts to cultivate useful connections. Like other baseball owners then and now, he offered free season tickets to a variety of city officials just in case any needs arose in which their office might be helpful to the club. A list of complimentary season passes compiled for the 1880 season included all of the city's aldermen as well as the city clerk, the commissioner of public works, the chief of police, and Carter Harrison, Chicago's mayor. The aldermen had to settle for general admission, while the higher-ups enjoyed box seats.[83] Although the records of the Chicago City Council indicate that the club's concerns did not frequently become the object of public policy, it clearly didn't hurt to cover all your bases.[84]

Spalding was also aware of the need to take care of his paying customers, particularly by making it easy for them to attend games. The league's prohibition of Sunday contests, coupled with a desire to attract an audience of middle-class businessmen willing to leave work in mid-afternoon in order to take in a game on the way home, encouraged Spalding in September 1884 to write to John Lake, superintendent of the West Division Rail Company, about ways to maximize business. For their "mutual interest," he told Lake, it was important to improve service on the Van Buren Street and State Street lines by providing extra cars and better scheduling on game days, so that patrons could get from the business district to the club's Lake Front Park in time to enjoy the afternoon's entertainment.[85]

Accessibility was only part of Spalding's concern. It was also important that the ballpark be an enjoyable and attractive place to spend an afternoon. Throughout his years as club president, A.G. devoted a good deal of time to designing, building, and financing ballparks. His first effort came in 1883 when the White Stockings moved into newly constructed grounds located at Randolph and Michigan avenues, on Lake Michigan, on land leased to them by the city. Accessible from midtown by streetcar, Lake Front Park, built "under the personal supervision of Albert Goodwill Spalding at a cost of $10,000," was billed as the finest baseball facility in the West. "Everything is entirely new," one Chicago paper noted. "The seats, fences, etc. are wholly built of new lumber, rendering them perfectly safe for large crowds," even if the park's 10,000-seat capacity was tested. While the average spectator was guaranteed unobstructed views, free scorecards, and the opportunity to rent seat cushions, A.G. provided a row of eighteen private boxes above the grandstand replete with "cozily draped curtains...and luxurious arm chairs" for "the accommodation of reporters, club officials, and parties of ladies and gentlemen." Spalding also equipped his private box with a telephone line to the clubhouse "to enable him to conduct the details of the game without leaving his seat."[86] Anson must have been thrilled.

Unfortunately for the White Stockings, their stay at Lake Front lasted only two seasons. A federal court injunction issued at the request of the U.S. government forced them out. Both Spalding and the city were parties to the bill of complaint, which argued that the land on which the park stood had been given to the city on terms that prohibited its sale, its use for profit, or the building of permanent structures on it.[87]

Undaunted, Spalding made plans for 1885 by securing a long-term lease on a square block of land on the west side of town, at Congress and Loomis streets. The Congress Street Park, refurbished for $30,000, boasted a twelve-foot-high brick wall around its perimeter, seating for 10,000 people, private roof boxes, facilities for cycling, track, and lawn tennis, and a "neatly-furnished toilet room with a private entrance for ladies." All in all, the New York *Clipper* reported, "President A.G. Spalding...is deserving of commendation for the enterprise he has displayed in its completion."[88] With the exception of the 1891 season, when Spalding scheduled half of his home games at a park on the south side of town, the White Stockings remained at Congress Street until 1893, when the club opened a new park on the west side in an exclusive native-born, white, middle-class neighborhood on land already owned by the club and within a seven-minute streetcar ride from downtown.[89]

On at least one occasion, A.G.'s desire to offer baseball as a legitimate entertainment to Chicago's white middle class prompted an idea clearly ahead of its time. Wiring A. G. Mills on June 30, 1883, Spalding asked that the White Stockings be allowed to play a "picked" nine, chosen from other league clubs, "in the evening under electric lights."[90] Although this "experiment," as he called it, never materialized, Spalding put his lights to use three years later when he rigged his ballpark with a toboggan slide, elevated to 65 feet, where, at night and under Anson's supervision, anyone with a quarter could travel over 700 feet "shooting between the pitcher's box and Anson's stamping ground...over Pfeffer's preserves" and ending up where "Gore is wont to come in for short hits to center-field." More sedate visitors could rent a pair of ice skates for the same fee and use them on a large skating rink laid out next to the slide.[91]

There were, of course, limits to the "experiments" A.G. was willing to undertake. In a society that increasingly restricted opportunities for its black citizens, baseball's establishment generally followed suit. Spalding was no exception. Finalizing arrangements for a July 20, 1884, appearance of the White Stockings against the American Association's Toledo club, Jonathan Brown, writing on Spalding's behalf, reminded C. H. Morton, Toledo's manager, of an earlier letter to Spalding in which Morton had agreed to keep Toledo's "colored man" off the field when Chicago came to town. The "colored man" was Moses Fleetwood ("Fleet") Walker, who long before Jackie Robinson was the first black man to play for a major league professional baseball team. Brown assured Morton that although "the management of the Chicago Ball Club have no personal feeling about the matter...the players do most decisively object and to preserve harmony in the club it is necessary that I have your assurance in writing" about Walker. Brown also warned that if Toledo went back on its word after Chicago arrived, the White Stockings would not take the field and nonetheless claim a $100 guarantee for their troubles.[92]

In 1887 a reporter for *Sporting Life* referred to this episode as "the first time in baseball history that the color line had been drawn," and he credited Cap Anson with doing so. Anson, an open racist, who casually referred to blacks as "chocolate-colored coons" and "no account niggers," no doubt agreed with the club's stand.[93] Regardless of who instigated the exclusion, demands like the one contained in Brown's letter took their toll. By the 1890s Walker and other black ballplayers were on their own teams and in their own leagues, keeping major league professional baseball lily-white until "baseball's great experiment" in 1947.[94]

In 1891, although still the White Stockings' principal stockholder, Spalding "officially" retired as club president. Not everyone, however, was convinced that A.G. no longer influenced club policy. Commenting on Chicago's management in 1896, for instance, a writer for the *Sporting News* noted, "[O]f course everyone knows Al Spalding, the owner of the Chicago Club. Al's mouthpiece is Jim Hart, the nominal president of the club. Al pulls the string and Jim spiels."[95] Cap Anson certainly felt that way in 1897, when, after a series of mediocre finishes, he was asked to resign as manager, despite Spalding's personal assurances that he would be retained. When Anson refused to submit, Spalding fired him and then offered to organize a testimonial dinner to honor Cap's contributions to the club. Bitterly, Anson refused the tribute, leaving his former boss momentarily embarrassed. As A.G. told one reporter, "I found myself something in the position of a politician who had announced his candidate, had the wires all set, convention packed, election assured, but my candidate would not run."[96]

Spalding's choice of metaphor aptly fit his role in Chicago baseball. Like many men of his generation, A.G. viewed his job as a serious profession. Aggressive, enthusiastic, and occasionally ruthless, he manipulated ballplayers, attracted publicity, and appealed for respectability as he shaped his conception of a professional sport that would allow both personal profit and public acceptance by a Victorian middle class. In doing so, Spalding unintentionally revealed a good deal about how others in his society felt about social mores, career, and status. Not surprisingly, A.G.'s critical role in guiding the destinies of the National League provided him equally and at times more striking opportunities to demonstrate such themes.

4

The Brains of the National League

In late January 1891 A. G. Mills, a New York lawyer, business executive, and former president of the National League, declined an offer from league officials to serve as chairman of the national board—a new executive position in the reordered world of professional baseball created in the aftermath of the Brotherhood War. Suggesting that the job called less for a lawyer than for "a representative baseball layman," Mills instead recommended his friend A.G. Spalding for the job. As Mills told it, here was "a man of known and approved executive capacity; a man of practical experience in and constant contact with the affairs of baseball; conversant with its legislation, its rules, and management. . . a man whose successful management of his own business. . . constitutes the highest guarantee of his fitness to advance the business interests of others." Just as important, Mills continued, "Spalding's lifetime from early boyhood has been devoted to baseball. His every relation to it has been characterized by conspicuous ability, skill, manliness, and honorable conduct." No man now alive, he concluded, has done more to promote baseball, a sport "justly recognized as the national game."[1]

Although flattered by the endorsement, Spalding refused this informal nomination and announced his retirement from league affairs, only three months before his resignation as president of the White Stockings. Eulogizing his own contributions to baseball, he praised the National League as that "strong, fearless, and well-governed central organization . . . essential to the success of professional baseball. I now retire with the consciousness that I have always tried to do that which I believed to be for the best interests, advancement, and elevation of professional baseball. In my efforts in this direction, my thoughts have been first, the National Game, then the National League, then my club, and lastly my personal interests."[2]

A.G.'s assessment, however self-serving, and Mills's glowing tribute accurately define Spalding's critical and continual involvement in the business of the National League. Always, it remained for him essential to baseball's success as the "National Game," as a business enterprise, and as a respectable entertainment for America's urban middle class.

Shaping and enforcing league policy, A.G. confronted potential competitors, rebellious ballplayers, and a demanding public in ways comparable to those used by other entrepreneurs in an industrializing, capitalist society. His efforts, like theirs, met with mixed results as he and other baseball men struggled to consolidate competition, stabilize markets, and control workers. Even those who sometimes disagreed with his tactics and design, however, acknowledged him as "the axle around which the National League . . . revolved," the man most responsible for making it "the foremost professional sporting association in the known world"—in short, "the brains of the National League."[3]

Even before Spalding became involved in the league in a manner that earned him his sobriquet, the organization's first leaders created and enforced policies compatible with their desire to stabilize professional baseball and maximize opportunities for profit. As an interested observer A.G. learned from these experiences. Much like his years as Chicago's president, they helped shape his approach to the game. He watched in awe, for instance, when William Hulbert in 1876 expelled the Philadelphia Athletics and the New York Mutuals from the league for failing to complete scheduled road trips to western cities at the close of the season. In 1877 he stood by when his mentor banned four Louisville players for life for fixing and betting on league games.[4] That same year Spalding supported Hulbert's "League Alliance," a plan by which nonleague clubs, for a $10 fee, could be assured that National League clubs would not go after their players.[5] And in 1879 A.G. witnessed the adoption of the league's first reserve rule, introduced by Boston's Arthur Soden, as a means of guaranteeing a ball club's control over its players.[6]

After Hulbert's death, in 1882, however, Spalding emerged from the background to become the key figure in the National League's efforts to regulate and control professional baseball in its best interests. Although he was hardly an original thinker or always the architect of league policy, A.G.'s flamboyant personality, insatiable ego, and knowledge of baseball marked him as the chief promoter, spokesman, and enforcer of the league's position on all matters regarding the professional game.

Spalding's election as Chicago's president coincided with the first of a series of challenges to the National League's announced hegemony over major league baseball. The league's adoption of the reserve rule and its constitution appeared to dictate where, how, and by whom the game could be played, but there was no law that prevented other enterprising capitalists from mounting competing teams and organizations. Just such a confrontation occurred in 1882 when a group of risk-taking entrepreneurs led by O. P. Caylor of Cincinnati and Chris Von der Ahe of St. Louis announced the formation of a six-team circuit known as the American Association with an approach that directly challenged the National League's view of the sport and its desire to control competition for markets and players. Although not party to the resolution of this conflict, A.G. became its most vigorous supporter and established himself as the man to turn to whenever league interests were at stake.

Labeled by its detractors as the "beer and whiskey league," in part because four of its club owners owned breweries, American Association clubs, unlike those in the National League, allowed alcoholic beverages to be sold in their parks, permitted Sunday baseball, and charged an admission fee of twenty-five cents, half the going rate at league contests. While association advocates defended these measures as a means of extending the benefits of spectatorship to the "poor laboring man," league officials, led by Hulbert, criticized them as detrimental to both the commercial and the social ends of professional baseball.[7] Writing in November 1881 to H. D. McKnight, the association's president, Hulbert warned that such "departure[s]" from National League policy "would cause havoc with the game. You cannot afford to bid for the patronage of the degraded, if you are to be successful you must secure recognition by the respectable." In another letter to McKnight, Hulbert reminded him that "the sole purpose of the League, outside of the business aspect, is to make it worthy of the patronage, support, and respect of the best class of people."[8] Compounding Hulbert's fears that the association's practices would dilute league standards, thereby making all versions of the game unattractive to a paying public, was McKnight's open invitation to league ballplayers to jump their contracts and join association clubs.[9]

Hulbert's concerns matched those of late-nineteenth-century entrepreneurs in other industries as diverse as meat-packing and railroads who worried that unregulated competition, particularly from competitors that did not conform to the standards of the largest firms in the industry, would destroy both the quality of the product and the stability of the marketplace. Responses to such challenges, no matter what the enterprise was, ranged from conciliation to destruction of rivals.[10] In the instance of the American Association, the National League opted for conciliation.

Initiated by Hulbert and completed in time for the 1883 season by A. G. Mills, who succeeded him as league president, the National Agreement bound the association and the league in a mutual pact designed to give both organizations protection of their labor force and their markets. By it, both organizations designated themselves as major leagues and also acknowledged the existence of the Northwestern League as a minor league and as a party to the accord. All three leagues adopted the reserve rule, guaranteeing the right of all clubs to protect as many as fourteen players, each with minimum salaries of $1,000. They also agreed to blacklist any players who attempted to work outside the system. Although no uniform rules regarding alcohol or Sunday baseball were made part of the agreement, a provision that gave each club "exclusive control of its own territory" prohibited the intrusion of competing franchises. The establishment of a board of arbitration, composed of three National League and three American Association representatives with power to create officers and committees necessary to enforce and modify the agreement, completed the compromise.[11]

Although Spalding originally opposed conciliation with the American Association, he soon recognized that the National Agreement not only facilitated the irksome task of finding and hanging on to quality ballplayers but also encouraged a healthy competition that proved profitable for clubs in both organizations.[12] In fact, down through 1891, by his work on committees and occasionally as a member of the board of arbitration for the National League, he emerged as the agreement's chief spokesman and most creative enforcer.

Working within its outlines, A.G., like organizers of other large-scale business enterprises, emphasized the rationalization of procedures and uniformity as important factors in maximizing opportunities for financial success. He arranged league and association schedules to minimize conflict, encouraged the adoption of uniform playing rules, equipment, and ticket prices, and promoted the idea that all visiting teams receive the same percentage of the gate regardless of where they played.[13]

Influenced by Hulbert's vigorous purge of Louisville players in 1877 and by his own efforts in Chicago to present his athletes as sober, respectable citizens, Spalding also urged all clubs bound to the National Agreement to impose similar standards on their charges. His 1882 baseball guide, for example, praised the use of the blacklist for players who "by gross acts of intemperance or insubordination...merited suspension. A professional ballplayer...who weakens his play by indulgence in liquor is a fool unfit for a position on any first class team. Such a man sober, would command...$1200 a year...with his drunken ways he is not worth $600; indeed ten dollars a week would be good pay for such a fellow." One year later A.G. continued his temperance campaign in somewhat different fashion when he successfully encouraged league officials to shut down a liquor stand run by the New York Giants at the Polo Grounds.[14]

In the spirit of the National Agreement, Spalding offered firm support for the reserve rule and its role in making professional baseball an attractive economic venture—beneficial, in his mind, to capitalist and ballplayer alike. The pages of his baseball guides, his public statements in the press, and his personal correspondence offer impressive testimony of his commitment to it. In the 1884 guide, for instance, A.G.'s editor and spokesman Henry Chadwick observed that without the reserve rule "the exorbitant demands" of players would "eventually bankrupt the strongest company in the professional arena." Noting that most ballplayers would be lucky to earn $10 a week while putting in fifteen-hour days as a "common day laborer," he questioned their demand for salaries as high as $2,000 for "six months services as a ballplayer in which...work is comparatively a pleasant recreation, requiring two or three hours of easy work each day." The reserve rule prevented such excessive demands, assured a player "a comfortable position in the service of a reliable company," and at the same time placed "a barrier to the reckless competition for the services of men who, outside of the ballfield, could not earn a tenth part of the sum they demand for baseball services."[15] In more frank and private appraisals, which clearly emphasized the reserve rule as management's advantage, A.G. called for tight enforcement, harsh penalties for players and clubs that tried to circumvent it, and the need for uniform player contracts to minimize potential problems.[16]

Spalding gave the reserve rule more than mere verbal support. Upset by criticism that his "stinginess" denied Chicago the services of able substitutes during their unsuccessful drive to capture the 1883 pennant, A.G. responded by organizing a rough equivalent of his own farm team for the 1884 season.[17] Known as the Chicago Reserves, its players were under contract to A.G. for the year and were subject to all of the provisions of the National Agreement, including the reserve rule.

Hopeful that the "Reserves" would provide a ready source of talent, Spalding and the club's manager, E. D. Clarke, attempted to arrange a schedule of games for them with minor league and amateur clubs in order to keep the players fit and ready for the White Stockings. But, as A.G. wrote to Mills in March 1884, other National Agreement clubs picked up on the idea and began organizing their own reserve clubs, making "this Reserve scheme that I started last fall. . .into a bigger thing than any of us anticipated." Seeking to make the most of it, Spalding went on to propose a "Reserve Championship" so that "teams will have something to play for."[18]

A.G.'s ambitious plan by which league and association clubs could assure themselves of ballplayers without expensive competition with each other did not survive the summer. In May, Spalding recorded that reserve games in Chicago, conveniently booked when the White Stockings were on the road, averaged only 500 spectators. On June 3 he wired Clarke that the St. Louis reserves had dissolved and that the whole venture was up in the air. Three weeks later, Spalding gave up on the scheme as a "financial loss" and, like the efficient capitalist he was, instructed Clarke to disband the team and cut losses by selling the contracts of all but a few players to other clubs.[19]

Although Spalding found compromise possible with the American Association, he did not shy from confrontation in dealing with interlopers that threatened the National League's control of professional baseball. The Union Association, organized in 1884, provided him with just the opportunity to display his impressive combative skills.

Challenging the National Agreement's control of players and markets, the Union Association placed six of its teams in cities where either American Association or National League clubs competed, and announced its intention to raid them for players. Led by Henry Lucas, a St. Louis railroad millionaire, Union Association clubs, true to their pledge, did battle with the established leagues throughout the 1884 season. Although unstable finances and uneven competition best explain its collapse, Spalding recognized his own efforts in Chicago and elsewhere as essential to the Union Association's defeat.

From the outset, A.G. labeled the new league's investors as irresponsible "adventurers," unlike the men of "considerable nerve and capital" of the National League who had turned baseball into a profitable business. Convinced that most cities could not support two professional ball clubs, he acknowledged that "the fittest only will survive."[20] Challenged on his own turf, he had no doubts about who the fittest were.

Key to the Chicago Unions' chances were its efforts to lure the White Stockings' ace pitcher, Larry Corcoran, into their fold. Larry counted on his pitching credentials in his 1884 contract negotiations with Spalding, and he was not against using the Unions' offer as additional leverage. Corcoran correctly assumed that neither the White Stockings nor the

National League would like to lose one of their stars to the new league. He was wrong, though, in his view of how A.G. would deal with the matter.

Hopeful that public controversy would work to his advantage, Corcoran started, as he told it in the pages of the New York *Clipper*, by asking Spalding for a $4,000 contract, "not because I thought I would get it but in hopes of inducing the management to give me my release." Larry was right on one count. A.G. denied the terms as well as a subsequent request for $2,500 and offered instead a contract for $2,100. Again in the press, on December 15, 1883, Corcoran announced that he had returned the contract unopened, signed with the Unions, and left it to "the public to judge of [his] action."[21]

Apparently, however, Corcoran forgot to tell his public that on December 7, in a telegram to Spalding, he requested A.G. to forward a contract along with a $400 advance. In letters to the league office, Spalding inquired whether Corcoran's telegram, "in the eyes of the League," was as valid as a written and signed contract.[22] When A. G. Mills, who coordinated the National League's assault on the Union Association, wired back in the affirmative, Spalding telegraphed Corcoran and warned him that he had already signed to play with the White Stockings in 1884. "If it is not performed," A.G. threatened, "you will be expelled. Mills will show you the new rules if you want to see them."[23]

Spalding's stern handling of a ballplayer's demands and the ease with which he claimed the right to act in behalf of the league were hardly unusual. Still, if Corcoran decided to risk blacklisting in the hope that the Union Association might succeed, A.G.'s efforts would be in vain. Having given his pitcher an ultimatum to sign the actual contract by January 6, 1884, he wired Cap Anson, who was on vacation in Philadelphia, and instructed him to hand deliver it to Corcoran at his home in Newark, New Jersey.[24] When Anson wired his boss that Corcoran had signed only two days before the deadline, A.G. could barely contain himself. Dashing off a letter to Mills he exclaimed, "Whoop-la! Corcoran has signed and the back of the Union Association is broken....I look upon this as a great blow to [it]...and a big victory for the League." With somewhat less exuberance, Mills, who had lent Corcoran $600 from league coffers to buy back his contract from the Chicago Unions, concurred. "Corcoran's defection," he noted, "will aid in breaking up the Union gang," but he added that there would be "hard work ahead" before it was "safely buried."[25]

Aside from doing battle in Chicago, Spalding talked strategy with Mills throughout the 1884 season in an effort to defeat the Union Association. A.G. urged Mills to obtain better newspaper coverage when the outcome was uncertain. He also suggested that the Reserve League might "add a few outside clubs and in this way keep them from affiliating with the Union Association." In turn, Mills asked Spalding's help in keeping certain players from jumping leagues. He even suggested the possibility that A.G. back a second club in Chicago, affiliated with the Northwestern League, to meet the Union Association challenge.[26] By September, when it was clear that hegemony had been maintained, Spalding gleefully expressed a sense of personal triumph in announcing that "the Chicago Unions are a busted community...a complete clean-out."[27]

The defeat of the Union Association strengthened American Association and National League control over professional baseball, but it hardly guaranteed them financial stability or success. Of the original eight franchises in the National League, for instance, only Chicago and Boston still fielded teams in 1890. Between 1877 and 1890, twenty-three different cities held franchises in a circuit that never contained more than eight clubs in any one year. Five of the six original American Association clubs were still around for the 1889 season, but ten other cities between 1882 and 1890 also started teams, with only those in New York and Brooklyn lasting more than two seasons. Although the Chicago *Tribune* correctly noted that the two major leagues were "endeavoring to perfect a baseball trust," their success, like that of efforts in other industries, was somewhat halting.[28]

Not that the enterprise lacked creative effort. Throughout the 1880s Spalding and other baseball magnates manipulated the National Agreement and proposed new schemes to enhance the possibilities for profit. One plan that surfaced several times involved dissolving the weakest franchises in both the league and the association and merging the remaining teams into one league. In response to continual stories in the press about his role as engineer of this proposal, A.G. told a reporter for *Sporting Life* in June 1887 that, although he "was not pushing any such idea," and had never discussed with other owners the prospects "of standing at the head of a monopolistic organization of any kind," it was nevertheless "in the natural order of things that the two leading organizations should eventually consolidate." What he forgot to add was that seven months earlier he had proposed just such a plan to A. G. Mills, along with the suggestion that Mills become head of the new league.[29]

Stories about Spalding's "pet scheme" for "one great stock company" and accusations that he was "a one-league monopolist" persisted throughout the summer. Pleased with the publicity, A.G. nevertheless minimized talk of consolidation, on the grounds that the National League was so much stronger than the American Association that it was not in its best interests to merge. As he told one reporter in July, the league was "without question the greatest athletic and amusement organization of its kind in the world today" and was in no danger of collapse. As to rumors that the association's St. Louis club might join the league, Spalding characterized them as "bull." "To the devil with such talk," he exclaimed; "it is cut absolutely from whole cloth."[30]

After the bloodbath of the Brotherhood War in 1890, one in which major league players organized their own league in an unsuccessful battle that saw Spalding as the chief architect of their defeat, A.G. welcomed the merger of association and league clubs into a new National League. For the moment, however, other proposals to shore up the finances of National Agreement clubs and their control over players and markets were more intriguing.

At the close of the 1887 season, for instance, in a letter to Charlie Byrne, owner of the Brooklyn club and secretary of the board of arbitration, Spalding rehearsed a more expansive version of Hulbert's league alliance as a way of generating new revenue. In the form adopted by the board, it permitted clubs in minor league associations to reserve a specified number of players each season, thus preventing major league clubs from luring them away. Each minor league accepting this plan would pay anywhere from $1,500 to $2,000 per season, depending on its size, for this privilege; the money was to be divided equally between the National League and the American Association.[31]

Even more elaborate were A.G.'s ideas about baseball governance, which he set out two years later and which aimed at enlarging the control already possessed by the league and the association under the National Agreement. Writing to Nick Young, then league president, in July 1889, he suggested an organizational structure headed by the two major leagues and followed by a four-tiered ranking of all other professional baseball leagues. Leagues would be classified in terms of the salaries they paid. Teams in class A leagues, for instance, directly below the National League and the American Association, could not pay monthly individual salaries that exceeded $200 or monthly aggregate salaries of more than $2,000. Class D teams were limited to monthly figures of $60 and $600, respectively. Although clubs and leagues in each category were assured protection by the reserve rule within their class, the plan provided that any player could move from a club in a lower division to a club in a higher one by giving one week's notice and by paying $250.[32]

A.G.'s plan for baseball's future failed to meet approval. Indeed, the advantages it offered to league and association clubs were not lost on either minor league officials or individual ballplayers who vehemently opposed Spalding's "baseball trust" as a "scheme for monopoly of the business...to serve [a] few capitalists' pecuniary interests."[33] More bluntly, as one player told a New York *Times* reporter, "this man Spalding is for himself all the time and...cares little or nothing for players."[34]

By the close of the 1889 season, similar attitudes prevailed among major league players, not only toward Spalding but toward all baseball magnates. Increasingly vocal about their opposition to the reserve clause, they organized themselves in 1885 into the National Brotherhood of Professional Baseball Players. Although the Brotherhood made no progress in repealing the reserve rule—described by its leader, John Montgomery Ward, as a "fugitive slave law"—it took pride in its growing membership and its formal recognition, in 1887, by baseball management. After talking to Brotherhood leaders at the National League's winter meetings that year, A.G. not only endorsed the organization but even told one reporter that if he were eligible, he might join the Brotherhood himself.[35]

The announcement of Spalding's abortive classification scheme in 1889 clearly limited his prospects for membership. Even more damaging, however, to any claims by members of management that they had the best interests of their players at heart, was an amendment to the National Agreement approved in November 1888 that placed all major league players into five categories on the basis of their "habits, earnestness, and special qualifications," with maximum salary for each one ranging from $2,500 to $1,500.[36] Stalemated throughout the 1889 season by intransigent club owners who refused to discuss either the reserve clause or these salary ceilings, the Brotherhood prepared for more dramatic action—the formation of its own Players League for the 1890 season, in direct confrontation with National League and American Association clubs and with Albert Goodwill Spalding.

While hardly as significant as any number of conflicts between labor and capital that characterized late-nineteenth-century America, the Brotherhood War dramatized various concerns that defined the emergence of an industrial society. To be sure, the struggle between competing groups of capitalists for control of baseball's marketplace, the demands of ballplayers and the risks they undertook to achieve them, and the ultimate triumph of the better-organized and better-financed side hardly matched the stakes or costs of workers or entrepreneurs in other industries. When major league ballplayers bolted their clubs to form their own league, however, they set the stage for events that announced, if less grandiosely, these significant themes. Most important, they also provided Spalding an unmatched opportunity to air his views about the development of professional baseball and to show the energy, determination, and skill he utilized to impress them on others.

Early signs of the impending struggle came in late summer 1889 when stories about the Brotherhood's intentions to mount their own league first appeared in the press. On September 22 the Chicago *Tribune* even detailed a proposed structure for the new league and hinted that A. G. Mills, the National League's second president, might become its first head.[37]

Spalding's response, the opening salvos in what he came to call "the battle royal for the control of professional baseball," were full of the confidence and bravado that were his trademarks. Scoffing at rumors about the Players League, he jokingly told one reporter that he had no plans to "retire...on account of the great plot." To another scribe he retorted, "[L]et 'em come if they think baseball is a bonanza, but before they start I would advise them to get a capital of $500,000. It will take that and more before any organization can successfully compete with the League." As late as November 2, A.G. publicly doubted that the "rumored revolt" would take place at all. "The players of the Chicago club have been paid off in full for last season," he noted, and "all expressed themselves as well-satisfied."[38]

Privately, however, Spalding voiced his concern. In August and September he wrote letters to A. G. Mills, urging him not to accept the presidency of any league the players might form and to side with the National League and American Association against any "visionary scheme" they might propose. On no authority but his own, he flattered Mills as "the natural leader of American Athletics" and offered him the nonexistent post of chief arbitrator in all disputes regarding professional baseball. Presumably, Spalding intended to create this position, from which, as he put it, "we can carry through any kind of scheme that seemed to us for the best interests not only of the National League but of the game at large."[39]

A.G. was not lax, either, when it came to protecting the interests of his own club. In early September, according to the Chicago *Inter-Ocean*, he had already sent an agent to visit ballplayers tied to the Western Association, in order to line them up for Chicago if his regulars left for the Players League. As one writer for the *Sporting News* took delight in noting, rumors about the Brotherhood had given Spalding "conniption fits," and he now "swears by the great hokey pokey that he will not only break up the conspiracy but land some of the conspirators in jail. Spalding makes one tired. Of all the boobies in the base ball world he is the biggest. Like the pig under the fence he squeals before he is hurt."[40]

A.G. did more than squeal, once rumors became reality. On November 4, 1889, John Ward issued the Brotherhood's manifesto, which declared formally its members' intentions to abandon their National League and American Association clubs and form their own Players League. In part, the players justified the move because club owners were "a combination among themselves, stronger than the strongest trust," who had bought, sold, and exchanged players "as though they were sheep instead of American citizens."[41] More to their liking were the novice baseball entrepreneurs who backed the eight teams that composed the new league— men like Edwin McAlpin, who made his money in New York City real estate, and John Addison, a Chicago contractor. Although these men certainly hoped to turn a profit by challenging those capitalists already in control of the professional game, they did agree to suspend the reserve rule, to offer three-year contracts at salaries equal to 1888 figures, and to divide club profits between themselves and their players.[42] No wonder that of the fifty-nine players who made up the rosters of the top four teams in the Players League, fifty-three had jumped contracts from major league clubs. Even the White Stockings' black mascot, Clarence Duval, signed on with the Chicago Players.[43]

Committed to the dominance of the National League that he had helped create, experienced in dealing with ballplayers, and a diligent and inventive worker in behalf of the National Agreement, Spalding was the obvious choice of club owners to crush the rebellion of the dissatisfied ballplayers. A.G. was caught up in the mood of an industrializing America that had recently experienced the bloody Haymarket riot, and he reflected the feelings of many middle-class Americans who associated labor unrest with fears of violence and revolution, when he mixed metaphors and tactics in combating the "hotheaded anarchists" who were out to overthrow "the established business of baseball."[44]

In a war in which, as Spalding recalled, the weapons were "printer's ink and bluff" instead of "powder and shell," the National League responded to announcements of the Players League with its own broadside.[45] After soliciting the advice of A. G. Mills, the league's three-member "war committee," chaired by Spalding, issued a statement that chastised the Brotherhood for questioning the "untarnished" record of the National League, the organization responsible for making professional baseball a dignified, honest business that guaranteed ballplayers "the dignity of profession and...[a] munificent salary." With due praise for the league's "stringent rules," "iron-clad contracts," and the reserve clause for making all this possible, it blamed the current unrest on the "efforts of certain overpaid players" out "for their own aggrandizement." If they were not stopped, the message concluded, "dishonor and disintegration" would befall "the most glorious and honorable sport on the green earth."[46]

By May, having failed in attempts to have courts issue injunctions barring league and association players from jumping to the Players League, Spalding prepared to meet the competition head on. "We will spend all the money that is necessary to win this fight," he told a reporter for the Chicago *Herald*. "From this point out it will simply be a case of dog eat dog, and the dog with the bull dog tendencies will live the longest."[47] Through the pages of the Chicago *Evening Post*, A.G. forecast that "if the players league lasts there will be 25 cent baseball, Sunday games, beer will flow in the grandstands, and the industry will be ruined by utter destruction." The National League, he promised, "will hold on until it is dashed to pieces against the rocks of rebellion and demoralization."[48]

Having "donned the war paint," as one observer noted, Spalding entered the battle with relish.[49] And a battle there was. With five franchises in National League cities and two in American Association towns, each manned with known talent from the major leagues, the Players League outdrew its rivals in the early months of the 1890 season. In mid-May the Chicago *Tribune* reported that sixty-six Brotherhood games had attracted 183,560 patrons, while seventy-one National League contests had drawn only 117,050. In Spalding's own backyard, the average attendance at Chicago Players' games stood at 1,654, compared with 828 for the White Stockings'.[50]

To counter these ominous signs, A.G. juggled club schedules, reported inflated attendance figures for National League games, and encouraged club owners to give away tickets in order to attract customers.[51] At home, where he instituted promotions such as "Professional's Day," an occasion when all actors gained free admittance to a White Stockings' game, George Munson, the business manager of the Chicago Players, complained that in Chicago free passes are "more plentiful than water."[52]

At the time, Spalding denied all charges of manipulation. In later years, however, he admitted that neither he nor the Players League "ever furnished to the press one solitary truthful statement" in their "fight to the death." Even he, however, expressed shock at the degree to which the truth was sometimes stretched in the service of the National League. As he recalled it, Jonathan Brown, his club secretary, once told a reporter that the number of spectators at one lightly attended Chicago game was twenty-four eighteen. When the newspaper man was out of earshot, Spalding asked Brown how, in good conscience, he could make such a statement. According to Spalding, Brown replied, "Why don't you see. There were twenty-four on one side of the grounds and eighteen on the other. If he reports twenty-four hundred and eighteen, that's a matter for *his* conscience, not mine."[53]

Whether or not the falsifying of figures reached such heights, Spalding and his compatriots offered more than numbers in pressing their case. Always available for an interview, A.G. never tired of accusing the Brotherhood's backers as "speculators from Wall Street" in appealing for popular support for the "conservative businessmen" who made up the National League. Proud of his own accomplishments as a business-man in baseball, Spalding ridiculed the inexperience of his counterparts in the Players League. They had embarked, he told a reporter for the Chicago *Evening Post*, on "a business of which they knew not the A.B.C. Observe what they do. They take all the risks; they make all the original investments; they advance all the money; they pay their employees fabulously high salaries and in addition to all that they divide with them the profits of the business half and half....A shrewd businessman would laugh in their faces at their temerity."[54]

Criticism of rash capitalists who, in their rush to make a dollar, jeop-ardized the dignity of the professional game did not rule out denunci-ation of the players who joined the new league. Labor organizations of any kind increasingly engendered suspicion among middle-class, urban populations in a society wracked by violent worker protest, at times tinged with revolutionary rhetoric. Not surprisingly, when National League defenders sought popular support by castigating the Brother-hood, they had no qualms about calling it subversive and undemocratic. With Spalding's blessing, for instance, Henry Chadwick devoted a long section in A.G.'s 1890 baseball guide to a history of the "National Game" in which he attacked the Brotherhood's leaders as conspirators who hatched their plans in "secret council" and announced them on Guy Fawkes Day—"the anniversary of the great English conspiracy." Only by employing "special pleadings, false statements, and a system of ter-rorism peculiar to revolutionary movements" were they able to get other National League ballplayers to abandon their true homes for the rene-gade Players League. Chadwick went on to show by "official statistics" that despite the Brotherhood's charges, National League owners had provided ever-increasing salaries to their players, thanks to "the justness and fairness of the much abused, grossly misrepresented, but beneficial Reserve Rule." Such information he hoped, "will open the eyes of the baseball world to the fallacies if not false statements of the Brotherhood combine."[55]

Unfortunately for the National League, however, the "baseball world," or at least those who paid admission to go to ball games, continued to favor the Players League.[56] Particularly hard hit by the Brotherhood's challenge were the New York Giants and the Boston Red Stockings, clubs in direct competition with two of the strongest Brotherhood teams, the latter led by Mike ("King") Kelly. Ever the leader in the fight against the insurgents, Spalding took the initiative in both cities to help the National League clubs.

New York posed the more serious problem. By July the club was virtually bankrupt. Spalding and other league club owners recognized that if the Giants collapsed, the Players League would claim an important victory in its struggle for legitimacy. Although A.G. and the Giants' owner, John B. Day, denied all rumors about such concerns, in early July, Spalding in New York ostensibly on sporting-goods business, met with the club owners of Boston, Indianapolis, and Philadelphia to resolve the problem. In the end, each bought a $20,000 interest in the Giants. Five years after the fact, Spalding revealed his participation in this venture. Always confident about the importance of his actions, A.G. admitted that although the bailout had been "pretty costly," it had "saved the National League and by saving it, the future of professional baseball in this country."[57]

Less successful were Spalding's efforts to lure King Kelly back to the Boston Red Stockings. Authorized by National League owners to offer the King whatever it took, A.G. set out to negotiate a deal. But even an advance of $10,000 and a guaranteed three-year contract with his old club could not budge the former Chicago star. "Aw, I want the ten thousand bad enough," Spalding recalled him as saying, "but I've thought the matter all over, and I can't go back on the boys. And neither would you." So impressed was A.G. with Kelly's "loyalty" and "sentiment" that he congratulated him on his decision and also lent him $500.[58]

Although Kelly remained loyal to the cause, the same could not be said for the financial supporters of the Players League. Unaccustomed to the cost and work involved in running a ball club and dismayed by fickle fans who stayed home in September, when the Brotherhood pennant race became a runaway for Boston, they were ready to talk compromise even if their players were not. Different versions of the intrigues between Players' League and major league club owners exist, but they all agree on two points—that the end result was the demise of the Brotherhood and that the chief undertaker was A.G. Spalding.

Fresh from a business trip to England, Spalding, now chief of the National League's conference committee, agreed to meet club owners from the Players League and the American Association in early October to talk things over. Barring players from the meetings because "they have nothing at stake," Spalding hoped that the sessions would allow him to assess how well the National League had fared in its struggle.[59] In that spirit, he suggested that all parties reveal their financial cards as a prelude to any discussions about how to end the conflict. Much to his surprise, according to most accounts, Brotherhood owners bubbled over with details of their financial woes and begged for mercy. Like any good capitalist, Spalding kept his mouth shut, took command of the situation, and began the process that led eventually to the collapse of the Players League.[60]

Fifteen years later, Spalding characteristically recollected things a little differently. Talking about the same October meetings, he noted that although he "was not President of the National League...as chairman of its 'War Committee,'" [he] was fully authorized to treat with those who came asking for terms." In that spirit he received "a delegation from the management of the Players League, bearing a flag of truce." Remembering nothing about original intentions to share financial information, A.G. instead recalled another tactic in what had all along been part of the two games the National League had been playing with the Brotherhood—"baseball and bluff." At this stage, he noted, "I put up the strongest play at the latter game I had ever presented. I informed the bearers of the truce that 'unconditional surrender' was the only possible solution.... To my surprise the terms were greedily accepted."[61]

It took a bit longer than Spalding remembered, but by late December all Brotherhood clubs had been bought up and dissolved by major league owners, who "allowed" the rebel players to return to their original teams. A.G. himself spent a good portion of November traveling from city to city helping to close the deals.[62] Although the Chicago *Herald* reported that Spalding's White Stockings lost $65,000 during the 1890 season, he still had enough cash left to buy out the Chicago Brotherhood team for some $19,000, with an additional $6,000 added on to cover players' contracts. Magnanimous to the end, A.G. even threw in complimentary tickets to the White Stockings' 1891 season for all stockholders in the Brotherhood club.[63] The Chicago *Times*'s comment that they meekly "surrendered...to the force of arms and brains which A.G. Spalding opposed them" only reinforced the opinion of the Philadelphia *Ledger* that the "baseball troubles" had been ended because of his "shrewdness and untiring energy."[64] Spalding concurred. "The Players League," he told one Chicago *Herald* reporter ("with all the unction of a sophomore delivering a valedictory"), "is deader than the proverbial door-nail. . . .When the spring comes and the grass is green upon the last resting place of anarchy, the national agreement will rise again in all its weight and restore to America in all its purity its national pastime— the great game of base ball."[65]

Naturally, A.G. presided over the resurrection. Traveling from one National League and American Association city to another, as the Chicago *Tribune* put it, with "the key to the baseball situation in his left pocket," Spalding, "the messiah of baseball," shaped a new National Agreement that bound together the two major leagues and the Western Association in ways that guaranteed even greater and more centralized authority for baseball management.[66] Included in it was the continuation of the reserve rule and the establishment of a national board composed of one member from each of the three leagues. Responsible for electing its own chairman, who would handle day-to-day business, the board also had broad powers to approve all player and umpire contracts and to serve as a court of last resort in any dispute involving leagues, players, or individual clubs.[67]

Spalding's efforts reaffirmed his continual desire to have monopolistic control of professional baseball rest in the hands of competent businessmen with full power and authority to regulate its every aspect, including the potential competition of other capitalists and the careers of its players. Although hardly perfected in his lifetime, his approach to the game set the tone for the development of professional sport in the twentieth century.

The Brotherhood War, however, had satisfied A.G.'s appetite for a steady role in that process. Although Chicago newspapers salivated at the prospects of their city's becoming the "Baseball news center of the World," and although A. G. Mills insisted that he take the job, Spalding, citing the press of personal business, turned down the offer to become chairman of the national board, "preferring," as the Chicago *Herald* reported, "his old Dunlap derby to the glittering crown of the baseball King."[68] Privately, he explained to Mills that he had "become satiated with this baseball business and nothing would please me better than to be out of it entirely. It is a constant source of bother, annoyance, and perplexity." "I feel like the old time politician," Spalding moaned, "who has become weary of political strife and glory and desires to retire to private life."[69]

A.G. did return to "private life"—as private as possible for a man who enjoyed public attention, who owned the largest sporting-goods house in the world, and who was intent on promoting popular acceptance of sport as a legitimate leisure-time activity for middle-class

Americans.[70] Indeed, some wondered whether his formal retirement from league councils meant any more than his resignation as president of the White Stockings. As one correspondent for *Sporting Life* observed in 1895, in regard to false rumors that Spalding sought election to the national board, "So A.G. Spalding is coming back into baseball, eh? Pray, when did he ever leave it? You may not have observed him but he was there all the time."[71]

A.G. was certainly there throughout the 1890s when it came to offering his views about the professional game and its proper conduct. He never failed to extol the necessity of "a strong central organization...to perpetuate baseball...keep it clean" and counter "those who conspire against it."[72] Nor did he withhold advice on how to cultivate the loyal fans who were essential both to the spirit of the game and to the ability to turn a profit. In 1894, for instance, responding to stories that several major league clubs were out to sign the newly crowned world heavyweight boxing champion, James ("Gentleman Jim") Corbett, he deplored this novel way of attracting patrons. "Baseball cranks are peculiar," A.G. emphasized. Although they might tolerate Corbett's ineptitude for a game or two, once his errors cost ball games, they would quickly protest. Drawing a distinction between baseball and "theatrical enterprises," Spalding went on to indicate that the "spectacular" had no place on the diamond. What counted was winning. "The people," he claimed, "do not care whether the play is perfect or not. They are interested not in the playing so much as the result of the contest. They go to the park to 'pull' for one or the other baseball team. Unless that feeling exists baseball cannot thrive."[73]

In Spalding's conception of the game, then, the means did not always justify the ends. Not surprisingly, when proposals to reorganize professional baseball to make it more competitive and profitable surfaced in 1901 that were not to his liking, he returned to the baseball wars in characteristic style to oppose them.

The issue that brought Spalding out of retirement was the attempt by Andrew Freedman, owner of the New York Giants, and by other magnates to establish what they called the National League Baseball Trust. Freedman, a New York city realtor, transit owner, and Tammany politician, bought a controlling interest in the Giants in 1895. Although he enjoyed a reputation as being irascible, devious, and hard-nosed, Spalding had warmly greeted his entrance into the game. "From what I hear," A.G. said, "Mr. Freedman is a clever businessman and will prove successful. I hope he makes a lot of money." Four years later, when his brother Walter resigned as a Giants official, because he could not tolerate Freedman's management or his manners, Spalding downplayed the break and referred to Freedman as an "amusing cuss" whom "you cannot take seriously." By 1901, however, when James Hart urged him to come east to fight Freedman's trust scheme, he was ready to stamp out the man he later called "the incarnation of selfishness supreme."[74]

Freedman's plan, supported by several other club owners, called for all clubs and players in the National League to be part of one large syndicate, whose elected and salaried officials would have the responsibility for locating franchises and relocating players, literally on a year-to-year basis, in ways that would maximize competition and profits. For Spalding, however, the "inordinate greed" of the Giants' owner threatened to destroy the National League and its mission "to perpetuate, establish and maintain the integrity of baseball" and compelled him to engage in "active struggle to protect the game from enemies in its own household."[75]

Similar familial imagery appeared in A.G.'s speech at the league's annual December meeting in 1901. There he formally joined the conflict with Freedman by standing for the presidency of the National League against the choice of the Freedman faction, the incumbent Nick Young. Declaring himself, along with William Hulbert, as one of the two founding fathers of the National League, Spalding claimed the right to speak to its councils. He then proceeded to give a long account of the history of the league, coupled with a tirade against those who now sought to destroy it purely for profit.[76] As he told one reporter, after presenting his speech:

> Think of a trust in baseball. Is it all commercialism? Is there no more of the glorious sentiment attached to our national sport? National League Baseball is a very sick patient today, and my God it has had some awful bad doctoring lately. The only salvation is to turn it completely upside down. A revolution. The fight is within, not without.[77]

For a man who sold King Kelly to Boston in 1887 because it was good for business and who was hardly above making expedient decisions solely in the interest of economic advantage, there was obvious irony in Spalding's criticism of his adversaries as mercenary capitalists who sought to introduce a system whereby "one man or a half-dozen men...might dominate the entire business—and with villainous brutality."[78] Certainly, his own attempts to shape the development of professional baseball had provoked similar charges.

Moreover, Spalding was aware that the National League was, as he put it, "a very sick patient" in need of attention. Having absorbed American Association clubs when that league collapsed after the Brotherhood War, the National League had operated precariously as a twelve-team circuit for a decade, with mixed financial results. Now it was also under siege by the newly transformed Western League. Led by Ban Johnson since 1894, it had established itself in direct and successful competition with the National League, raided it for its best players, and demanded full recognition as a major professional baseball league. Indeed, prior to the Freedman controversy, rumors circulated that Spalding himself had unsuccessfully discussed with Johnson a compromise by which the two rival leagues would merge into one.[79]

Nevertheless, A.G.'s appeal to sentimentality was not incompatible with his denunciation of "commercialism." In his mind, Freedman was no better than the irresponsible "adventurers" who had launched the Union Association or the "speculators from Wall Street" who had backed the Brotherhood. Proud of his career as a ballplayer and his role in creating and shaping the National League, he took seriously its self-proclaimed responsibility as "the guardian of a nation's sport." Unhesitatingly, he distinguished himself and others whose careers were inseparable from the development of professional baseball from opportunistic capitalists who cared nothing for tradition or the game's higher purpose and who entered baseball simply to make money. Much like Teddy Roosevelt, his favorite president, who distinguished between "good" and "bad" capitalists and who by working with the former and crushing the latter earned the reputation of trust-buster in an era of unprecedented business consolidation and monopoly growth, A.G. made a similar distinction between baseball men and acted accordingly. Just as in the past, he explained, anyone who tampered with the National League in ways that challenged "the *integrity* of Base Ball had to be stopped."[80]

Freedman and his allies, however, were formidable opponents. Whereas in the early years of the National League, Spalding had confronted gamblers and irresponsible ballplayers, he now saw himself "for the first time...face to face with a situation full of graver menace...because those who were seeking its ruin...were men of real power, men of ability, men of acute business instincts—an enemy that knew how to fight."[81] Although he failed to acknowledge anything of himself in this portrait of his enemies, A.G.'s own actions in combat with them suggest he was at least their equal.

Supported by Jim Hart of Chicago, Charlie Ebbets of Brooklyn, John Rogers of Philadelphia, and Barney Dreyfuss of Pittsburgh, Spalding allowed his name to be placed in nomination for the league presidency, from which he hoped to deny Freedman's efforts and to force the "traitor" and "marplot" out of baseball.[82] After a series of election ballots in which Spalding and Young each received four votes, the owners of the clubs supporting Freedman withdrew, allowing the remaining owners to illegally declare a quorum and elect Spalding to office. A.G. responded by accepting the post and, in an early morning "raid" on Nick Young's hotel room, by seizing league records in his possession.[83]

Freedman was hardly pleased with the news of Spalding's ascendancy. "Spalding is an interloper," he told one reporter, who "is scheming to help himself and not baseball." Referring to the illegal maneuvers of the four owners who had brought A.G. to office, the Giants' owner discounted their efforts: "Those four have no more right to direct the affairs of the National League than they would have to direct the affairs of the Steel Trust."[84]

In a similar spirit, the New York *Clipper* called Spalding's seizure of the league's records and his bogus election "not only farcical but...the crudest thing that was ever attempted at a baseball meeting."[85] Through it all, however, it was hard to deny, as one scribe put it, that "Mr. Spalding is the sensation of the meeting." That is how A.G. remembered the proceedings: "All I had to do was to speak four words to a reporter, and it was good for a column in his paper." "A sentence," he noted with all the immodesty he could muster, "was sufficient for a page of Base Ball literature."[86]

In the end the National League continued without Spalding as its president and without Freedman's baseball trust. A succession of court proceedings terminated in April 1902 with a decision against Spalding's election. Announcing his "resignation" from a post he never held legally, he made no mention of the ruling. Rather, A.G. offered the resignation in hopes that it would end the league's "factional" political warfare. Although the *Sporting News* noted that Freedman gloated over the news, by July he was out of baseball, having sold the Giants for $725,000.[87] Indeed, when the *Sporting News*, in December 1902, offered its readers pictures of officials who were "National League Celebrities," neither he nor Spalding was in the group portrait of five.[88]

Spalding's triumph over Freedman was a fitting climax to his career in baseball. Consistent with his age's penchant for professionalism and his own identification as a progressive, A.G. poured his creative energies and his ego into the National League—that "bulwark of professionalism," as he called it, the organization responsible for determining standards of excellence and decorum and for governing the marketing, promotion, and progress of professional baseball. By instituting reforms and by fighting off those who tried to challenge the National League's authority, he had time and again helped, he believed, mold baseball into America's "National Game" while making it attractive entertainment and profitable business.[89]

Competing capitalists and exploited ballplayers could rightly question whether A.G.'s efforts in behalf of baseball were as benign as he claimed they were. Men like Henry Lucas, Edwin McAlpin, and Andrew Freed man could ask whether Spalding was any less concerned than they were with consolidation, efficient operation, control of ballplayers, and profit. Members of the Brotherhood or of the Chicago White Stockings could not take at face value Spalding's pronouncements that those who favored the reserve rule really had the best interests of the ballplayer at heart. Clearly, A.G. understood who benefited most from it. Underneath his fulsome praise of ballplayers and the "dignity of their profession" was the potential for ruthless action against what he considered to be their outrageous demands, which went against his vision of the game. Indeed, much like other progressive reformers who attempted to order and improve a rapidly changing society, Spalding brooked no challenge from those with different visions or with motives he found threatening or suspect.

In one of his last public statements about professional baseball, Spalding returned to the same themes that he had sounded throughout his career. Acting in his capacity as owner of the American Sports Publishing Company, he wrote an open letter to his baseball guide for publication in the 1915 edition. In it, he made clear that the policy of all "Spalding baseball publications" will be "to ignore all leagues, clubs, and players who are fighting organized professional baseball." Until such individuals and associations come under the jurisdiction of the National League, he asserted, "our publications will not recognize recalcitrants in any way." Anyone familiar with the history of professional baseball, he argued, will see the necessity of such policy: it was "strong men supported by efficient organization" and "the power of organized effort" that time and again saved the game from conspiring players and misguided magnates.[90]

Spalding did not bother to mention himself as one of the "strong men," nor was it necessary to do so. Regardless of how much his actions reflected personal needs for public attention and whether everyone agreed with his methods or purpose, Spalding's critical role in the development of professional baseball was undeniable. His efforts not only pointed the way for others who tried to turn sport into business in the twentieth century but also marked him as a product and a shaper of late-nineteenth-century American culture.

Albert Goodwill Spalding, age three (1853). Photo from *The Reminiscences of Harriet I. Spalding*.

Albert Goodwill Spalding, age twelve (1862). Photo from *The Reminiscences of Harriet I. Spalding*.

J. Walter Spalding, age nineteen (1875). Photo from *The Reminiscences of Harriet I. Spalding*.

Harry Wright, manager of the Boston Red Stockings, 1871-75. Photo courtesy of the NBL, Cooperstown, New York.

The champion Boston Red Stockings of 1874. A.G. stands second from the left, ball in hand. Photo courtesy of NBL, Cooperstown, New York.

The Chicago White Stockings, 1876 National League Champions. Photo courtesy of the NBL, Cooperstown, New York.

Adrian "Cap" Anson, manager of the Chicago White Stockings, *ca.* 1886. Photo courtesy of the NBL, Cooperstown, New York.

Billy Sunday, *ca.* 1885. Photo courtesy of the NBL, Cooperstown, New York.

The Chicago White Stockings of 1884, 1885, and 1886. Photo courtesy of the NBL, Cooperstown, New York.

THE MONARCHS OF THE SPHERE.

The St. Louis Browns, Champions of the American Association, 1886. Photo courtesy of the NBL, Cooperstown, New York.

A.G. Mills, 1882. Photo courtesy of the NBL, Cooperstown, New York.

Mike "King" Kelly in his Boston uniform after being traded by A.G. Spalding in 1886. Photo courtesy of the NBL, Cooperstown, New York.

John Montgomery Ward, captain of the New York Giants, *ca.* 1886. Photo courtesy of the NBL, Cooperstown, New York.

A.G. Spalding, age twenty-nine (1879). Photo from *The Reminiscences of Harriet I. Spalding.*

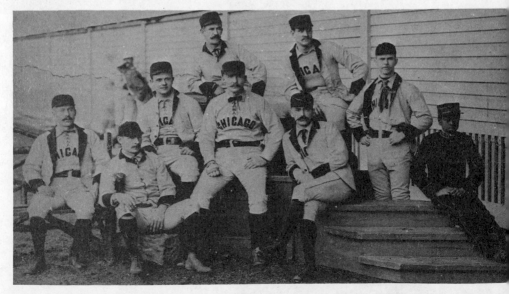

Spalding's baseball tourists at the Sphinx, February 9, 1889. A.G., wearing a pith hat, stands alongside his mother in the middle of the picture. Photo courtesy of the NBL, Cooperstown, New York.

The Spalding residence at Point Loma, California. Photo courtesy of the Archives of the Theosophical Society, Pasadena, California.

A.G. and Mrs. Elizabeth Spalding in their Locomobile at Point Loma, California, *ca*. 1900-1905. Photo courtesy of the San Diego Historical Society, Ticor Collection.

A.G. Spalding, *ca*. 1910.   Photo courtesy of the Archives of the Theosophical Society, Pasadena, California.

Harriet Spalding, age sixty (1881).
Photo from *The Reminiscences of Harriet I. Spalding*.

A.G. and Mrs. Elizabeth Spalding, *ca*. 1910.   Photo courtesy of the Archives of the Theosophical Society, Pasadena, California.

ALBERT GOODWILL SPALDING

ORGANIZATIONAL GENIUS OF BASEBALL'S
PIONEER DAYS. STAR PITCHER OF FOREST
CITY CLUB IN LATE 1860'S, 4-YEAR
CHAMPION BOSTONS 1871-1875 AND
MANAGER-PITCHER OF CHAMPION
CHICAGOS IN NATIONAL LEAGUE'S FIRST
YEAR. CHICAGO PRESIDENT FOR 10
YEARS. ORGANIZER OF BASEBALL'S FIRST
ROUND-THE-WORLD TOUR IN 1888.

A.G. Spalding's plaque in the Baseball Hall of Fame, Cooperstown. Photo courtesy of the NBL, Cooperstown, New York.

Announcement of A.G. Spalding's death on the front page of the *San Diego Union*, September 11, 1915. Photo courtesy of the NBL, Cooperstown, New York. Reprinted with permission by the San Diego *Union*, copyright 1915.

Typical advertisements for Spalding products appearing in their publications. Photo courtesy Spalding, Chicopee, Mass.

5

A. G. Spalding and Brothers: The Business of Sport

Only twelve years after Mrs. O'Leary's cow touched off the great Chicago fire, the Chicago *Inter-Ocean* published a brief promotional history of the city that celebrated its progress and accomplishments since 1871. In typical booster fashion, its first chapter, entitled "The City of Surprises," asserted that Chicago rightly deserved to be called the "Sporting Capital" of the West. Central to the paper's argument were the city's "parental position" as the birthplace of the National League and of professional baseball and the success of the Chicago White Stockings both on the field and at the box office. The editors did not forget Albert Goodwill Spalding, as baseball man and as sporting-goods entrepreneur, in making their case. "No man has done so much to encourage and stimulate outdoor sports in Chicago and the West," the *Inter-Ocean* exulted, as "Mr. A. G. Spalding, the President and Manager of the Chicago Base Ball Club... the patron saint of the base ball fraternity in the West," and the founder of "A. G. Spalding and Brothers... the rendezvous and headquarters of the sportsmen of Chicago and the Northwest." Similar accolades for Spalding, his business, and his city also appeared in a survey of Chicago's architecture, published four years after the *Inter-Ocean*'s paean. Accompanying a woodcut of A. G. Spalding and Brothers' "mammoth" Chicago store was the announcement that "in Chicago we claim everything, and the claim is made that every man, woman, and child in this country has heard of baseball; then they have heard of A. G. Spalding and Bros., as they... equip the world of sports with all of its supplies."[2]

Spalding must have been pleased with the praise and the publicity offered by this special attention, much more elaborate than the brief notices that had appeared in Chicago newspapers in 1876 acknowledging the opening of his "baseball and sporting-goods emporium."[3] Pleased, yet not surprised, for armed from the outset with a logo of a large baseball over the door and a motto on his desk that read "Everything is possible to him who dares," he consciously sought to capitalize on his reputation as a famous ballplayer and baseball magnate, both to capture and to extend an expanding market for athletic equipment among middle-class Americans.[4] Although it was hardly on the same scale as the more renowned and sometimes infamous businesses that bring to the last quarter of the nineteenth century sobriquets like "the age of enterprise" or "the era of the robber barons," A. G. Spalding and Brothers' successful domination of a sporting-goods industry it had helped shape nicely illustrates Spalding's own role in the process as well as the major tendencies of business expansion in these years.

Calculation always entered into important decisions in A.G.'s life, and the attempt to launch a business that catered to a growing demand for sporting goods was no exception. Even as a young man following the exploits of the Cincinnati Red Stockings, he made careful note of Harry Wright's attempt to combine a successful career as a professional ballplayer and manager with that of a supplier of baseball goods. By the time he decided on a similar course, there was ample evidence that such a venture was a risk worth taking. Even a casual reader of the New York *Clipper* in 1875 could hardly ignore the abundance of advertisements for businesses specializing in the manufacture and sale of athletic equipment. Located mainly in the East, firms such as Peck and Snyder, Ryan and Davenport, James Master, and the Wright Brothers urged potential buyers to purchase their "professional deadballs" and bats.[5] And purchasers there were. In 1878 the *Clipper* noted that anyone doubting the popularity of baseball "would open their eyes in astonishment" at "the business transacted in baseball goods. Bats are being made by the 500,000, balls by the thousand gross; uniforms by the thousand, and baseball material of all kinds in the same ratio."[6]

Spalding was not the only ballplayer who responded to such prospects. In 1882 Ross Barnes, his friend and teammate since their days with the Rockford Pioneers, joined with Louis Mahn to specialize in the production of baseballs. In that same year, the New York *Clipper* recognized the success of Al Reach, often reputed to be the first paid professional ballplayer of the 1860s, who thanks to his "temperate habits, genial disposition, and sterling integrity of character...has risen from his position as a professional [ballplayer] and worked his way up by steady industry to the proprietorship of...the leading sporting-goods emporium of Philadelphia."[7] Eventually, however, A.G. outstripped all his rivals, overwhelming several of them, in pursuit of the American dream.

At the outset, Spalding's national reputation as the best pitcher in baseball enhanced his possibilities for economic success. Not only the name of the new company but also the partnership agreement he devised with his younger brother in February 1876 explicitly acknowledged that fact when it specified that Walter, then a bank teller in Rockford, be responsible for giving full attention to the management of the firm. A.G., on the other hand, while involved in such matters, would continue to play ball in order to provide publicity for the company.[8]

Family connections of other sorts also facilitated the opening of the young capitalists' business at 118 Randolph Street in March 1876. Above all, there was Harriet, who witnessed her sons' agreement and, as one of her granddaughters remembers, "stood alone with her children," despite the protestations of her friends, and advanced them their entire starting capital of $800. Although publicly Spalding never denied stories that depicted his rise to wealth and fame in rags-to-riches fashion, privately he recognized his debt, "with filial devotion," to "the real founder of our Company."[9] Nor was Harriet's support of her sons' venture limited to cash outlay. At least on one occasion, at a time when company management also involved physical labor, she helped Walter sew the name *Indianapolis* on the front of a set of knit shirts ordered by that baseball club, as she recalled it, "with great difficulty."[10]

Albert's sister, Mary, also took a hand in the firm's early success. She not only served as the company's first bookkeeper but also married William Thayer Brown, the son of a local Rockford banker, described by one observer as a "young man of promise" from a wealthy family. It was Brown who provided the capital that allowed the Spaldings to become owners of their first bat factory—in Hastings, Michigan, in 1879— and that compelled a change in the company's name from "Brother" to "Brothers."[11]

A.G.'s own situation with the White Stockings and his family ties obviously influenced his decision to open his business in Chicago. So, too, did his sense of the city's economic potential. Chicago's reputation as a major city was well established long before Spalding set up shop there. Known for trade in grain and lumber and for its meat-packing industry, the city was a major terminus for a growing network of railroads, which destined it to be a national commercial center. Even the great fire failed to stifle its amazing growth and vitality. Between 1871 and 1881 its population rose from slightly under 300,000 to 500,000, and the value of its trade increased from $387 million to $700 million. By

1883 the number of its people employed in manufacturing had reached 114,457—almost double what it had been five years earlier. And between 1878 and 1881 alone, the city's banks recorded a startling measure of Chicago's economic growth by doubling the amount of their clearings, from $1 billion to $2.25 billion.[12] In 1876 Spalding did not yet identify himself with business leaders like Potter Palmer, Marshall Field, Philip Armour, George Pullman, or Gustavus Swift, whose activities directed Chicago's economic progress. He clearly hoped, however, to take advantage of it by turning his store, as he told one reporter, into the "headquarters for...Western Base Ball clubs."[13]

While Spalding and others lauded Chicago's economic promise, at least one observer was also aware of a darker side to the city's development, one that in a different way may have contributed to A.G.'s decision to enter the sporting-goods business there. In March 1873 a reporter for the Chicago *Tribune* offered mixed reviews of Chicago's recovery from the 1871 fire. "Chicago was set forward ten years by the fire," he noted. "The mingled town and village aspects are gone.... The tendency is to the metropolitan in everything—buildings and their uses, stores, and their occupants." Somewhat regrettably, the column concluded that "village notions are passing away.... We are getting to be a community of strangers. No one expects to know...half the audience at the church or theatre, and as to knowing one's neighbors, that has become a lost art."[14]

In Chicago and elsewhere, as the *Tribune*'s reporter intimated and as other commentators have verified, the urban transformation of late-nineteenth-century America created a whole range of new problems for city residents, not the least of which was the need to come to terms with the strangeness of their new surroundings and the lack of familiar reference points. These "city people," as one historian calls them, sought new outlets for their energies and new cultural forms to replace the sense of community that "village notions" formerly provided. Indeed, despite baseball's description in the 1890s as a thoroughly modern game— one that symbolized for Mark Twain and others the "raging, tearing, booming nineteenth century"—many observers of baseball's history think it grew increasingly attractive as a spectator sport in these years precisely because it reminded city dwellers of a nostalgic, rural past that they had left behind in search of the excitement and economic rewards of urban life.[15]

It is impossible to know whether Spalding's return to Chicago in 1876 rekindled memories of the adolescent insecurity that marked his early years in Rockford and that his discovery of baseball alleviated. There is no question, however, that, whether promoting the game or his business, he offered involvement in sport, both for spectator and for participant, as a new means to counter the social dislocation and personal anxiety associated with a rapidly changing American landscape. Such efforts surely served both his business interests and his personal demand for popular attention. Moreover, they did not become prominent until after he had established himself as a successful entrepreneur and baseball magnate.[16] Still, location in Chicago, "a community of strangers," may well have heightened his sensibility to concerns that ultimately defined his special contribution to American life—an awareness of the needs of his society and the ability to offer sport as one outlet for them.

A. G. Spalding and Brothers' first storefront was located only a few doors down from the headquarters of the Chicago White Stockings. By 1883, after Spalding assumed the club's presidency, both the business and the baseball club shared the same new address on Madison Street.[17] Obviously a matter of choice, the proximity of A.G.'s major interests underscores that along with personal reputation, family support, and geography, his early role in baseball management and his close ties with William Hulbert were critical factors in bringing stability and success to his fledgling sporting-goods enterprise.

Whatever meaning Spalding's consistent support for the National League might evoke, his early enthusiasm for it clearly reflected his business's stake in its existence. In 1876, the first year of both enterprises, league officials, at Hulbert's insistence and Spalding's request, awarded his firm an exclusive contract to publish the "official League Book." Under Spalding's aggressive direction, this privilege provided its own financial gain while serving as a catalyst for business expansion.[18]

Ever aware of opportunities for profit and publicity, A.G. almost immediately supplemented publication of the league book with an annual volume modestly entitled *Spalding's Official Baseball Guide*. In case a potential buyer was unsure of who Spalding was, each guide included a full-page picture of the handsome, robust, mustachioed fellow, complete with his autograph.

Although his guide was not an official league publication, A.G. did not hesitate to assure its readers otherwise. Indeed, the inside covers of the early guides reprinted a letter from Nick Young, then the league's secretary, announcing that the National League had granted A. G. Spalding and Brothers the exclusive privilege of publishing the "league book." Although Young's letter referred to the book and not to the guide, Spalding did not bother to make that distinction clear to his audience.

Only when A. G. Mills assumed the National League's presidency, in 1882, was any effort made to stop Spalding's subterfuge. Persuaded by Mills's threat to deny the firm the publication rights to the league book, Spalding acceded to his request that he no longer pass off the guide as an official publication. By then, however, both the guide and the book were synonymous for most followers of baseball with Spalding and the National League.[19]

While the book contained only the league's rules and constitution, the guide supplemented this material with descriptions of the preceding season's play, records of individual players and clubs, instructions on how to play baseball, minutes of league meetings, and increasingly over time, editorial opinion consistent with Spalding's views on organized baseball and his role in its development. Most important, from a business standpoint, both publications, especially the guide, also became powerful vehicles for promoting and selling a growing line of Spalding athletic products and for creating in the public mind the inseparability of the Spalding name from interest in baseball or, for that matter, in sport generally. Harry Wright, Spalding's mentor at Boston, and by 1876 a business competitor, recognized these themes as early as 1877. Writing to Charles Fowle, president of the National League's St. Louis team, about the expulsion of players from the Louisville club for gambling, Wright noted that the league's constitution demanded such action. "Check it out in the 'League Book' (beg pardon, 'Spalding's Advertiser')," he suggested, sarcastically poking fun at the identification of Spalding, his business, and baseball that became commonplace over time.[20]

The guide not only promoted Spalding and his wares but also became a marketable item itself. In 1884 A.G. claimed a national circulation for it of 50,000 and actively solicited other businesses to advertise in it. In a form letter sent to a variety of enterprises, he emphasized "the value of Spalding's Base Ball Guide" as a national advertising medium, while offering rates at $50 a page to potential customers. Occasionally he made a more specialized appeal. Writing to the proprietors of a Baltimore hotel, he encouraged them to advertise in the guide because "it is the recognized standard authority of the National Game and will fall into the hands of all travelling base ball clubs," some of whom would presumably be stopping in Baltimore. Closer to home, Spalding made the same pitch to the manager of Chicago's Clifton House in 1884, adding a hot tip that a brisk hotel trade was in the offing since twice as many clubs would be visiting the city in the upcoming season than in 1883.[21]

Although Spalding spent less time with these mundane but important matters as his business became more established and as his personal reputation grew, in 1884 he was still personally soliciting customers for the guide and taking a hand in its layout and production. Concerned with the format of that year's edition, he wrote to O. P. Caylor, the editor of the American Association's book, and reneged on a previous agreement that called for an exchange of league and association club records for publication in each other's guides. Not only would they take up too much space, Spalding noted, but it would "make too much statistics for the good of the book."[22] A.G. also sent off a series of letters to National League officials, chiding them for not promptly returning copy and then page proofs for the 1884 guide. Their tardiness, he reminded them, threatened to delay publication until after a mid-March target date and to allow "the American Association book [to] get some advantage over me by being in the field earlier."[23]

No less important than the guide to the early success of Spalding's sporting-goods business was its contract to provide the National League with baseballs for all league games in exchange for the exclusive designation as the maker of the league's official ball. Year after year, at league meetings attended by Spalding in his capacity as secretary and then as president of the White Stockings, his firm was awarded the honor. Like any talented businessman, A.G. made the most of it. The 1879 guide, for instance, carried a letter from Nick Young, then the league's secretary, which certified the adoption of the "Spalding League Ball" for the 1880 season.[24] One year later the guide offered answers to a series of questions presumably sent in by readers that both justified and reinforced the exclusivity of the Spalding ball. "Why does the League adopt a special ball for all their games and what one has been selected for 1880?" the ignorant fan asked. "To insure uniformity and guard against fraud," the guide answered, adding that the "Spalding League Ball" had once again been chosen. To the query whether other baseballs could be used when National League clubs played nonleague games, the guide adamantly but incorrectly replied in the negative. Only "Spalding's official League ball. . . *must* be used in *all* games played by League clubs, whether with League, professional, or amateur clubs."[25]

Consistent with Spalding's own image as a baseball expert and the elevation of the National League as the organization that set the standards for all those who played the game, these promotions were obviously aimed at a mass audience who would never play in the National League but who desired to purchase the same ball that the professionals used. Invariably, the guide harped on this theme, adding testimonials from other quarters whenever possible. The 1884 guide, for instance, informed its readers that not only the National League but also the Northwestern League, the American College Baseball Association, the Louisiana Amateur Baseball Association, and even the Iron and Oil

Association had all adopted the Spalding ball for official use in their contests. By 1890 a more sophisticated appeal was also included: a brief history of the baseball, culminating with a detailed description of the state of the art—the new Spalding League Ball, revolutionized by the use of a patented plastic cement that "makes it more elastic...soft to the hands, and at the same time...retains its perfect shape."[26]

Exclusive rights to the league's book and ball, ably manipulated by A.G. and Walter, gave them an edge over their competitors, which they used to full advantage. Somewhat less successful was the firm's attempt to exploit a contract awarded in 1882 to furnish all National League clubs with their uniforms. As he had done with the rights to the ball and the book, Hulbert played an important role in securing this plum for Spalding. At A.G.'s request, he also persuaded league officials to adopt color-by-position uniforms. Everyone wore white pants, belts, and ties but each team wore different colored stockings as distinguishing marks. After that it was color-coordinated chaos. The color of your cap and shirt, regardless of whom you played for, was determined by your playing position. Pitchers in baby blue, catchers in scarlet, first basemen in scarlet and white, second basemen in orange and black, maroon short-stops, gray right fielders, left fielders in white, third basemen in blue and white, and center fielders in red and black had to look to their ankles to see whether they belonged to the Boston "Reds" or the Worcester "Browns."[27]

Spalding's experiment in couture and his uniform contract lasted only one season. Still, A.G. encouraged anyone else looking for uniforms to come to the place where the professionals shopped. Not only would customers have the privilege of having their outfits made by the firm that served the National League; they would also have them cut from "superior flannel...not possessed by any other house in the country," in a department supervised by "an expert in designing and cutting...baseball and athletic uniforms." "Don't make the mistake," the 1882 guide warned, of allowing "local dealers whose experience...is necessarily small" to make your uniforms; rather, "send them directly to us and get a good, cheap, and satisfactory outfit."[28]

Despite the failure of flamboyant uniforms, National League connections clearly provided Spalding an initial advantage in his efforts to dominate the sporting-goods industry. More significant in the long run, however, were the firm's decisions to manufacture its own products, offer a wide diversity of wares, acquire control of goods already on the market, buy out competitors, and develop its own marketing and production systems.

A step that set the tone for A. G. Spalding and Brothers' future was the opening of the Spalding and Wilkins Manufacturing Company in Hastings, Michigan, in November 1879. With their brother-in-law's money, A.G. and Walter bought into an existing croquet-and-baseball-bat company, owned by James Wilkins, which had been in existence since 1876. Incorporated as a new firm in 1879 with a capital of $20,000, the business listed as stockholders the men who became its chief officials: Albert as president, Walter as vice-president, William Brown as secretary-treasurer, and James Wilkins as superintendent. In 1881 Wilkins sold his shares in the company, and it was renamed the Spalding Manufacturing Company.[29]

Located on three acres, with separate factories for baseball bats, croquet implements, ice skates, and fishing gear, Spalding and Wilkins employed close to 100 men in a community of some 2,500 residents. According to one local observer, the business was "the most extensive of its kind in America." Although Spalding did not claim quite as much, he did devote the inside cover of the 1880 guide to a full-page woodcut of the Hastings plant. He boasted that because of this facility, located "in the heart of the finest lumber land in the West" and outfitted with "the most approved modern machinery...we are the *only* sporting-goods house in America that pretend to make their own goods...."[30]

A.G.'s assertions, at least in regard to his own company, were quite justified. Indeed, in 1887 the *Sporting News* reported that the firm was producing over one million bats a year to meet the demands of a baseball-starved public.[31] Whether or not these figures were accurate, there is no question that Spalding had more in mind than just selling baseball goods over the counter in one Chicago store. Even a summer fire that swept through Hastings in that year—destroying the bat factory along with the town's opera house, grain elevators, and hotel—did not diminish the brothers' aggressive pursuit of an expanding market. Only weeks after the fire, a new plant opened in Chicago at a site conveniently near the Rock Island Railroad lines. One year later, advertisements directing "wagon-makers" to send their ash lumber by freight to Spalding headquarters in Chicago, for production of "our special black band League bats," testified to the vitality of the new operation.[32]

Within a decade, "Spalding headquarters" managed more than a Chicago bat factory. "Determined to manufacture their own products," A. G. Spalding and Brothers, according to a story in a March 1896 issue of the *Sporting News*, had by then developed a national web of specialized factories that made it a "sure winner" in an industry it shaped. In some detail, the *News* sketched the extent of the empire. Spalding and Credenza bicycles that "dazzled competitors" were produced in Chicopee Falls, Massachusetts, in the "best-equipped factories in the country by the most skillful workmen from the best material." Also located there was a skate factory, a "golf gymnasium and factories for the various goods in which steel predominates." Chicago remained the center for bat production, but other athletic equipment made from wood, including tennis racquets, dumbbells, and Indian clubs, was now produced in Chicopee Falls. Spaldings' Philadelphia plant concentrated on leather goods, and a new factory in Ogdensburg, New York, manufactured a variety of boats formerly produced by the St. Lawrence River Skiff and Canoe Company, which the firm had recently acquired. And in Brooklyn, Spaldings' "monster business" controlled the George Barnard Company, "the largest manufacturer of athletic and sportsmen's wear in the world" that "manufactures exclusively for A. G. Spalding and Brothers." Here, in a new, four-story building of 40,000 square feet, up to 1,000 workers turned out "bicycle shoes, stocking caps, football shoes, football pants, jackets, hunting goods of all descriptions, hunting clothes, and everything necessary for athletes' or sportsmen's wear." Altogether, the story concluded, the Spaldings' "mammoth business" employs over 3,500 workers and "aggregates several millions a year."[33]

"Mammoth" and "monstrous," the Spalding enterprise, as the *News*'s reporter suggested, benefited as much by expanding its own facilities as by buying out or controlling potential competitors like the St. Lawrence boat company or Barnard's clothing house. The Spaldings' first merger with James Wilkins, in 1879, proved to be a minor achievement compared with these efforts or with the absorption of the Lamb Bicycle Company and the purchase of Peck and Snyder's retail business in 1894, the acquisition of a major interest in A. J. Reach's substantial retail trade in 1889, or their silent partnership with the firm of Wright and Ditson in 1891.[34] Indeed, in 1895 the *Sporting News* made clear the connection between the firm's success and its ability to monopolize the industry when it noted that "supervised by A. G. Spalding, the history of the house has been marked by progressive prosperity. Smaller concerns have been absorbed in many fields," and "A. G. Spalding and Brothers are without a rival."[35]

This assessment of the vitality of the firm only reinforced its own sense of well-being. Only three years earlier, like any smart businessmen then or now, A.G. and Walter took advantage of state laws that offered tax breaks for corporate enterprise and reincorporated their company in New Jersey with a capitalization of $4 million. Spalding listed himself as president, Walter as treasurer, and William T. Brown as vice-president. In the space of sixteen years, a modest $800 speculation had become a multimillion dollar business and made its namesake a millionaire. "The money," as A.G. said at the time, "is all in the family."[36]

Although proud of their growth and determined in their efforts to control the marketplace, the Spaldings were also sensitive to increasing public concern over monopolies and trusts. Consequently, they sought little publicity for their mergers and often allowed companies they controlled to continue to sell their products under their own labels. If a tale in an 1886 issue of the *Sporting News* is any indication, however, most people in the business knew what was going on. As the *News* "reported" it, two unnamed professional ballplayers, experts in their field, swore they could tell the difference between Spalding and Reach baseballs just by touching them. "The joke of all this," the story went, "is that the balls...are made at the same factory and of the same material. One basket is marked 'Spalding' and another 'Reach.' This is the only difference between them."[37]

Although bats and balls remained staples of the Spalding line, the extent and nature of the firm's industrial plant highlight its efforts to offer a complete line of sporting-goods equipment. Whether designing the first basketball used by James Naismith in Springfield, Massachusetts, introducing and then manufacturing golf clubs for the country club set, or inventing the first automatic umpire indicators, A. G. Spalding and Brothers' reputation for diversity, innovation, and enterprise was well deserved.[38]

Diversification depended on more than invention. From the outset, the Spaldings aggressively sought control of existing products as a means of broadening their own appeal and limiting that of potential rivals. As early as 1876, for instance, they arranged a deal to have L. H. Mahn produce baseballs that would carry the Mahn patent and the Spalding label. They pushed on in these endeavors throughout the 1880s, with such items as "Bright's Baseball Turnstiles," "the Bray Fly Book" (a convenient holder for fish flies), and "Gray's Patented Chest Protector." So successful was their approach that by 1888 they advertised their ability to control and market the inventions of others. "In the past two weeks," they proudly announced in *Sporting Life*, "we have secured control of an article which promises to make almost a furor...a linen silk stocking, a patented article....It is a Yankee's invention of course. Who else but a Yankee would have had the ingenuity to invent such an article, and sense enough to put it in our hands to distribute."[39]

On one occasion, in 1886, the brothers' efforts to acquire tested products got out of hand, when they introduced a catcher's mask that infringed the patent rights of its inventor, F. W. Thayer. Thayer sued the firm in the U.S. district court and, after two years of litigation, won his case and back damages. Undaunted, A.G. noted the proceedings in his 1889 guide alongside an advertisement for his company's own mask. In the next year, the firm recouped some of its catcher business in traditional fashion by picking up the patent on Harry Decker's safety catching mitt and establishing it as the standard glove for those who risked injury to their bodies behind the plate.[40]

One could minimize risk, of course, by learning how to catch from a Spalding manual on the subject, for, in addition to producing every piece of athletic equipment imaginable, the firm provided an equally impressive range of publications that offered instruction and encouragement for athletic participation. Begun in 1885, its Library of American Sports series aimed at "educat[ing] the readers in each particular game or sport." Initially, the series offered thirteen short volumes, ranging in price from ten cents to a quarter and available "at newsstands throughout the country."[41] Anticipating a "national circulation," Spalding sent out a form letter to potential advertisers in January 1884 informing them of the company's goal to "print and mail directly to individuals, from 100,000 to 300,000 copies" of specialized pamphlets relating to hunting, fishing, baseball, and bicycling. Quoting rates at $10 per column, four columns to a page, it noted, "[I]f you desire to reach this class of people, we believe it will pay you to insert a card."[42]

By 1892 the publishing end of the business had become a separate concern, the American Sports Publishing Company, owned by A. G. Spalding and Brothers and managed for them by James E. Sullivan, who later became president of the Amateur Athletic Union. Under Sullivan's leadership, the Library of American Sports was reorganized into Spalding's Athletic Library, which was inaugurated with a run of 300 separate publications on sport and physical activity. The firm's claim that it was "the greatest educational series on athletic and physical training subjects that has ever been compiled" was no exaggeration.[43] For 1916 the series listed sixteen groups of publications arranged by activity, including "Baseball," "Skating and Winter Sports," and "Home Exercising." Each group contained numerous titles, ranging in price from the ten-cent "Blue Cover" series to the twenty-five-cent "Red Cover" series. For only a quarter you could learn "How to Live 100 Years." Ten cents would buy you "Ten Minutes Exercise for Busy Men."[44]

The wide array of products made available by Spalding clearly had much to do with the firm's success. No less important, however, was the development of a national retail and wholesale marketing system to move its goods. While the main store in Chicago serviced the West, in

1884 and 1885 the brothers opened first a wholesale and then a retail store in New York City to handle "eastern customers." In a pinch, the New York facilities could even meet other needs. When a fire virtually gutted the Chicago store in October 1884, A.G., as the New York *Clipper* astonishingly reported, "at once rented a storefront at 164 Madison St. and reopened on October 27th, having telegraphed east to have his stock duplicated."[45]

Major branches in Chicago and New York serviced a growing network of "depots" that carried the Spalding line. Each year the firm's publications noted the addition of new cities and towns where Spalding products could be purchased by individual consumers and at wholesale, not only in America but throughout the world. Somewhat boastfully, the 1889 *Guide* categorized them by western, southern, eastern, and foreign depots, including under the last heading offices in Alexandria and in Cairo, Egypt. In 1909 the Spalding firm listed thirty American cities and six foreign ones where a sports enthusiast could find a storefront bearing the Spalding name.[46]

Unrelenting in their pursuit of profit, the Spaldings continually sought new ways to attract both the general public and other businessmen to their banner. In this spirit, they announced the "Spalding Policy," aimed at the introduction of sporting-goods departments into existing retail businesses. The April 1899 issue of the *Sporting Goods Gazette*, a professional trade magazine, carried an early promotion for it that encouraged businessmen to write directly to A. G. Spalding and Brothers for the details. "Americans are evoluting into a fresh-air people," the notice said. "They are being converted to the gospel of EXERCISE." For adventurous capitalists, the firm offered an opportunity to cash in on it. "We can interest you," the advertisement concluded, "if you will meet us half-way."[47]

At its core the "Spalding policy" aimed to control competition by having the company sell to all retailers directly and at the same price, in return for their assurance that they would sell the Spalding line at prices determined by the firm. As A.G. said in 1908, it would accord retailers and consumers fair treatment. In addition, having a guarantee of stable markets, he and his brother would continue purchasing the very best raw materials in order to insure the consistent production of quality goods. "In other words," he concluded, invoking the spirit of Teddy Roosevelt, "the 'Spalding Policy' is a 'square deal' for everybody."[48]

Although Spalding's testimonial to his own scheme emphasized a concern for the consumer and retailer, the policy originated in a desire to increase business, stabilize market situations, and eliminate price-cutting. His commitment to its continuation eleven years after its inception confirms its success, apparent to his brother as early as July 1899. Commenting on it after only six months of operation, Walter told a *Sporting News* reporter that "there had been a wonderful increase in their athletic goods business" and that price-cutting had virtually ended. Only twenty-five retailers had refused to mend their ways, and their relations with Spalding had been terminated. As the reporter noted, this was "not bad, considering they have over 20,000 accounts on their books."[49]

The keen interest of retailers in the Spalding line rested on the public's increasing identification of the Spalding name with quality athletic goods, a connection pursued assiduously by the firm's innovative advertising. Much like P. T. Barnum, the Spaldings understood that late-nineteenth-century Americans were attracted to displays of extravagance and to bold claims of greatness, power, and wealth. Just as Barnum advertised his circus as "the Greatest Show on Earth...the World's Largest, Grandest, Best Amusement Institution," they promoted their products as "the Standard of Comparison the World Over." Or as a 1904 newspaper advertisement put it, "First be sure it's a Spalding—then go buy."[50]

An early effort to promote the firm as the leader in its field was its introduction, in 1877, of the Spalding trademark—a picture of a baseball with the name *Spalding* printed between the seams—stamped on every product it manufactured as assurance of its worth.[51] By 1895, according to its own advertisements, this seal of approval had come to guarantee its entire line, "from the cheapest to the highest priced, as the very best that can be produced for the money." In order to help the consumer distinguish among the variety of goods it offered, the company went one step further by identifying the top of the line for each item—the best of its eighteen bats, the most expensive of its nine golf balls, or the finest of its fifteen baseballs—with an additional trademark, "The Spalding, Highest Quality." Anyone purchasing a product with this handle, as the Spaldings told it, owned something manufactured from "the very highest grade of material, workmanship and finish...the most perfect in design past experience enables us to produce."[52]

In upholding their firm's reputation, A.G. and Walter at times made full use of their middle-class audience's fascination with professional experts and their role in setting standards and guiding the uninitiated. A 1908 advertisement for "the Spalding policy," for instance, offered a long discussion of trademarks and the idea of "standard quality" as a means of attracting interest in their wares. After defining "standard quality" as an "appellation...conceded to be the criterion to which are compared all other things of a similar nature," the notice cited as example the "Gold Dollar of the United States," whose integrity was protected against "counterfeiting and other tricks" by a "Secret Service Bureau of

Experts." Imaginative copywriting quickly helped the confused consumer understand the connection between the gold standard and Spalding's sporting goods. Thanks to thirty-three years of "integrity...responsibility [and]...rigorous attention to 'Quality,'" Spalding products, identified by their trademark, were known to be "as dependable in their field as the U.S. Currency is in its field." Tediously pursuing the analogy, the advertisement continued that without a secret service at the company's disposal, the only way to insure the continuation of the Spalding name as the guarantee of "Standard Quality" was for consumers to purchase only Spalding products.[53]

Sales pitches asking customers to uphold standards went hand in hand with others that warned them of the unfortunate consequences if they chose the inferior goods of "unscrupulous" competitors. In 1884, for instance, the baseball guide cautioned unsuspecting catchers against purchasing "cheap" masks rushed on the market by manufacturers with "no reputation to sustain." Warning ballplayers that such items were "worse than no protection at all" and were "liable to disfigure a player for life," the advertisement urged them to trust their faces only to Spalding cages.[54]

Expressed concern over fraudulent competitors was not total fantasy, manufactured by the Spaldings as a promotional device. Commenting on the state of the industry in 1899, the *Sporting Goods Gazette* underlined a specific version of the problem when it noted how "the prominent makers in the trade" have often been bothered by "unscrupulous small concerns" who turned out inferior products and marketed them under well-known labels. Only recently, in Philadelphia, the *Gazette* noted, Spalding had gone to court to stop a bicycle outfit in that city from selling their product as a "Spalding."[55]

Although no effort was made to exploit this particular episode, at other times similar tales served as good copy for Spalding advertisements. As a precaution against disreputable businessmen, the firm often warned consumers to beware of counterfeit merchandise and to purchase only products stamped with the Spalding trademark. In 1886 it even began packaging its baseballs in red, sealed boxes while instructing buyers to make sure that the seal had not been broken before purchase.[56] Against this backdrop, with no details that could be verified, the 1896 baseball guide carried a promotional piece on the Spalding ball that told the story of a conniving "ball-maker...in an out-of-the-way place, making counterfeit Spalding League balls." Not only did the cad possess "a full line of stamps" to imprint the Spalding name on his baseballs; he even stitched the seams with the same color thread used on the "genuine" Spalding article, and boxed them in red boxes sealed with counterfeit labels. "With considerable expense and difficulty," the Spaldings tracked down the scoundrel and brought him to justice. Playing the melodrama to its fullest, the story concluded that although "tears and entreaties by his family saved him from State Prison," A.G. and Walter made him destroy all his counterfeiting paraphernalia and exacted from him a sworn statement that he would never engage in such activity again.[57]

Not every Spalding advertisement relied on morality plays or pronouncements about standards to lure customers to its products. Appeals that emphasized innovation, novelty, and workmanship—all written with a flair for hyperbole, no matter where they appeared—most frequently characterized the firm's promotions. Typical was a series of newspaper advertisements for individual products that appeared in the June 1893 issues of the *Sporting News*. Each week, located in the same space, a pencil sketch of a baseball player announced the copy devoted to particular items, ranging from chest protectors to uniform bags. "DOUBLED UP" read the caption of one illustration that dramatized the unfortunate results of a young catcher bent over in pain, hat askew, who had been hit in the stomach by an errant toss. "If only the poor lad," the copy exclaimed, "had purchased any one of a number of models of Gray's patented Catcher Protector, now manufactured solely by A. G. Spalding and Company, such fate could be avoided."[58] Even more catching in its attention to detail and innovation was a newspaper pitch for Spalding's "neck-protecting mask," designed specifically for catchers and umpires who were afraid of taking a foul ball in the Adam's apple. Long before Steve Yeager of the Los Angeles Dodgers popularized the feature in the 1970s, the Spaldings had encouraged the purchase of a catcher's mask that included a padded extension from its bottom, "filled with goat hair and faced with the finest imported dogskin, which, being, impervious to perspiration, always remains soft and pleasant to the face."[59]

By 1886, with the Library of American Sports in place, the promotion of Spalding products had nearly become a business in itself. Every volume in the series not only advertised the Spalding equipment necessary to play the game or amusement it described, but also contained abundant news about the variety of products that carried the Spalding seal. Similarly, every one of the company's annual guides covering sports, from baseball to international polo, also highlighted the fecundity of the Spalding enterprise. The 1900 bicycle guide, for instance, included twenty-two pages of advertisements that covered the gamut of needs, from the sophisticated ones of professional bicycle racers to those of the interested middle-class lady or gentleman about to take up golf or tennis. There was even one page devoted to four models of the "Whiteley Exercisers, an ideal gymnasium for home use," available for both men and women and carried exclusively by A. G. Spalding and Brothers.[60]

If, by chance, potential customers failed to find what they were looking for in newspaper advertisements or in the back pages of Spalding publications, they could always order directly from the Spalding catalogue. In the pages of the 1886 baseball guide, the firm announced that it had just "issued the largest and most complete Sporting Goods Catalogue ever published, containing over 1,000 separate illustrations." Available for only a quarter, each catalogue included a certificate entitling the holder to a twenty-five-cent discount on any item that cost at least one dollar.[61]

This magnanimous-sounding come-on preceded another that caught the attention of the New York *Clipper* in April 1886, when it reported that the Spaldings would offer $100 to anyone who, by June 1, could correctly predict the order of finish of the eight National League clubs at the close of the 1886 season. To avoid potential bankruptcy at the hands of lady luck, the firm stipulated that if there was more than one winner, the prize would be divided equally among all those who guessed correctly. To enter the contest, all you had to do was send your prediction and twenty-five cents to A. G. Spalding and Brothers, who would forward, in return, "one of their 180 page catalogues."[62] Whether anyone either entered or won the contest was never recorded in the press. Nor was a similar promotion again advertised. But the catalogue itself, like everything else associated with the Spalding company, continued to grow. Indeed, by 1888 even this phase of its business had become so specialized that, according to the *Sporting Goods Gazette*, it now published separate ones for fishing tackle, guns, bicycles, tennis equipment, baseball supplies, gymnasium apparatus, and general athletic furnishings.[63]

Although catalogues and advertisements encouraged consumers to buy Spalding products, equally important in promoting the line was A.G.'s reputation as America's leading sportsman. Helpful here was his constant visibility in the affairs of professional baseball and the care he took to exploit any opportunity to gain public attention.[64]

In 1896, for instance, Spalding organized a nationwide celebration in honor of Harry Wright, marked by fifteen benefit baseball games played throughout the country on the same day, to raise money for a monument in his memory. Assured that all Rockford demanded his presence, A.G. returned to the town of his boyhood and, at the age of forty-six, donned "a suit of immaculate cream" to pitch a one-inning game for the survivors of the Forest City team with which he had begun his career. Needless to say, his team won this first old-timers' contest, providing publicity for himself and for his business.[65]

A.G.'s involvement in the Olympic Games of 1900 and 1904 brought even greater exposure. In 1900 a fellow Chicagoan, Ferdinand Peck, then commissary general of the United States, appointed Spalding to lead American athletes to the Paris Exposition. Commenting on his selection, the *Sporting Goods Gazette* noted that there was "no better choice." "As founder of the largest sporting-goods house in the world," the paper continued, he "has passed through all stages of business and has a fund of knowledge which will make him...invaluable."[66] Indeed, Spalding not only led his charges to a number of victories in the second modern Games but also found time to supervise the firm's display of athletic goods and apparel, which won a grand prize at the Paris show.[67]

So successful was Spalding that in December 1901 he accepted the charge to serve again and, as he noted, to help make the 1904 Games, planned for Chicago, "the greatest event that has ever occurred in athletic sports."[68] Although the Games eventually took place in St. Louis, in conjunction with the Louisiana Exposition, A. G. Spalding and Brothers designed the stadium, organized the track-and-field competition, provided the necessary athletic equipment, and once again won awards for the quality of its products. Not surprisingly, the firm's advertisements capitalized on these achievements by encouraging the public to buy products officially recognized as the best by experts in the field of athletics. As one of their advertisements put it, Olympic officials "selected Spalding Athletic implements for exclusive official use...because of their acknowledged superiority, reliability, and official standing."[69]

Although less newsworthy, promotions other than Spalding's participation in the Olympics provided publicity for himself and his products. A.G. offered "Spalding" trophies for amateur baseball teams that won tournaments sponsored by the firm in England, Canada, and the Philippines. In 1897 he traveled to England to present personally the Spalding English Cup.[70] Sponsorship of similar competition in Canada, as the 1893 baseball guide pointed out, demonstrated both the popularity of the Spalding line and A.G.'s role in promoting it. In regard to the rules governing baseball tournaments there, the guide noted that Spalding did not "demand that...balls and bats of his own make be used in the championship contest, but these implements of baseball warfare are in such general use that this clause was scarcely necessary."[71]

Although these ventures assured Spalding public recognition of his role in athletics and contributed to the success of his business, on occasion he took the opportunity to underline this connection. Commenting on his own contribution to baseball in the 1908 baseball guide, for instance, he pointed out that his sporting-goods business rested on his "athletic reputation" and on his "national prominence in the realm of sport."[72] After A.G.'s participation in another old-timers' game in September of that year, a reporter for the Boston *Herald* went Spalding one better. "Next to Abraham Lincoln and George Washington," he announced, "the name of A. G. Spalding is the most famous in American literature." "It has been blazing forth on the covers of guides to all sorts of sports, upon bats and gloves...for many years. Young America gets its knowledge of the past in the world of athletics from something that has Al Spalding on it in big black letters, and for that reason as much as any other, he is one of the national figures of our times."[73] A.G. couldn't have agreed more. Dutifully, he reprinted the story in the pages of his 1909 baseball guide.

Despite such acclaim, Spalding's "family" business clearly required more than his energy and reputation to make it work. Like others in the late nineteenth century who experienced the transition of their firms from small family concerns to large corporate enterprises, he and his brother recognized the need to involve other individuals in its operation. To be sure, as he had from the very beginning, Walter presided continually as general supervisor of the company's varied activities. Recognizing his role in 1897, the *Sporting News* described him as "a splendid type of businessman" and a major "factor" in the firm's success.[74] Over the years, however, A. G. Spalding and Brothers increasingly relied on others with special talents, from proprietors of its retail outlets to managers of its factories, to guarantee its fortunes.

Julian Curtiss, for instance, who became the firm's president in 1920, graduated from Yale in 1879 and embarked on a management career in industry as an employee of a manufacturing company that did business with Spalding. In 1885 he joined the Spalding firm as A.G.'s business secretary. By 1898 he had worked his way up through the ranks to become second vice-president, having already achieved notoriety in 1892 for introducing English golf equipment to Americans and initiating that part of the Spalding line. While he rose to the firm's presidency, Curtiss also served as a director of the U.S. Chamber of Commerce, confirming his place as a prominent businessman.[75]

Curtiss was not the only Spalding employee who occasionally merited public attention from an appreciative business audience. Commenting on the company's domination of West Coast markets in 1888, the *Sporting*

Goods Gazette gave the credit for the Spalding success to its general representative, F. N. White, a "rattling hustler." As White himself put it, in a spirit that A.G. would have admired, "what trade [I] did not secure on baseball and athletic goods was not worth having, and don't you make any blooming error."[76]

Spalding was well aware of the importance of men like Curtiss and White to the success of his business. In a 1915 article in the *Spalding Store News*, a company magazine, he lauded his employees' achievements and the system that encouraged them. In language that reflected his era's fascination with organization, efficiency, teamwork, and expertise, A.G. noted that "managers and other employes [sic]" in the firm secured their positions because "after long years of devoted service they have demonstrated peculiar personal fitness" for their jobs. Noting that the firm played "no favorites," he added that all who showed "efficiency" and loyalty to management would find fulfillment there. Relying on metaphors with which he was comfortable, Spalding emphasized that success in the business was like success on the diamond. Spalding employees learned the importance of teamwork, recognized the need "to hit the ball rather than knock the organization," and knew they were "part of a machine, which in order to produce...must have all its parts working in perfect harmony." Just as "a slouchy, incompetent, unfaithful ball player is relegated to the commons," he concluded, any Spalding employee found to be "indifferent...dishonest...or disloyal" would soon give way "to the other and better kind."[77]

Spalding's appreciation of a corporate outlook, consistent with the requirement of an increasingly complex industrial plant and marketing system, did not rule out the opportunity for individual excellence or notoriety, particularly if it involved himself. A.G.'s involvement with the bicycle, as much as with any single business venture, highlights his own role in the success of his business and the nature of its operation.

The growing popularity of the two-wheel safety bicycle among middle- and upper-class urban Americans in the late 1880s was not lost on Spalding. In the summer of 1890 he traveled to Chicopee Falls, Massachusetts, and negotiated an agreement to market bicycles produced by the Overman Wheel Company, the firm that had first introduced the safety bike, in 1887.[78]

By 1894, when bicycling was fast becoming a "craze," A.G. had more than retail trade in mind. Court proceedings terminated the Overman connection, after both companies sued each other for breach of contract,

Spalding contending that Overman produced too many defective bicycles.[79] At the same time, he and Walter bought out the Lamb Bicycle Company and installed A.G. as president, moving the firm directly into production of its own line of bicycles.[80] Within a year they had become the standard in the field. "Eastern customers," the *Sporting News* noted in December 1894, eagerly awaited the Spalding's 1895 editions because they already accepted their "superiority to the many wheels which can now be classed as has beens." In later editions the *News* noted that the company's standard model—"The Spalding," priced at $100, and winner of awards at both the Chicago and New York cycle shows—"is now coming to the front as a favorite with all lovers of cycling." Indeed, as the *Sporting Goods Gazette* succinctly put it in April 1895, in bicycles, " 'Spalding' is winning its way."[81]

As with that of their entire array of sporting goods, the success of the Spalding bicycles in part depended upon careful advertising. Although the wide range of Spalding publications provided ample space for advertisement, the firm also put out an *Official Cycle Guide*, replete with copy and photographs of its bicycles, sweaters, and shoes.[82] Interspersed throughout the guide, readers also found articles on specifications and repairs as well as accounts of professional racing competition and training. Aware of women's growing interest in cycling, it also carried occasional columns aimed exclusively at a female audience. One item, "Advice to Lady Bicyclists," appearing in the 1898 *Guide*, assured "our lady friends" that "all our pages are addressed to them, equally with their husbands and brothers." It also cautioned that no woman should ride "unattended by a male relative or friend."[83]

Complementing the printed word were public displays of the Spalding line. At cycle shows held annually in New York and Chicago, the Spalding exhibits consistently evoked praise as the grandest and most attractive. Particularly pleasing to Spalding was the fact that large numbers of the "finest people," the kind, as he put it, "that any branch of sport would be pleased to attract," paid attention to the Spalding line.[84] For potential customers who wanted to try bicycling before buying and for others who wanted a safe place to ride, the firm opened a bicycle academy in New York on the roof of Madison Square Garden in March 1895. Two months later the academy moved downstairs to the Garden's amphitheater, which boasted fifty instructors and facilities for over 500 "wheels" at one time.[85]

Bicycle schools were not the only gimmick Spalding used to stimulate business. In 1895 the firm acquired the rights to the Christy anatomical saddle. Within two years this seat had become standard equipment on Spalding bikes and quite common on those produced by domestic and foreign competitors. Just to insure continued interest and sales, however, Spalding in 1897 announced a competition in the _Sporting News_, open only to doctors, for advertisements that best presented the medical reasons for using the Christy saddle. After sorting through "hundreds" of entries, a jury consisting of the editor of _Metropolitan Magazine_, the advertising manager of the New York _Times_, and Julian Curtiss, then manager of the New York store, announced the winners in the May 15 issue of the _Sporting News_. The winner received a prize of $50. All contestants, the _News_ reported, received a free saddle for demonstrating "conclusively that the doctors of this country are very much interested in the saddle question."[86]

Experts on anatomy were not the only professionals to present testimony. Just as King Kelly and John Ward offered their praise of bats and baseballs, professional road racers like Fred Titus, Walter Sanger, and L. D. Cabanne lauded the quality of their Spalding machines while urging the public to purchase what the professionals rode. A.G. took a personal hand in this promotion by signing the three men to contracts in 1894, which required them to use Spalding equipment whenever they raced. Wearing racing shirts with the words _The Spalding Team_ emblazoned across the front, the trio dominated the League of American Wheelmen's professional circuit in 1894, allowing the Spaldings to take full advantage of their efforts to attract business. Eager to cash in on their riders' celebrity status, A.G. and Walter featured them in their advertisements and trotted them around to store openings and cycle shows as company representatives. Having re-signed the three and hired a team trainer for the 1895 season, the firm used the news to interest new marketing agents in the Spalding line. "AGENTS!" began the copy in a January 1895 issue of the _Sporting News_, "SANGER, TITUS, and CABANNE will ride the Spalding Bicycle. They will help push a good thing along. Write for terms."[87]

The Spalding team lasted only two years and in the end caused real embarrassment for A.G. and for his business. In September 1895 Titus and Cabanne were accused of fixing races during a St. Louis meet. Their suspension by the League of American Wheelmen brought an immediate protest from Spalding, who demanded the reinstatement of his riders pending an investigation. As he wrote to George Gideon, the league's chairman, "serious business wrong has been done them and us by this sudden suspension without opportunity for defense."[88] Defense proved to be no guarantee of vindication. In December 1895, after a closed hearing, the league permanently suspended the two riders, squashing any plans to maintain the team.[89]

Spalding's personal involvement in the bicycle business went beyond sponsorship of his racing team. In January 1895 A.G. was elected president of the National Board of Trade of Cycling Manufacturers, an accomplishment noted in the *Sporting News* as justifiable tribute for America's best-known sports figure.[90] Taking office at the first New York cycle show sponsored by the group, Spalding encouraged his colleagues to work together in nurturing a growing market, available to all competitors. Apparently at a loss for an appropriate baseball analogy to describe the opportunities he envisioned, he reminded his audience that "a decade ago, the dozens of wheels...in the world could be counted on the fingers of your hands. Today, the hairs on your head are inadequate."[91]

During his one year as president, Spalding established permanent board offices in New York City, increased its membership from 75 to 225 firms, organized regional and national cycle shows, consulted with League of American Wheelmen officials to coordinate the interests of manufacturers and professional racers, and devised lobbying strategies at the local and state levels aimed at improving and constructing roads and bike paths.[92] Through it all A.G. denied every claim that the board planned to control prices and markets. "In no way," he told one reporter, was it "a trust, combination, or monopoly."[93]

By 1899 decreasing profits and fierce competition from small companies had compelled Spalding and other large manufacturers to reconsider their approach to the industry. The result was the formation, in May 1899, of a giant trust, the American Bicycle Company, created by A.G. and large enough to satisfy even his ego. Comprising forty-eight companies and having assets valued at $22 million, ABC, as it was called, issued its own bonds and stock to purchase control of these concerns. Spalding earned a modest profit for handling all the transactions and served briefly as its first president.[94]

Initially, bicycle dealers and manufacturers looked to ABC as the savior of a faltering industry. Testifying before a U.S. Senate commission on trusts and industrial combinations in 1901, Albert Pope, president of the Pope Bicycle Company, acknowledged Spalding's critical role in buying out individual companies and selling them to ABC. As he saw it, the trust would end "cut-throat" competition, make for "efficiency of management," reduce production costs, and increase profits. Spalding's own 1900 cycle guide praised ABC for providing confidence in the trade and for insuring the exercise of "care in the quality of their goods than any smaller or less responsible company would." An unnamed bicycle dealer quoted in the *Sporting Goods Gazette* reiterated similar sentiments in calling the formation of the company "the best thing [that] ever happened to the bicycle business." Noting the restoration of "stability" and "confidence," he concluded that "consolidation was just what the business needed to keep it from slipping off the earth."[95]

In fact, what the business needed was consumers. By 1900, however, demand was virtually nonexistent. Commenting on the "decline of the bicycle," the New York *Times* noted in September 1900 that "even the most popular of toys must have its day and pass." "Society seems to have given it up altogether," the paper continued, "and now it is chiefly used as an article of utility, to get clerks and workmen to and from their business and occasionally to carry former bicycle devotees to the golf grounds."[96]

Despite all the confident rhetoric about ABC and its virtual monopoly of the business, less than two years after its formation, the firm defaulted on $260,000 interest due its bondholders and went into receivership. Reorganization and collapse followed, but by then Spalding's personal association with the company and with bicycles had long since ended.[97]

Spalding's flirtation with the bicycle was his last major activity as president of A. G. Spalding and Brothers. Although, in this case, his aggressive pursuit of new business, clever advertising, and attempts to control the market failed to salvage a dying trade, the Spalding empire continued to prosper. Caught up in war news in August 1915, Julian Curtiss offered one measure of its extent when he compared the " 'far flung'...Spalding commercial battle line" to the " 'far flung' " battle lines of Europe. In some detail he talked about a Spalding agent in Argentina installing playground equipment for the government, the New York store manager traveling in France in search of new specialty items, factories in Brooklyn and Chicago gearing up to make knapsacks for Russian soldiers, the Philadelphia warehouse "packing baseball goods for the Philippines," golf heads being forged in Scotland, leather tanning in Leeds, and the Spalding plant in London "making tennis and golf for India and Egypt" while other Englishmen did battle "for their country in the trenches in Flanders." Enmeshed in the British Empire, Curtiss alluded to it one more time in mentioning his own pride as a Spalding man: a member of "an organization on which the sun never sets."[98]

Curtiss's description of the Spalding domain and his own identification as a company man suggest how far A. G. Spalding and Brothers had come from being a family business run by two young aspiring entrepreneurs out of a Chicago storefront in 1876. The company's success in this venture, in part tied to A.G.'s identity as the most recognizable figure in American sport, depended upon its ability to seize the opportunities offered by an urbanizing society in ways that effectively responded to its leisure-time needs. Creatively nurturing a new industry in sporting goods, Spalding was moved by the same impulses to control competition and the marketplace that governed his approach to baseball and that directed the activities of businessmen in other industries caught up in the rapid development of a corporate industrial economy. Like them, he recognized the advantages of modern concepts of industrial organization, emphasized innovation and diversification, and took pride in his firm's ability to dominate its competitors. So successful were he and his brother, that, over time, it became increasingly difficult for Americans not to think of the Spalding name when the urge to participate in athletics came over them.

6

Touching Bases Around the World: The Social Promise of Sport

Speaking before a banquet of baseball aficionados in Philadelphia at the turn of the century, Francis Richter, editor of *Sporting Life*, extolled the "steady progress" the game had made as business and sport since the inception of the National League. "Every patron of the sport," he began, "knows that baseball is a fixed and stable business which has been maintained continuously for two generations." Richter scoffed at claims that it was "mere recreation" and declared that baseball was "a great sport, representative and typical of the people who practice it...one that stimulates all the faculties of the mind; keenness, invention, perception, agility, celerity of thought and action, adaptability to circumstances—in short all the qualities that go to make the American man the most highly-organized, civilized being on the earth."[1]

Those listening to Richter's remarks and knowledgeable about baseball's "steady progress" could not have helped thinking of Albert Goodwill Spalding in connection with the development of the game as a stable, well-organized business enterprise. Nor would they have been wrong to identify his voice as one of many of his generation that promoted baseball and sport in general as a means of sustaining American progress.

Historians are just beginning to appreciate what late-nineteenth-century observers of American society understood firsthand. In a variety of ways, involvement in sport, whether as spectator or as participant, received encouragement as a vehicle believed capable of mitigating some of the problems inherent in the transformation of the United States into a modern industrial state.[2]

For those individuals who attributed that process to an emphasis on organization, efficiency, expertise, and teamwork, sport became an activity that prepared men for their roles as society's leaders or, as Teddy Roosevelt more viscerally suggested, readied "a man to do work that counts when the time arises."[3] Compatible with this view were intellectual impulses at home and abroad and readily available in popular form. American writers, for instance, took to heart the ideas of a young Wisconsin historian, Frederick Jackson Turner, who in 1893 argued that the now closed western frontier had for two centuries served both as a natural cultivator of American democracy and values and as a safety-valve for the frustration and discontent of those who could find neither happiness nor economic success in the more settled regions of the nation. Writers were aware, too, of the English author Thomas Hughes and his fictional character Tom Brown, who was molded by his exploits as a rugby player into a "muscular Christian"—the epitome of the kind of leader whom free societies required. In articles, books, and stories, they depicted sport as an acceptable substitute for what no longer existed. It was a new frontier, "artificial adventure, artificial colonizing, artificial war"—an activity that would produce a "more stalwart and better formed race."[4] Anyone accepting this message would not be surprised to find one writer for the *Outlook*, obviously familiar with both Turner and Hughes, extolling the growth of the country club in 1901 as a "safety-valve of an overworked Nation," quite as responsible for the American victory in the Spanish-American War as "the Rugby gridiron" had been for the British triumph at Waterloo.[5]

The *Outlook*'s reference to "an overworked Nation" also suggests another perspective that informed a growing acceptance of sport, and indeed of what some called a "gospel of relaxation" among middle-class Americans in these years. Attributing them to the rapid pace of American life and its emphasis on excessive work and to the urban comfort and "overcivilization" that resulted from it, a number of observers recognized increasing signs of nervous tension and anxiety among those very people who enjoyed the benefits of American progress. The condition was labeled neurasthenia and was characterized by a whole range of neurotic symptoms, among them a paralysis of the will. Described in such works as *Wear and Tear: or Hints for the Over Worked* and *American Nervousness*, it enjoyed the status of a "national disease" among middle-class Americans.[6]

The search for antidotes that would revitalize the individual's physical and moral fiber while offering new opportunities for developing the character and values required for continual personal and national growth was wide-ranging.[7] Increasingly, it included an acceptance of sport as an activity appropriate to the task. For urban, middle-class Americans, in particular, the last quarter of the nineteenth century witnessed a virtual explosion of popular interest in sport. Whether measured by the bicycling craze of the 1890s, by the growth of organized, professional baseball, or by the astounding success and expansion of the sporting-goods industry—activities all close to Spalding's heart—the emergence of sport as a legitimate leisure-time pursuit and as an activity that served a significant social purpose in a society undergoing dramatic change was manifest these years. Indeed, for a man like Charles Ives, who became one of America's most distinguished composers, participation in baseball was one way of asserting his manhood. According to a biographer, Ives, concerned that his musical interests might make him appear effeminate, participated in amateur baseball well past adolescence in order to dispel any doubts about his masculinity. Once asked as a boy what he played, Ives proudly replied, "Shortstop."[8]

Although Spalding was hardly original in articulating these connections between sport and social purpose, no one expressed them with more flair or style than he. He did not talk about "the play impulse as an aid in the rational and efficient conduct of life," as one author did in a 1913 *Outlook* piece entitled "Baseball and the National Life," but he could declaim alphabetically that baseball was "the exponent of American Courage, Confidence, Combativeness; American Dash, Discipline, Determination; American Energy, Eagerness, Enthusiasm; American Pluck, Persistency, Performance; American Spirit, Sagacity, Success; American Vim, Vigor, Virility."[9] A.G., however, was not a professional reformer, social critic, or moralist. Although he shared many of the sentiments and goals of such people, he was above all a flamboyant entrepreneur, out to enhance his personal fortune, a man who recognized that it was good business to promote sport in terms of its social promise. He consistently offered Americans the idea that sport, while a profitable business and an amusement, also built character, encouraged order and discipline, and produced the type of citizen necessary for continued American greatness. Because his was the most recognizable name in American sport, his efforts, however self-serving, had a dramatic impact on the emergence of sport as a significant social institution in American life.

No episode better demonstrates all these tendencies than A.G.'s world tour of professional baseball players, undertaken between October 1888 and April 1889—an achievement that Henry Chadwick called "the greatest event in the history of athletic sports."[10] Although less aggressive and more modest than other late-nineteenth-century adventures in American imperialism, Spalding's gambit clearly aimed to extend an American presence in the world.

Viewing himself and his ballplayers as missionaries—"representatives of the great Western Republic"—A.G. hoped to spread American manliness and virtue by introducing baseball to the world in dramatic style.[11] Baseball was also his business, and Spalding intended to mix idealism with practical calculation. As he bluntly told one reporter, he went to Australia "for the purpose of extending [his] sporting goods business to that quarter of the globe and to create a market for goods there." Recognizing the risk involved in the venture, Henry Chadwick encouraged his boss and predicted that Spalding's "characteristic Western pluck and energy" would make it a "noteworthy success."[12]

On Spalding's original itinerary Australia was the only major international stop on the tour. Plans also called for a visit to Hawaii and a series of exhibitions in the United States both in order to cover expenses and, as he noted, "to make enough noise in this country so that...Australian people...will have no difficulty in hearing us long before we reach their shores."[13] Leaving detailed arrangements for the American portion of the tour to James Hart and for the Australian excursion to a professional theatrical manager, Leigh Lynch, Spalding devoted his attention to assembling his entourage and publicizing his mission.[14]

As president of the Chicago White Stockings, A.G. had little trouble securing the services of his regulars. Although he had fervently hoped that his boys would win the pennant in 1888 so that he could advertise his expedition as including the champions of America, he had to be content with a team that finished second to New York. Still, it did include Cap Anson and Jimmy Ryan, who together held just about every National League batting title for the season, and a young substitute pitcher, John Tener, who doubled as tour secretary and who later was to become president of the National League and governor of Pennsylvania.[15]

Opposing the Chicago nine were the "All Americas," drawn predominately from other National League clubs. Although the team fielded Monte Ward and Eddie Crane from the first-place New York Giants, the *Sporting News* unfairly charged that Spalding had signed fourth-rate ballplayers because he was too cheap to offer the kind of money that would attract the best. Charlie Comiskey, then playing for the St. Louis Browns, noted that if he had been extended "anything like a fair inducement," he might have gone. As it was, the "figures were not even enough for cigar money."[16] Spalding scoffed at such criticism, noting that the paper attacked him because he had withdrawn his business advertisements from it. Besides, as he remembered years later, the chief criteria in picking Chicago's opposition had to do with their character and deportment. "It was absolutely essential," he claimed, "that all who...go should be men of clean habits and attractive personality, men who would reflect credit upon the country and the game."[17]

Having assembled his ballplayers, Spalding offered his own contribution to the orchestration provided by Hart and Lynch. With the help of Frank Lawler, an Illinois congressman, A.G. obtained a brief farewell meeting for himself and the White Stockings with President Grover Cleveland at the White House. Although disappointed in not receiving a formal presidential endorsement for his adventure, he did come away with an ink drawing of the event, from which he had 5,000 copies made "for use upon the trip."[18]

Returning to Chicago, A.G. barely had time to say good-bye to his wife and family before departing on his international quest. After pitching in the opening exhibition of the tour, on October 20, Spalding and his entourage of thirty-five gathered at Union Station for what the Chicago Times described as the "noisiest...leavetaking...the depot ha[d] seen in years."[19] Included in the party that boarded railroad cars bedecked with banners announcing "Spalding's Australia Trip" and bound for San Francisco were the wives of several players; Spalding's friend Harry Palmer, a newspaper correspondent; reporters from the Chicago Inter-Ocean and the New York Sun; Irving Snyder, of the sporting-goods firm of Peck and Snyder; Carter Harrison, the former mayor of Chicago; Hiram Waldo, Spalding's longtime adviser from Rockford; and Harriet Spalding, A.G.'s mother. Always the businessman and with an impresario's sense of showmanship, Spalding also hired a hot-air balloonist, one "Professor" Bartholomew, to accompany the party, just in case baseball itself was not enough to bring out crowds of the uninitiated.[20]

On the way to San Francisco, the White Stockings also had the good fortune to "recover" their mascot of the preceding season, a young black named Clarence Duval, who had deserted them in midyear. The employment of mascots as crowd pleasers and good-luck charms was a common practice among major league ball clubs. Widespread, too, were the racist attitudes of their all-white rosters toward those mascots who happened to be black. Whether he was noticed by newspaper writers or by ballplayers, every mention of Duval, from his "capture" in Omaha to his return to the United States, unfailingly referred to him in ways that an American white public, bent on Jim Crow and segregation, could appreciate. The "pickaninny," "nig," "coon," or "darkey mascot," as he was invariably called, deserved attention, one observer noted, "because his grin is broad, his legs limbre and his face as black as the ace of spades. ...Whenever anything goes wrong, it is only necessary to rub Clarence's wooly head to save the situation, and one of his celebrated 'double shuffles' to dispel all traces of care, even on the gloomiest occasion."[21]

No such occasion apparently arose during the baseball missionaries' month-long swing through the West, which saw them play eighteen games with each other as well as a series of exhibitions with local California clubs. Enjoying, as the Chicago *Tribune* noted, the "novelty of traveling in nabob style," Chicago, dressed in light gray shirts, knee britches, and black stockings, and the "All Americas," dazzling in white flannel with a silk American flag draped over their shoulders, brought out the crowds from Omaha to San Francisco in such numbers as to more than cover Spalding's projected expenses for the entire Australian trip.[22] Pleased with his success and concerned about getting the best from his players, Spalding capped the tour's arrival in San Francisco by offering the winning team in each subsequent game $5 per man. As John Ward reported for the Chicago *Times*, A.G. also assured them that he would share any profits with those whose "deportment and play" deserved recognition."[23]

Although the *Sporting News* objected to any notion of Spalding's generosity and continued to berate the "fakir" for his miserly behavior, most observers offered nothing but praise for the man and his enterprise.[24] In comments at a farewell banquet that A.G. hosted for California baseball people at the Baldwin Hotel in San Francisco on November 16, Ward noted that "given Mr. Spalding as the host, it is unnecessary to say that the affair was gotten up in the most elaborate style." Another reporter added that "Pomery and Perrier Jouet flowed freely" while guests feasted until 4 A.M. on such delicacies as "pêtits pâté à la Spalding" and "eastern oysters on the Home Run." They could not, moreover, take their eyes off a confectionary centerpiece at the head table shaped like "a tripod of baseball bats upon a base . . . upon which rested a league ball," all beneath a suspension of "a catcher's mask . . . incrusted with sugar crystals."[25] Somehow everyone survived the affair, and the next morning, A.G. and his boys set off for Hawaii, on course for the land down under.

Spalding's careful plans for the American "visitation" to Australia were not in vain.[26] Enthusiastic receptions, complete with greetings from local dignitaries, parades, and bands playing "Yankee Doodle Dandy," preceded baseball games and cricket exhibitions from Sydney to Melbourne during the tourists' three-week stay there.[27] Although one Australian suggested that Professor Bartholomew's balloon ascents provoked more interest than the exploits on the diamond, most observers were more appreciative. After witnessing the first game played in Melbourne, on December 22, before 10,000 people, a reporter for the Melbourne *Age* celebrated the tour as a "striking illustration of American promptness in business," one marked by an "enterprising spirit...vastness of conception" and attention to detail so characteristic of "Our American cousin." Even more decisively, a correspondent for the Melbourne *Punch* commented that the "life and dash" of baseball would make it popular among his countrymen. He added the hope that baseball's arrival in Australia would be but the "first link of a mutual friendship between the two island continents." Describing his own country and the United States as nations of "go," he referred to America's ability to "stand against the world" and hoped that baseball's acceptance by his country would guarantee that America "will always be on our side helping us on the onward path."[28]

American commentators offered similar appraisals. Newton MacMillan, in his Christmas Day story for the Chicago *Tribune*, praised Spalding for having achieved "a distinct coup for himself, his game and his country. The red, white, and blue are the fashionable colors here just now, the baseball bat is mightier than the cricket paddle, and the Americans are the princes of jolly good fellows." In the "short space of a fortnight," he concluded, American baseballers had convinced Australians "after all that America must be a great country."[29]

Spalding did not ignore these sentiments when he attempted to market his wares. A.G. dedicated a special Australian version of his 1889 baseball guide to the "sportsmen of Australia" and reminded them that "all those essentials of manliness, courage, nerve, pluck and endurance, characteristic of the Anglo-Saxon race," were embedded in baseball. Hopeful that Australians busy developing a large country would find baseball a quick game conducive to developing such traits, Spalding filled the guide with detailed playing instructions, advertisements for his baseball guides, and the addresses of stores designated as exclusive agents for his products.[30]

The remaining portion of A.G.'s around-the-world trip proved cause for less ambitious plans. In the works since November, but not announced publicly or to his ballplayers until December 29, 1888, Spalding proposed to introduce America's national game to "crowned heads, nobles, and peasantry in the Old World" by gallivanting through Ceylon, Egypt, Italy, France, and the British Isles.[31] One Chicago columnist greeted the announcement with snide praise by comparing Spalding to touring "actors and entertainers" adept at gathering up "the coin of the realm." An account in the Chicago *Times*, in far more complimentary tone, characterized his "determination" to continue around the world as a "bold move...that redounds to his credit, because it shows that he is willing to risk a good deal to spread the fame of his game" without any real hope of personal profit.[32] Both observers correctly identified Spalding as the risk-taking capitalist, flamboyant impresario, and dedicated baseball man that he was. Regarding the outcome of the tour, however, the *Times*'s reporter proved far more prescient.

At best, the post-Australian excursion brought mixed results. After leaving Melbourne in early January, the tourists suffered through a three-week journey across the Indian Ocean to Colombo, Ceylon, that beset them with boredom and rough seas. Hot weather, according to one reporter, left them "panting in the sun like so many lizards." Their arrival went virtually unnoticed, although a five-inning exhibition they played brought out some native spectators who "looked at us as though we were so many escaped inmates."[33]

Only Spalding's fascination with rickshaws offered any compensation for the abortive attempt to introduce baseball to the Cingalese. According to Samuel Goodfriend of the Chicago *Inter-Ocean*, so "infatuated" did A.G. become with them that he wondered whether Spalding might not organize a rickshaw company on returning to Chicago. Although the ladies in the party chided him for allowing young boys to pull around so large a man, A.G., said Goodfriend, coiffed in a pith hat "with a brim broad enough and an upper section high enough to use for his contemplated new Chicago ground and grandstand...lolled back in state...look[ing] serenely calm and acclimated" as he sashayed through the streets of Colombo.[34]

From Colombo it was on to Cairo and a game at the Pyramids, before "long-sheeted Bedouins" and "white-robed sons of the Desert." After the game, as Spalding recalled, the players climbed onto the Sphinx for photographs, much "to the horror of the native worshippers of Cheops and the dead Pharaohs." No less disconcerting must have been the unsuccessful efforts of those ballplayers who tried to throw baseballs over the sacred Egyptian tombs.[35]

Apparently, the presence of Clarence Duval evoked more of a response from the Egyptians than baseball did. Several ballplayers forced him to wear a catcher's mask and gloves and then paraded him about the Cairo railway station, tethered by a rope, "as if he were some strange animal let loose from a menagerie." As one reporter described it, the natives, unaccustomed to seeing a black man, ran in "abject terror" at the sight of him. "One could scarcely blame them," another noted, "for could a disciple of Darwin have seen the mascot in his impromptu make-up, his host would have bounded with delightful visions of the missing link."[36]

Spalding's desire to publicize his venture by playing baseball at historic sites met frustration in Italy, the next stop for his entourage. Astonished archaeologists and Roman officials resisted his resourceful efforts to book a game in the Colosseum. Even an offer of $5,000 and the donation of gate receipts to local charity were of no avail. An attempt to obtain an audience with the pope also failed. The best A.G. could hustle was an exhibition played before the Italian king, his court, and the American legation on the stately grounds of the Villa Borghese, in Rome.[37]

Games followed in Florence and Paris, but Spalding's thoughts were fixed on England. Rekindled were memories of 1874 and his participation in Harry Wright's futile attempt to convince the British that baseball was a better game than cricket. Although this second effort proved more elaborate, the results were the same.

Altogether the Chicagos and the "All Americas" played eleven games during their two-week stay in England, Ireland, and Scotland. Throughout their visit, the ballplayers themselves enjoyed warm receptions, first-class accommodations, honorary membership in the elite Century Club, special acknowledgment in the House of Commons and at Westminster Abbey, and even a meeting with the Prince of Wales.[38] For some, there were also opportunities to meet relatives they had never seen. Jim Manning, for instance, the "All Americas' " third baseman, from Kansas City, relished his visit with an uncle and nieces in the town of Callon, in Kilkenny. As Manning told it, the entire village turned out for his arrival, greeting him "as though [he] might have come out of the clouds." Manning's relatives decorated their house with his pictures and bombarded him with questions about baseball, incredulous that "a man could earn a living by playing" a game. "Of course," the American observed, "I had a delightful time, and everything in Callon, even the scores of pretty Irish girls, was mine."[39]

Less well received, however, was baseball itself. Although Londoners turned out "at the feet of Mr. A. G. Spalding's base-ball players," they remained at best lukewarm to the sport. Typical were the remarks of a British reporter who pronounced baseball unquestionably inferior to cricket and "as much out of place in England as a nursery frolic in the House of Commons."[40]

Spalding saved these clippings for his scrapbooks but offered no comment at the time about his return to England. Twenty years later, however, he reminisced publicly about his British experience, calling it a means of drawing attention to himself and his beliefs about baseball and American democracy. Recounting the first game in England, played at London's Kensington Oval and attended by the Prince of Wales, he noted the Prince's admission that baseball, while not superior to cricket, was indeed "an excellent game." More telling was A.G.'s remembrance of his personal encounter as a representative American with British royalty. Stationed in the royal box to provide expert commentary, he found it awkward to bend down constantly in response to queries about the action on the field. "Under these circumstances," as he recalled, "I did the perfectly natural thing for an American sovereign to do—just what I would have done had President Taft been witness of the game and needed instruction—which, of course, he would not." All this verbosity in the display of American notions of equality to explain Spalding's decision to sit down paled before his need to defend himself for touching royalty on the shoulder after the Prince had slapped him on the leg in his excitement over a triple by Anson. "If I violated the code of court etiquette," A.G. asserted, "I must plead that I was not at court, but at an American ball game. If I sat in the presence of Royalty, it is certain that Royalty sat in mine. If I tapped the future King of Great Britain on the shoulder, it was nothing more offensive than a game of tag." "If British Royalty honored us by its presence, which I am willing to concede, we repaid it by a splendid exhibition of our National Game. No," the proud American concluded, "I am not able to see wherein honors were not quite even."[41]

However unsuccessful Spalding's efforts were at convincing the British of baseball's virtues, America's response to the tour's homecoming softened the blow. National League and American Association clubs were well into their spring exhibitions when the travel-weary band of baseballers arrived in New York on April 6, after a six-month trek involving forty-two games played before an estimated 200,000 people. Nevertheless, their tour contract mandated participation in a two-week swing through nine eastern and midwestern cities before they could return to their regular jobs.[42]

A.G., who delighted in public adulation, enjoyed every parade, banquet, and testimonial from New York to Chicago. Arriving in New York to a harbor reception reported as unequaled in the city's history, Spalding joked about how happy he was to be "back in the land where I can eat pie."[43] More seriously, he told one reporter that having "travelled...over the entire world...supped with royalty in Australia...eaten currie in India...gazed on the ruined palaces of the ancient Romans...looked into the siren eyes of Parisian beauties...grasped the hand of men who are in line for Kingly thrones...[and]...wept at the scenes of poverty in Ireland...I never fully appreciated anything nor experienced such keen delight in all my travels as that which swelled through my breast this morning when I stepped ashore. I am Proud to be called an American...."[44]

An exhibition baseball game and a night at the opera followed, but as a man who cultivated the company of society's finest and who strongly believed in the role of baseball as an incubator of American character, Spalding must have been particularly pleased with the "notable gathering of American manhood and brain," assembled by A. G. Mills, that celebrated the tour's return at a banquet at the exclusive Delmonico's, in Manhattan. Walls decorated with large photos of the ballplayers in Rome and Egypt reverberated with the applause of 300 guests, including Teddy Roosevelt, Mark Twain, local politicians, baseball officials, Yale undergraduates, and "popular members of the New York Stock Exchange," as they paid homage to Spalding's "feat of pluck."[45]

Perhaps overwhelmed by a dinner "served in nine innings," A.G. did no more than reiterate his pleasure at being home. A host of toastmasters, however, praised his exploits in ways consistent with its intended purposes of promoting sport's social value and of extending an American presence in the world.[46] Proclaimed as "representatives of American manhood and citizenship" and as "gladiators...covered with their American manhood," the players received praise as devotees of "manly sports" and as men "a country that holds liberty dear must have...men of athletic spirit," who make "a race fit for peace and war." One speaker suggested the possibility that they had "perhaps paved the way to new commercial relations."[47] More amusingly, Mark Twain commented on the incongruity of bringing baseball, "the very symbol, the outward and visible expression of the drive and push and rush and struggle of the raging, tearing, booming nineteenth century...to places of profound repose and soft indolence." He also thanked the baseballers for unraveling the mystery surrounding the imaginary line around the world known as the equator. The "boys," as he put it, had made it visible, by "stealing bases on their bellies" around the world, "leaving a nice deep trench along the way."[48]

Speakers at other stops on the homecoming were not able to match Twain's wit or eloquence, but their remarks consistently praised Spalding's efforts, his game, and the social promise of sport. Typical were those of A. K. McClure, of the Philadelphia *Times*. At a banquet in his city, McClure applauded the character and morality displayed by the Chicagos and "All Americas" and by baseball itself for nurturing such traits. "I bid you Godspeed," he told the ballplayers, "for an institution that teaches a boy that nothing but honesty and manliness can succeed, must be doing a missionary work every day of its existence. It will not only make a high standard of baseball men, but the world better for its presence."[49]

Chicago provided the last stop on the homecoming, and the city turned en masse to greet the returning heroes. Arrangement committees, manned by "prominent businessmen, bankers, and even wearers of ermine" and determined to celebrate Spalding's triumphal return as Chicago's "first foreign Apostle" of the 1893 Columbian Exposition, organized a demonstration unlike any ever accorded a group of American athletes until that time.[50]

Spalding and his entourage arrived in Chicago at Union Station on the evening of April 19. Illuminated by a display of fireworks, a huge escort of representatives from over 130 business and athletic organizations—among them cricketers, lacrosse players, 1,000 bicyclists "mounted on their metal steeds," and a special honor guard composed of employees of A. G. Spalding and Brothers—accompanied the world tourists as their carriages wove along a parade route crowded by an estimated 150,000 people on the way to the Palmer House for one final round of speech making and revelry. As the Chicago *Tribune* described it, "the streets were thronged" with a crowd that "represented all classes. Businessmen were in it, toughs and sports . . . also a great many ladies. And they went fairly crazy."[51]

A.G.'s response to this public outpouring, concluded over expensive cigars and fine brandy at a reception attended by Chicago's elite, was equally expansive. After admitting that his "attempt to Americanize Italy" had failed, he eschewed prepared remarks on the topic of "Baseball as a National Amusement" and offered instead a tribute to his city. "There may be some great and good places in the corners of this earth," he noted, but Chicago, with its "bustle and life, is the sweetest, dearest place on this globe."[52]

As at other stops on the homecoming, Spalding left it to others to draw the proper lessons from his missionary venture—those that reinforced notions about the social purpose of sport that he believed in and that promoted his interests. More than equal to the task was Henry L. Turner, a major in Chicago's national guard, who praised the ballplayers for doing "grand work in attracting men away from offices and desks out into the light to breathe heaven's pure air." Invoking baseball's role in making "men that we are proud of," Turner called America "a country mighty in people of courage" and urged his audience to "help . . . God in building up a country of men all powerful in protecting a country such as this. Long life to baseball and athletics. Long life to the National Guard. Long life to America, the freest land on earth."[53]

Not every stop on the homecoming proved as exhilarating as those in New York, Philadelphia, and Chicago. Particularly disappointing was a brief visit with Benjamin Harrison, the newly elected president. Described by Anson as being as "cool as an icicle," he reportedly to Spalding that it was beneath the dignity of his office ever to be see a ball game. In a comment on the episode, a reporter for the Chicago *Times* ridiculed the baseballers' unrealistic expectations to be "treated as national heroes." Viewing the tour solely as a commercial venture, he applauded Harrison's resolve not "to satisfy the whimsies of a passing showman and suffer himself to be used as an advertisement for some fellows who have salaries to harvest and gate money to gather in."[54] Predictably, the *Sporting News* joined in, noting that Spalding's profit-making scheme "met with the fate it deserved—dire and dismal failure."[55]

Although Spalding did lose $5,000 on the tour, he never doubted its success. Financially, he and others expected it to increase the popularity of professional baseball at home and to expand his sporting-goods business abroad.[56] Moreover, he saw nothing wrong in promoting his own fortune by a venture that in his mind introduced the world to the superiority of American values and culture. Indeed, with characteristic immodesty, his 1889 baseball guide praised his leadership in undertaking "a bold and plucky" tour that "did in six short months what as many years under ordinary circumstances would have failed to accomplish."[57]

Spalding's missionary venture to Australia and beyond was the most prominent, but hardly the only, way in which he sought to promote his beliefs, his business, and himself. Through his involvement in the organized-play movement, his orchestration of the mythology surrounding Abner Doubleday and the invention of baseball, and the writing and promotion of his autobiographical history of baseball, *America's National Game*, he continually encouraged middle-class Americans to accept baseball and other sports as legitimate leisure-time pursuits that provided positive social purpose, while making him rich and famous.

Like the men who extolled the world tour as proof of American exceptionalism and baseball's role in advancing it, the individuals who were prominent in the organized-play movement viewed active participation in sport as a way of training proper citizens for that special society. Yet Luther Gulick, Jr., G. Stanley Hall, Joseph Lee, and others, whose ideas and actions spawned organizations like the YMCA, the Playground Association of America, and the Public School Athletic League (PSAL), also spoke directly to real fears about America's future. These men firmly believed that children's play rehearsed particular aspects in the evolutionary process of the human race. For them, a careful, rational supervision of youthful pastime, directed toward the development of character traits deemed essential for society's continued progress, provided a major opportunity to shape the children of a generation of middle-class

Americans that had severe doubts about its own future. They understood these people's fears about their physical and moral states and shared the belief that the banality and "overcivilization" of American life had contributed to them. They were mindful, too, of the appearance of increasingly large European immigrant populations, whose very presence, to say nothing of their involvement in celebrated violent struggles between labor and capital, suggested a potential for social disorder and unrest. No longer able to rely on the frontier experience as a means of acculturating either these people or, for that matter, their own kind, play advocates offered sport as a new experience that would serve such a purpose.[58]

Although A.G. was not an active participant in the organized-play movement, its message reverberated strongly with his own personal experience and the importance of sport to his own development from a frightened, unconfident schoolboy to a prominent public figure and successful businessman.[59] Its progressive emphasis on experts, trained in psychology and recreation and responsible for organizing activities, establishing procedures, and setting standards for others to follow, also reminded him of his own contributions to the growth of professional baseball. Certainly, its belief that organized athletic competition taught proper values—the motto of the PSAL, for instance, was "Duty, Thoroughness, Patriotism, Honor, and Obedience"—appealed to a man who saw baseball as America's national game and a developer of American character.[60] Above all, however, Spalding recognized the possibilities for profit and public attention in any activity that heightened popular interest in sport. That his goals dovetailed with those of professional play reformers only served to benefit both parties in ways that helped establish sport as a significant institution in American life.

Spalding's link with the organized-play movement was Luther Gulick, Jr. A.G. first met him when Gulick taught physical education at the International YMCA Training School, next door to Chicopee Falls, in Springfield, Massachusetts. Acting under the auspices of the New York City Board of Education and enjoying the financial support of Andrew Carnegie, John D. Rockefeller, Jr., and J. Pierpont Morgan, Gulick in 1900 established the PSAL. Programmed through the city's schools, the PSAL offered athletic competition for schoolboys, by grade, in track and field and in baseball, medals and trophies being awarded for individual and group achievement. Together with James Sullivan, who served as chairman of the organization's game committee and who had hired him to write for the Library of American Sports series, he urged Spalding to become involved by donating trophies for the baseball competition.[61]

In ways that promoted his business and at the same time gave him opportunities to win public adulation and to express his views about the social purpose of sport, A.G. cashed in on the offer. In 1906 he donated the A. G. Spalding "Play Ball" trophy to the best elementary school baseball team in New York City. By 1911 the "Play Ball" trophy, and a similar version for high school teams, was being offered in PSAL leagues established in Chicago, San Francisco, and Cleveland. In addition, smaller cities where leagues existed were able to compete for the Spalding "Chain" trophy plaque.[62]

Public announcements of such doings, replete with appropriate photographs of trophies and teams, appeared regularly in Spalding's baseball guide and in the official PSAL guides, edited by Gulick and published by the American Sports Publishing Company. Included as well were words of wisdom from A.G. himself, first offered at public ceremonies at which he personally presented his awards.

A.G.'s message was clear and consistent with the objectives of the organized-play movement and with its view of the world. As he told schoolchildren at P.S. 46 in Manhattan in May 1906, "we live in a strenuous age, and our American boys and youths should be educated and developed along lines that will enable them to meet and cope with these conditions." Athletics, especially baseball, he informed his youthful audience, was the best way to "fit a boy for the rough and tumble business life of today." Making the connection between muscles and morality, as men like Gulick regularly did, he elaborated, in what must have been a tedious experience for the boys and girls in the school auditorium, on baseball's ability to nurture physical strength as well as the mental and moral faculties. Confidence, concentration, aggressiveness, alertness, ingenuity, and self-poise were all to be developed on the ball field. Commenting on the game's ability to control antisocial behavior, he added that the contest itself so sapped "a boy's youthful vitality" that "after a hard fought game" he had "no inclination for anything except a good meal and...bed." A.G. closed with an appropriate reference to Teddy Roosevelt, "our first Athletic President," and emphasized that his "sportsmanlike qualities, energy, and 'square deal' brand of integrity" inspired the nation's youth and were available to them through the PSAL.[63]

In 1910 John Foster, then editor of Spalding's baseball guide, published a long article in that year's edition that both summarized and exaggerated his employer's association with that organization. Recognizing "the good growing out of organized baseball," A.G., as Foster told it, acknowledged the PSAL to be the "perfect system" through which to offer a similar experience to American schoolboys, not only "for athletic purposes, but as a disciplinary method of instruction and formation of character." According to Foster, "Mr. Spalding has well said...that competition on the athletic field" prepared a boy for "the battle that he is shortly to fight when school days are over and the struggle for existence must begin...." Foster proceeded to focus on baseball and offered a list of benefits the game provided, freely expatiating on Spalding's remarks given at award ceremonies in various cities. Paying attention to the play reformers' belief that sport harnessed aggression and ambition to the demands of an urbanized society without causing chaos, he noted that baseball taught not only aggressiveness and concentration but also "the absolute necessity of self-control" and the need to play by the rules, be it those of baseball or the more important ones of society. After all, the game's "basic principle," said Foster on behalf of his boss, is "subordination to the rule."[64]

Although Spalding hardly disagreed with this analysis, Foster's effort to present A.G. as a professional play reformer is as problematical as those people's optimistic expectations that schoolchildren would respond to their programs as predicted. Whether or not participants in the PSAL and in similar organizations used bats and balls to achieve the desired results of the recreationists, one thing is certain: A. G. Spalding and Brothers benefited from the attempt.[65] However sincerely Spalding believed in the social promise of sport, from his perspective no better measure of the success his participation in the organized-play movement brought could be offered than a brief notice appearing in the *Spalding Store News* in May 1915. Thanks to the determination of the firm's Baltimore outlet, the *News* reported, that city's PSAL, which supervised 184 basketball teams, 98 soccer squads, and "one hundred playground teams," had just adopted for official use "the Spalding No. 14PB Official Playground Ball."[66]

Spalding's efforts to prove the native origins of baseball demonstrated a similar mixture of practical calculation, desire for attention, and expression of sport's higher purpose. As A.G. saw it, if baseball truly had a special contribution to make to the shaping of American character, its pedigree had to be impeccably American. He did not doubt that the attempt to prove the point, if carefully managed, might provide good publicity for himself and his business.

As a young man, Spalding accepted the arguments of Henry Chadwick that baseball originated from the English game of rounders.[67] Over time, however, he became convinced that a game so fundamentally representative of American values had to be American in origin. By 1905 he was ready to make his case in grand style. Using the pages of his baseball guide as his major vehicle, A.G. meticulously took apart, without a shred of evidence, Chadwick's "rounders theory." Noting the umbrage that Englishmen, Scots, or American Indians would take if told that their games of cricket, golf, or lacrosse had originated from rounders, Spalding argued that it was even more absurd to suggest that baseball had similar roots. Instead, he offered the opinion that baseball had evolved from a colonial American game called one old cat, maturing into its present form thanks to the ingenuity and creativity of succeeding generations of American youth.[68]

Acting on no authority but his own, Spalding called for the appointment of a national board of baseball commissioners to collect all available evidence and to come to a definitive decision "as to the origins of baseball." As its secretary, he suggested James E. Sullivan. Also named as members were Al Reach, his business associate; George Wright, Harry's brother; Nick Young, the man Spalding unseated as National League president in 1901; two United States senators, Arthur Gorman of Maryland and Morgan G. Bulkeley of Connecticut, each of whom had served as president of the National League; and A. G. Mills. All agreed to serve, and with Spalding's help this handpicked body of baseball experts went about its business.[69]

From the outset, Chadwick, whose arguments about English origins were the butt of Spalding's attack, recognized the insignificance of the question. As he put it, although he was certain that baseball began in England, that fact did not "detract one iota from the merit of its now being unquestionably a thoroughly American field sport, and a game too, which is fully adapted to the American character...."[70] No matter. Over the next two years, several hundred pages of testimony filtered into Sullivan's office from across the United States, each with its own peculiar contribution to the great historical debate. The *Sporting News* contended that much of it was pure fabrication. Commission members apparently thought so, for in the end they relied primarily on evidence suggested by Spalding to settle the issue.[71]

Writing to the commission in July 1907, Spalding called its attention to a letter from Abner Graves, a mining engineer in Denver, Colorado, who claimed "that the present game of Baseball was designed and named by Abner Doubleday of Cooperstown, New York, in 1839." Graves recollected that Doubleday, his schoolmate, had interrupted a game of marbles behind the local tailor shop to draw a diagram in the shape of a baseball diamond while he explained the game and gave it a name. As a witness to this event, Graves was certain that Doubleday had invented baseball, although he admitted that "there is not one chance in ten thousand that a boy's drawing...would have been preserved."[72] Drawing or not, Spalding urged the commission to give "serious consideration" to Doubleday's progeny. Reminding its members of Doubleday's exploits as a northern officer during the Civil War, he added that "it certainly appeals to an American's pride to have had the great national game of Baseball created and named by a Major-General in the United States Army."[73]

A. G. Mills, who had served as part of an honor guard in 1893 when Doubleday's body lay in state in New York's City Hall, found Graves's letter particularly intriguing. He also wondered about the possibility of connecting Doubleday to the famous New York Knickerbocker baseball club that Mills associated with baseball's beginnings. Writing to the city's customs collector in December 1907, Mills inquired whether a former employee of that office, one Mr. Wadsworth, had grown up in Cooperstown at the same time as Doubleday. If so, he hoped it was the same man mentioned in testimony received by an original Knickerbocker who had in 1845 given the club a diagram of a baseball field that altered the way they played the game. Could it be that this diagram had been the one originally drawn by Doubleday in 1839? "Should this prove to be a fact," Mills concluded, "the connecting link between Doubleday at Cooperstown and the beginning of the game in New York would be established....Perhaps in the years to come, in view of the hundreds of thousands of people who are devoted to baseball, and the millions who will be, Abner Doubleday's fame will rest evenly, if not quite as much, upon the fact that he was its inventor...as upon his brilliant and distinguished career as an officer of the Federal Army."[74]

Whether the press of business as vice-president of Otis Elevator Company or his inclination to support Graves's testimony held sway, Mills decided to draft the commission's final report before he received a reply. Signed by its members and submitted to Sullivan on December 30, the report concluded that baseball originated in the United States and that "the first scheme for playing it, according to the best evidence obtainable to date, was devised by Abner Doubleday at Cooperstown, N.Y. in 1839." Special "indebtedness" was also directed to A. G. Spalding for the acquisition of "a circumstantial statement by a reputable gentleman" that had directed the commission's attention to Doubleday and Cooperstown.[75]

Almost without exception, the decision of Spalding's commission received universal acceptance when it was announced in the pages of his baseball guide in March 1908.[76] Henry Chadwick held fast. In a note to Mills he commented that "your decision in the case of Chadwick vs. Spalding...is a masterly piece of special pleading which lets my dear

old friend Albert escape a bad defeat." "The whole matter," he concluded, "was a joke between Albert and myself."[77]

Joke or not, Spalding's plea for baseball as America's immaculate conception only served to underline his personal feelings about baseball's
important contribution to American development. Some thirty years
later, in 1939, as testimony to the persuasiveness of his beliefs, the
Baseball Hall of Fame opened at Cooperstown and celebrated baseball's
mythological centennial by posthumously admitting A.G. as one of its
charter members.[78] Anyone familiar with baseball lore who attended
that event should have known that if it had not been for Spalding there
would have been no festivities at all to commemorate the one hundredth
anniversary of the "invention" of America's national game.

No one today, not even baseball's officialdom, recognizes Abner Doubleday as the inventor of baseball.[79] Yet baseball's continual hold on the
American public as more than a game owes much to Spalding. Throughout his long career as a baseball man and entrepreneur, his every public
action and pronouncement reiterated themes concerning the game's role
in developing character and its demonstration of the importance of organization, professionalism, and individual strength for achieving success in late-nineteenth-century America. These themes also dominated
A.G.'s own history of baseball, *America's National Game*.

Eager to transmit his message to future generations, to turn a profit,
and to insure his own place in the annals of the game, Spalding at first
wanted to commission Henry Chadwick to do the job. Chadwick, still
editor of Spalding's baseball guide, and well into his eighties, responded
positively when A.G. first raised the subject, in November 1905, and
asked him whether he was physically up to writing a book on "the
Origins and History of Baseball."[80] Chadwick once described Spalding
as a "stirring Western merchant, full of...nerve, pluck, independence,
and push." He must not have been surprised when, three days after he
expressed interest, he received a lengthy reply. Reminding Chadwick
"that you are not going to live forever," A.G. ordered him to drop all
other work and "*get busy, get action* and give me the manuscript for a
first class history on Baseball, both professional and amateur, in this
country and the rest of the world."[81]

To insure that Chadwick's prose matched Spalding's intentions, A.G.
provided an outline for the book. It called for a series of chapters on the
development of baseball from the "Knickerbocker Era" to the "National
League," with special emphasis on "Baseball Revolutions" that at-

tempted unsuccessfully to challenge the structure of the organized game. "Keep the book free of statistics as much as possible," A.G. advised; if any are necessary, "let them be...League or club...rather than of players....In other words, make it a history of the game with principal reference to its government and development." Finally, to a man who had been his chief baseball writer since 1878 and who was nationally acclaimed as the father of sports journalism, A.G. offered firm directions about the preparation of the manuscript itself. Instructing him to use full-size paper and to leave spaces between lines to facilitate corrections, he requested that Chadwick send him carbon copies of each section "to show me how you are handling the work" and to provide an opportunity "now and then...to make a suggestion as we go along."[82]

Chadwick died before he had a chance to follow these instructions, so Spalding wrote the book himself. Dedicated to Henry Chadwick, "The Father of Baseball"; to William Hulbert, "The Savior of a Nation's Pastime"; and to the "National League of Professional Baseball Clubs," *America's National Game* first appeared in 1911, published by Spalding's own house. In the foreword he noted that he had undertaken the task at the frequent urgings of "admirers of our National Game" and at the special behest of Chadwick, who in his will had left him his baseball library "in the hope that I would write...a book on Baseball." The result, he hoped, was "the simple story of America's National Game as I have come to know it," with special attention to the establishment of "a form of government...which has wrought the salvation of the game and made it the cleanest, most scientific and popular pastime known to the world of sport"—all done in a way that disclaims "any desire to exploit my name, my views, or my achievements."[83]

Spalding batted .500, by writing a book that emphasized the role of the National League in baseball's growth as an acceptable leisure-time activity but one that hardly ignored his own imprint on the game. Indeed, the book is as much A.G.'s autobiography as a history of baseball—a pastiche of personal reminiscences, narrative history, and pointed opinion.

Advertisements for the book stated that Spalding's chief aim was to detail the history of organized baseball and the successful fight "by strong men" against degenerate forces that threatened its survival. A.G. devoted more than half of his 600-page tome to this effort. Spiced throughout with traces of evolutionary flavor, the book chronicled baseball's development, always stressing professionalism and proper organization as the key ingredients in its progress. Commenting on the success of the Cincinnati Red Stockings in 1869, for instance, a success that had much to do with his personal decision to become a professional ballplayer, Spalding noted that it marked "the dawn of a new era in Base Ball." Cincinnati's accomplishments forced the public to recognize that "professionalism had come to stay; that by it the game would be presented in its highest state of perfection; that amateurs could not hope to compete with those whose business it was to play the game—and play it as a business."[84]

A critical factor in the successful transformation of baseball from a playful pastime to a business enterprise was the emergence of the National League as an organization capable of maintaining standards and efficiently managing the game's affairs. Success, however, did not come without struggle. Integral parts of Spalding's story were accounts of the degenerate forces and evil men who did battle with the league and its leaders. From the gamblers who threatened baseball's integrity in the 1870s to the anarchist Brotherhood of 1890 and the infamous Freedman of 1901, every villain is accounted for, at times even in a lively and readable fashion. In the end, thanks to baseball magnates willing to go "at a pace that kills," not only were these obstacles overcome but players, according to A.G., were relieved "of all care and responsibility for the legitimate functions of management," enabling them to give "the very best performance of which they were capable in the entertainment of the public." The results were status and profit for the owner, the presentation of the game in its highest form, a satisfied public, and for the ballplayer "the dignity of his profession and . . . munificent salary."[85]

Spalding's deliberate emphasis on the role of professional experts supported by efficient organization in baseball's rise to glory clearly celebrated his own, personal contributions in that process. Yet the constancy with which he harped on these matters belies more than predictable attempts to satisfy his insatiable ego. A fascination with efficiency, rationalization, and organization monitored by experts to bring order, control, and progress to virtually every realm of American life marked the diverse efforts of businessmen, politicians, and social reformers throughout his lifetime. A reliance on trained professionals to improve the lot of the urban poor, to clean up corrupt government, or to rationalize the operation of business enterprise was a hallmark of this era. In this context, Spalding's identity as a progressive comes as no surprise, nor does his insistence on reiterating that claim. So strong was his belief in the National League and its system of government as the "organization" that was baseball's foundation, for instance, that he once noted that even "if Jay Gould were to come to life and join forces with all the capitalists of the nation in forming an organization in opposition to the

National League, I believe even then the latter would come out victorious."[86] In *America's National Game*, A.G. offered a powerful refrain to this same song.

It is not surprising that a man who saw virtue in promoting sport as a new incubator of values and character essential to continued American greatness also emphasized the special ability of baseball to serve such ends. With typical bombast, A.G. suggested at the outset that there was no need to "prove that Baseball is our National Game" or that "it has all the attributes of American origin [and] American character." To do so would be "to undertake the elucidation of a patent fact...it is like a solemn declaration that two plus two equals four."[87] Nevertheless, from the first chapter to the thirty-eighth, in and out of narrative accounts of the history of organized baseball, through chapters on baseball literature, religion, the game in the Army and the Navy, the world tour of 1888–89, and those on baseball around the world, A.G. relentlessly stated the case.

Spalding boldy asserted, rather than argued, that baseball was the quintessential American game. "The genius of our institutions is democratic," he noted, and "baseball is a democratic game."[88] Pointing to the "brilliant array" of "men of eminence in all professions and in every avenue of commercial and industrial activity" who had played ball, A.G. underscored that the game prepared young boys for success in life.[89] The ability of the game to provide a legitimate outlet for man's aggressive drive while at the same time encouraging respect for authority and submission to discipline also deserved mention.[90]

Touching every base, A.G. even relied on the words of his old baseball comrade A. G. Mills in order to emphasize baseball's role in alleviating anxiety about an unfit, sedentary middle-class population lacking outlets to develop the character necessary to meet the demands of a modern world. Thanks to baseball, Mills noted, "the deterioration of the race has ended and the rising generation is better equipped for the duties, the conflicts, and the pleasures of life than were their fathers or mothers." For both Mills and Spalding, baseball, "whether played on the village common or the splendidly appointed grounds of the modern professional club...satisfies and typifies the American idea of a manly, honest, entertaining recreation."[91]

Any reader who had difficulty following Spalding's picaresque account of baseball's contributions to American development could focus on the book's last chapter. Here he offered a summary of his thoughts by reprinting an interview that he had given to Edward Marshall, a reporter for the New York *Times*, and that had first appeared in that paper on November 13, 1910. In response to a series of questions about the "psychology of baseball," A.G. referred to baseball as a "man maker," a game that "elevates and...fits the American character" and that gives "a growing boy self-poise, and self-reliance, confidence, inoffensive and entirely proper aggressiveness," and "general manliness." Noting that "an able boy's blood always runs high," Spalding added that the game taught that "the first thing he must learn, if he is to win success, is to control it." Proud of baseball's ability to prepare youth for careers in business by teaching "quick thinking," A.G. called the game "a man as well as a soul builder." "The psychology of Baseball?" he responded to Marshall, "it is the psychology of success."[92]

Personal reminiscences of his own career in baseball underlined his message about baseball's social value. Whether describing his discovery of the game in Rockford as a frightened adolescent, his exploits with Boston, his years in Chicago, the world tour, or his encounters with Andrew Freedman or the Brotherhood, Spalding made clear that baseball had provided him confidence, self-esteem, and success. Intentionally or not, he held out similar possibilities to a generation of middle-class Americans anxious about their own changing world and their place in it.[93]

America's National Game was scarcely alone in suggesting that sport, particularly baseball, was a new outlet capable of relieving anxiety while shaping society's leaders. Because Spalding had the most recognizable name in American sport, however, his promotion of the social promise of sport carried special import.

A.G. and the American Sports Publishing Company certainly believed this to be so. "Profusely illustrated with one hundred full-page engravings and sixteen cartoons by Homer Davenport," the book was offered to the public for $2.00.[94] Although no official sales reports exist, the New York *American* noted that a first edition of 5,000 copies sold out in two months, and the Los Angeles *Times*, in an editorial that referred to it as an "adequate textbook" on the game, informed its audience that over 90,000 copies had been sold during its first six months on the market.[95] Whatever the actual count, it is clear from the firm's advertising blitz that Spalding had every intention of making money while spreading his message and satisfying his own craving for publicity.

Supervised by James Sullivan, the campaign for *America's National Game* relied on testimonials, mass newspaper exposure, and direct mailings. Prior to the book's publication, Sullivan sent out complimentary copies personally autographed by A.G., to at least seventy-five individuals either prominently connected with organized sport or well known for other achievements. Included in the group were William Howard Taft, a noted baseball fan and president of the United States; Pierre de

Coubertin, founder of the modern Olympics; Walter Camp, Yale's famous football coach; Luther Gulick; Pope Pius X; the crown prince of
Sweden; and the athletic director of Purdue University. Each person was
asked to acknowledge receipt of the book and to offer his appraisal of
it. While President Taft and the pope left it up to their aides to make a
perfunctory response, a good many individuals (some only after receiving a follow-up letter inquiring as to their delay in replying) did provide
Sullivan with appreciative comments. Luther Gulick, for instance, in
praising the book, wrote that baseball expressed "the National spirit
more perfectly than" did "our form of government" or "any other institutions." He also noted that it owed everything to A. G. Spalding,
who "deserved to rank with other great men of the country." The sporting editor of the Boston *Globe* simply referred to *America's National Game*
as "a classic in American history."[96]

Sullivan made good use of these testimonials, sending them, along
with his own promotional copy and the book itself, to some 200 newspapers throughout the country. In a covering letter he asked each editor
to review the book, noting that they might choose to use any one of the
"number of press notices" he had conveniently provided.[97] Whether or
not every editor read the book, a number did accede to Sullivan's request.
The editor of one California paper went so far as to thank him for his
"forethought in including press matter.…It ma[de] such fine copy that
when the foreman yelled, I grabbed the shears and paste pot."[98]

Showing initiative that Spalding would have been proud of, Sullivan
also sent similar mailings to the superintendents of public libraries, together with assurances that *America's National Game* deserved a place in
every one in order "to meet a demand that is sure to increase with the
passing of the years."[99] To the managers of all Spalding stores, Sullivan
provided four-page advertisements, instructing them to place a copy in
every book of the American Sports Library they sold as well as in every
envelope or package they mailed. He also suggested that they encourage
their salesmen to "call at the local bookstores, public libraries and clubs
or Y.M.C.A.'s…and try and induce orders for the book." Careful to
explore every potential market, Sullivan even sent out a form letter to
managers of baseball teams at every level, requesting the addresses of
their players so that they might be contacted about the book. As Sullivan
concluded, "the purpose for which we desire these names is in connection with an entirely baseball matter and one to which no one would
object."[100]

Pleased with the flow of tributes orchestrated by his own company,
Spalding collected them for his scrapbooks. None could have touched
him more than a personal note he received from Francis Richter, who

even suggested serializing *America's National Game* in the pages of *Sporting Life*. Richter praised the book as "an honest effort to crown a life devoted to Baseball...a supreme tribute which will outlast all of your work." "Frankly," he went on, "you have chosen the very best way to immortalize yourself in connection with the National Game."[101]

But A.G. had already left his mark. Rarely separating one concern from another, he promoted sport in ways that not only served his own personal and material interests but also helped solidify the place of sport in American life.

7

Retirement to California: Theosophy and the U.S. Senate

In 1902, a short time after the public announcement that A. G. Spalding had become a member of the Raja Yoga Theosophical Society, located outside of San Diego, at Point Loma, an eastern newspaper reporter interviewed Irving Snyder, Spalding's business associate and world-tour companion, about his friend's apparent retirement from the worlds of business and baseball. Remarking that "Mr. Spalding goes into every-thing that interests him with his whole heart," Snyder did not doubt A.G.'s new involvement in an experimental, religious community. "But," he added, "you may depend on it. He will be back East in the summer as usual, with an eye to his large business affairs" and to "things of importance in the sporting world."[1]

Snyder's prognostication proved only partly correct. A.G. occasionally did return to Chicago and New York to attend World Series games, check on business matters, present "Play Ball" trophies to schoolboys, and talk baseball with old friends. For the most part, however, after 1901 Spalding no longer took an active role in either the management of his company or the world of sport. Instead, he spent the last fifteen years of his life, as he put it, surrounded by "many educated, cultured, refined and most genial people...out in the quiet" of Point Loma.[2]

For a man whose actual encounter with Italy and the Mediterranean had consisted of unsuccessful efforts to play baseball in the Colosseum and to promote his business and his ego in Egypt and elsewhere in 1889, Southern California, "America's Mediterranean," seemed an unlikely place for retirement. Warmed by tropical sun, washed by the Pacific sea, cooled by its breezes, and nestled in the shadows of mountain ranges stretching from Santa Barbara to San Diego, the region, as one emigrant remarked, beckoned Americans who sought "to recover the joy and serenity which their manner of life denies them elsewhere."[3] For Charles

Dudley Warner, whose *America's Italy*, written in 1891, popularized the Mediterranean metaphor, the region's climate and beauty seemed destined to make it "a corner of the Union where there will be a little more leisure, a little more of serene waiting on Providence, and abatement of the restless rush and haste of our usual life." "This may be altogether fanciful," he acknowledged, "but I have sometimes felt, in the sunny moderation of nature there, that this land might offer for thousands at least a winter of content."[4]

Southern California provided more than quiet and serenity. The entire area offered fertile soil for dynamic economic growth. Indeed, A.G.'s years in San Diego coincided with its development from a small coastal town of 19,000 inhabitants, located somewhere south of Los Angeles, into a national tourist attraction and bustling port city of close to 100,000 people.[5] San Diego brimmed with a booster spirit that must have reminded him of his early years in Rockford and of the energy and drive that raised Chicago from the ashes of the Great Fire. Both the promise and the spirit of this California setting suited Spalding's needs.

A.G. liked to think of himself as an "elegant and cultured gentleman" who rose "from the ranks" to his "exalted position in the business communities of America and baseball." In Chicago he always belonged to the right gentlemen's clubs and occasionally made the social register. A resident of the fashionable Kenwood neighborhood, he also maintained a seventy-five-acre summer estate known as Meade Lawn, on New Jersey's prestigious south shore. Complete with its own ball field and "a palatial dwelling," it offered, in Henry Chadwick's words, "a picture of elegant refinement...a homestead an Astor or a Gould might be proud of." And yet, Spalding's wealth and stature paled before those of the Marshall Fields, the Ferdinand Pecks, and the Potter Palmers, who dominated Chicago's business and civic elite and left A.G. no more than a fringe player's role. While they designed and presided over the 1893 Columbian Exposition, built opera houses, reformed city government, engaged in cultural philanthropy, and directed Chicago's "higher life," Spalding played in benefit baseball games and entertained visiting Australian baseball players. San Diego and Point Loma changed all that, providing opportunities for social, civic, and economic leadership denied him elsewhere.[6]

For all that California eventually offered Spalding, his decision to settle there arose from other considerations. In July 1899, while on vacation at their New Jersey estate, Josie, A.G.'s wife, died suddenly. In an obituary that was more about Spalding than about his wife, the *Sporting News* described their marriage as "one of affection and prosperity," a union of two souls who were "devoted to and fitted for each other in temperament and attainments."[7] Within two years, Spalding found himself married again—this time to Elizabeth Mayer Churchill, a widow, and a childhood acquaintance of his from Rockford. The two had been secret lovers for years, and their liaison had produced a son. The boy, named Spalding Brown Spalding, had lived with A.G.'s sister. Now he formally recognized his patrimony and renamed the child Albert Goodwill Spalding, Jr. Along with him and their sons from their first marriages, A.G. and Elizabeth moved to Point Loma to start a new family life.[8]

Without Elizabeth, Spalding would not have "discovered" California. She had been a personal pupil of Madame Blavatsky, the popularizer of theosophy, and a believer in the religion's message long before her marriage to A.G. Devoted to Katherine Tingley, America's leading theosophist and founder of the Point Loma community, Elizabeth became a member of her cabinet and the general superintendent of a worldwide network of children's Sunday schools in 1898. The move to Point Loma, where she was to become its first musical director, was her chance for an even fuller commitment to the movement. Surprisingly, the curious world of mysticism, self-improvement, social reform, and performing arts that the Spaldings found there also provided A.G. new opportunities for public attention and social leadership.[9]

Katherine Tingley offered her followers a complex amalgam of Indian religion, social gospel, and a touch of the occult, all aimed toward the achievement of nirvana—the recognition of the "essential divinity of man." For her, individual perfection, attained by merging one's purified soul with a mystical Divine Essence, would result in a life of individual contentment and a world full of harmony, brotherhood, and perfection. These goals, however, were not easily reached. First, people had to accept responsibility for their actions and to realize that a person's karma, the consequences of such actions, had to be accounted for before they could achieve inner harmony and peace. The opportunity to accomplish this necessary and arduous task was offered by reincarnation. Tingley believed that a person's soul would be reborn in other forms, indeed as many times as was necessary, in order to allow the individual the chance to work off his or her karma by leading a good and socially responsible life.[10]

The "Purple Mother," or "Purple," as Tingley was fondly called, made original contributions to theosophy less in the area of doctrine than in the matter of implementation. Although not unconcerned with worldwide pilgrimages to secure converts and to legitimize her connections with Indian mystics, her major efforts focused on establishing an ideal community, organized, structured, and controlled by her benevolent but autocratic hand. There, she would train and educate a new class of people, free from negative impulses and prepared to show others the road to human perfection. As she put it, her vision was to "fashion a city and bring the people of all countries together and have the youth taught how to live, and how to become true and strong and no-ble...forceful warriors for humanity." Her "white city," as she called it, was Point Loma.[11]

By all accounts, Tingley's "white city," a demonstration of "theosophy in practice," was remarkable both in appearance and in operation. Spread over 330 acres on a jut of land overlooking San Diego and the Pacific, its architecture was an eclectic blend of Greek and Egyptian styles that caught every visitor's attention. Ray Stannard Baker, who visited the place in 1907 and wrote about it for the *American Magazine*, described the Homestead, the society's main building of ninety rooms, circled by an enclosed rotunda 300 feet around and 85 feet high, as "a huge struc-ture of indescribable architecture, surmounted with domes and globes...which by daylight shine in the sun and by night are always illuminated." Equally spectacular were the Temple of Aryans, complete with an amethyst Egyptian gateway, and an open-air Greek theater, dramatically set at the top of a canyon overlooking the Pacific.[12]

Built and maintained by the donations and "love offerings" of its members, this entire enterprise, at its peak populated by 300 children and 200 adults, was Tingley's domain. As one observer noted, "from changing the milk-bottles of the newest baby to laying the last shingle on a bungalow, her desire equals a Czar's edict."[13]

For Tingley, the community's design and her dominance facilitated the operation of the society's centerpiece, its controversial Raja Yoga school. Here, children, recruited from all over the United States and the world, lived apart from their parents, practiced the rule of silence and discipline as they went about their tasks, and learned, by practice, the beauty and meaning of theosophy. Their education emphasized music and art and involved them in apparently sophisticated and locally pop-ular productions of Greek plays, Wagnerian music, and Shakespearean drama. Under the direction of the society's Isis League of Music and Drama, not only the children but also a curious public could hear the timeless philosophical messages Tingley thought were inherent in such material. Indeed, in her hands even *A Midsummer Night's Dream* could teach that "falling in love with a beast is still much too common" or that "Quince and his fellows still cry aloud in the dullness of their distorted ideals, to those of higher station for help to understand themselves."[14]

Although Spalding denied that he believed in theosophy, he clearly supported his wife's interest in it.[15] In 1901 he purchased a large tract of land next to the Homestead and built an elaborate family residence with its own glass dome and exterior spiral staircases. Judging from family photographs, both the house and the setting seemed to have offered a fair amount of contentment. With the two younger boys enrolled in the Raja Yoga school and Elizabeth busy with the society's work, A.G. found time to construct and enjoy his private nine-hole golf course, which played out from behind his house down to the shores of the Pacific. There were also opportunities for outings with his wife, often taken with Spalding behind the wheel of his Locomobile, which he had shipped out from Chicago; quiet moments on the veranda of his house with his children; and sociable evenings with the society's more prominent benefactors such as Lyman Gage, himself a former Chicagoan and secretary of the treasury under William McKinley, and Clark Thurston, president of the American Screw Company.[16]

A.G.'s involvement in Point Loma went beyond these pleasures. However mystical theosophy's message might have seemed, its emphasis on shaping and controlling character in pursuit of an ideal world was hardly unique at the turn of the century. Reformers of all kinds focused their energies on similar concerns as they struggled to make the values and culture of immigrants conform to the demands of American society and to maintain the character and vigor of their own kind. Certainly, its philosophy was not altogether unfamiliar to a man whose own success depended upon convincing others that participation in sport served a similar purpose. Although he did not really seek the part, when circumstances compelled a defense of Point Loma's work in 1902, A.G. found himself embroiled in a controversy involving it that provoked national attention.

At issue was the status of eleven Cuban children who had left Santiago bound for Madame Tingley's Raja Yoga school. Arriving at New York's Ellis Island in November, the children and their theosophist chaperon were denied entry into the United States and detained by immigration officials charged with investigating claims against Tingley's Universal Brotherhood. Joining forces against Lomaland were rival theosophists disenchanted with the Purple Mother and officials of the Society for the Prevention of Cruelty to Children (SPCC). The SPCC firmly believed in its mission to better society not only by combatting the physical abuse of children but, in typical progressive fashion, by reshaping and altering character. Its disagreement with Tingley was less over ends than over means. Simply put, its position was that she was neither financially solvent nor morally capable of providing for the Cuban immigrants.[17] In pressing its case, the society initiated five weeks of public hearings, state and federal investigations of the Point Loma enterprise, extensive and at times sensationalist newspaper coverage, and the ultimately successful and dramatic transfer of the children to California in time for Christmas. Once caught up in these proceedings, A.G. relished both the battle and the attention it provided.

In New York for the National Cycle Show, the Spaldings received word of the detention from Olaf Tyberg, an ardent theosophist and a Point Loma neighbor, who urged them to attend a board of inquiry scheduled for November 2 at Ellis Island. Describing the session to Tingley in a letter the following day, Spalding reported that Elizabeth and Tyberg offered solid testimony in behalf of Point Loma. He added that he, too, had "testified as to the responsibility of the institution" and taken a forceful role in insisting that the children be removed to Long Island Hospital until their fate was decided.[18] When, on November 5, immigration authorities agreed to reexamine their initial decision to deport the children to Cuba, Spalding responded more boldly. "Have opened up broadside," he telegraphed the Purple Mother. "Have entire matter well in hand, legally, morally, financially, and otherwise, and there will be no let-up until the children are on their way to California and the nigger in the woodpile is unearthed." Expressing similar sentiments to a New York *Times* reporter, Spalding wondered whether the SPCC was half as energetic "in providing homes and educations for worthy children of poor parents as they are in preventing others from doing so." Characteristically, he announced his determination, having "been brought into this controversy," to "go to the end of it."[19]

The rehearing offered an immediate opportunity for A.G. to demonstrate his concern. In cross examination by Commodore Elbridge Gerry, a founder of the SPCC, Spalding, according to one account, "walked up and down...his hands in his pockets, his frame shaking with a rage which he tried hard to suppress," as he responded to a series of questions aimed at exposing Tingley as an eccentric mystic who taught children that her dog contained a human soul and that plants marry and have children. Indeed, the New York *Times* correspondent covering the event noted that at one point he moved as if to hit Gerry but instead "pounded the desk" in frustration.[20]

Disgusted with proceedings that allowed innuendo and hearsay as evidence and that denied him the chance, as Tingley's representative, to question witnesses, A.G. walked out of the hearing. In a telegraph to the mayor of San Diego, he urged official support for the Raja Yoga school "located in your city, whose citizens of prominence so unanimously and unqualifyingly endorse [it] as in every way responsible and respectable." For his own part, he asserted that "it is time for men to act. I have decided to take...this case into my own hands....I am determined that these eleven little Cuban children should soon be on their way to Point Loma, and all the Gerry societies this side of Hades can't stop them."[21]

Spalding had expressed a similar faith in the actions of "strong men" when discussing his own role in saving the National League from the likes of Andrew Freedman. Indeed, as in his support of one group of baseball capitalists over another, in defending Tingley against an organization out to "injure and besmirch [her] reputation and character," he had no trouble distinguishing which of two sides presumably pursuing similar goals deserved his support.[22]

For all of their boldness, however, Spalding's expostulations did not translate into immediate action. Although a second hearing resulted in a unanimous decision to send the children back to Cuba, public support for Point Loma from San Diego citizens, the mayor of Santiago, and federal officials in California who had offered their own evaluation of Tingley's school compelled F. P. Sargent, the commissioner general of immigration of the United States, to conduct his own investigation. In California to study Chinese immigration problems, Sargent visited the school and conducted interviews; much to the dismay of the SPCC, his investigation focused on Tingley's financial responsibility rather than on her moral character. His strong endorsement of Point Loma resulted in a December 6 decision by New York immigration officials that overturned their earlier verdict and admitted the Cuban children, "Lotus Buds," as the press now called them, into the country.[23]

Spalding, considered by one reporter "the most energetic New York agent of the Tingley side of the struggle," felt personally vindicated by the news. "I know the Raja Yoga School and know the good work it is doing," he told the New York Times, "and I feel that my course in the matter of coming to the defense of the school and these eleven Cuban children has been approved by the decision."[24]

The decision also gave A.G. a final opportunity for action. Rumors that the SPCC would attempt to kidnap the children placed Spalding "center stage" in organizing the trip of the "Lotus Buds" to Point Loma. Full coverage of the escapade, complete with photographs of the children, A.G., Katherine Tingley, and Point Loma in the December 8 edition of the New York Herald, referred to it as a "mild melodrama" that was "a spectacular climax to a little international drama which has aroused almost worldwide interest." Making use of secret plans, chartered tug-

boats, special Pullman cars, a dozen private detectives (each in charge
of one child with an extra one for "good measure"), Spalding, with the
help of James Sullivan, engineered the successful "escape" of the children to Point Loma. With the children on their way, A.G. returned to
his apartment at the Hotel Albemarle and, pleading exhaustion and cold,
refused to talk to reporters, regarding "the incident as closed." Later,
however, in characteristic style, he issued a press release describing his
role in the escape, in which, as one reporter noted, "no sensational
incident of the day was overlooked."[25]

Although on other occasions Spalding expressed praise for the Purple
Mother and her mission, the Cuban-children incident offered by far the
most dramatic expression of it.[26] While Tingley benefited her own, sometimes controversial cause by encouraging public identification of it with
well-known figures like A.G., he clearly enjoyed his part and the recognition as a defender of social and civic causes it afforded him. Even
more than Lomaland, however, San Diego's development provided continual opportunities for similar activities.

San Diego's success as a regional and national tourist attraction known
for its climate and beauty hinged, according to its most prominent business and political leaders, on its accessibility by railroad and highway.[27]
Spalding, whose interest in "good roads" antedated his move to California, could not have agreed more. Convinced by his travels that Eu-
ropeans built "impressive" roads and concerned that his bicycle interests
required similar facilities in the United States, he suggested as early as
1899 that bicycle manufacturers—indeed, "the makers of all vehicles"—
hold an annual convention to encourage "the advancement of road making." Endorsing a plan that called for government involvement at every
level and eventually for "national legislation" to construct a national
road system, A.G. urged all "good citizens" to join the campaign for
good roads. "It is one," he noted, "which only requires able leadership
to bring about an effective solution that will do much to advance the
prosperity of this country."[28] San Diego gave Spalding his chance to
practice what he preached.

In 1906 the city's chamber of commerce appointed a committee of
distinguished citizens to make recommendations regarding San Diego's
roads and streets. At the committee's suggestion, voters approved a
$75,000 bond issue to improve highways connecting San Diego to out-
lying coastal spots, including La Jolla, Mission Valley, and Point Loma.

Appointed as assistant superintendents of streets to oversee this project were Spalding, John D. Spreckels, and E. W. Scripps.

Spreckels had made his fortune in beet sugar and was a member of the San Francisco family that controlled the "sugar trust." A resident and promoter of San Diego since 1889, Spreckels involved himself in railroad and waterworks development and owned the city's streetcar system, two of the city's three newspapers, the *Union* and the *Evening Tribune*, and the Hotel del Coronado. Scripps owned the city's other paper, the *Sun*, and was well on his way to developing a national chain of newspapers. Described by the San Diego *Union*, hardly an impartial observer, as "three of the largest property owners and most prominent men in the city," the three millionaires, as they were also called, successfully carried out their mission.[29]

Two years later the three found themselves involved in a more ambitious project. Encouraged by a state law authorizing counties to issue bonds for highway improvements, San Diego County supervisors appointed Spalding, Spreckels, and Scripps to newly created posts as county road commissioners and charged them with developing a comprehensive plan. Known as "the Triple-S commission," they took a year to come up with a blueprint for what one reporter called "one of the finest systems of county highways...in the entire country." They recommended and successfully promoted the passage of a $1.25 million bond issue to repair existing surfaces and to construct some 450 miles of new county roads. Under their direction, rights-of-way were purchased and engineers hired to do the job. Indeed, Spalding received special mention in the press for personally hiring the chief engineer for the project while on a trip to New York.[30]

San Diego's newspapers, owned and operated by Spreckels and Scripps, offered nothing but praise for the commissioners and their plan. County voters, who approved it by an overwhelming margin, also showed their support. Not everyone, however, applauded their intentions or style. Some people expressed concern that the plan benefited only the property interests of the "three millionaires." When A.G. tendered his resignation from the commission, in 1909, a county supervisor eagerly urged its acceptance. As he put it, he was "tired of the abuse of these people" and no longer desired "to be rifraffed by these millionaires because I'm a poor rancher."[31]

Spalding's resignation from the county road commission did not diminish his interest in road building or in other activities that might enhance San Diego's image. As America's leading sports figure and one of San Diego's best-known citizens, he was a natural choice, along with

Rufus Choate of the city's chamber of commerce, to represent San Diego at a 1911 meeting of the Ocean to Ocean Highway Association, an organization devoted to connecting southwestern and midwestern states by highways.[32] Coincidentally, Spalding also lent his name to the Panama-California Exposition Company, organized to ready San Diego for the 1915 Panama-California Exposition, the city's celebration of the completion of the Panama Canal and its bid for national recognition as a center for trade and tourism. Although Spreckels and others supervised the city's preparations, Spalding's contributions to the event included service as president of the company and the private development, at considerable expense, of his own land at Sunset Cliffs. According to one account, A.G. spent $2 million on Japanese-style gardens, benches, and cobblestone paths on his land overlooking the Pacific, all winding down to a wading area, carved in sandstone and known as Spalding's Pond.[33]

A.G.'s interest in San Diego's development was not entirely altruistic. In 1891 he had turned a nice profit in Chicago after promoting the development of land he owned south of the city into "the great model manufacturing town of America." Although Harvey, Illinois, did not become another Pullman, Spalding sold over 700 acres of land for $700 an acre only three years after he had purchased it for less than $100,000.[34] Similar intentions marked the organization of the San Diego Securities Company, established in January 1912 with A.G. as its president.

Capitalized originally at $1 million and subscribed by Spalding, Scripps, Spreckels, and "other men of large affairs," it sought to develop more than 1,000 acres of land on the coast near Point Loma that had first been acquired by Spalding in 1908. In offering a fifth of its stock for public sale, the company emphasized that its foundation was the land and the future.[35] "The man who believes in San Diego," its booster advertisement rang, sees "a glorious future in the construction of new railroads, in the municipal acquisition of our splendid harbor, in the building of the Panama-California exposition, in the development of highways, and in new life along every avenue of our unprecedented activities." Encouraging people to invest in a sure thing, the company lauded its officers, especially its president, as successful "in the strenuous activities of legitimate competitive business" and as men who were not "so old as to have forgotten the days" when they were poor. Apparently, a good many people accepted these claims. Within a month of the announcement of the company's public stock offering, it was oversubscribed.[36]

Spalding's most prominent activities as a San Diego civic leader had to do with its commercial prospects. Occasionally, however, he became involved in other matters. In 1912, for instance, he served as a director of the YMCA.[37] That same year, when the city fathers authorized battle against members of the International Workers of the World over ordinances prohibiting their right to public gatherings, Spalding joined them in approving the violent actions of citizen vigilante groups that had physically attacked the Wobblies, chased Emma Goldman out of town, and brutalized her companion, Ben Reitman.[38] Not a central figure in this controversy, A.G. received far more attention that same year when he joined other San Diego businessmen who sought to secure a baseball franchise in the Pacific Coast League.[39] Three years later he found his name associated with a public enterprise of a far different nature: he was the initiator, along with his wife and Katherine Tingley, of a petition in San Diego to save the life of Leo Frank, an Atlanta Jew falsely convicted of murder in an anti-Semitic controversy that gained national attention.[40]

Whether defending Lomaland, promoting San Diego, developing his properties, or dabbling in social and civic affairs, A.G. enjoyed his status as a member of the gentry class. For Henry Chadwick, he was "a model of a professional ball player in retirement," surrounded by "financial prosperity . . . social happiness in his home life, and the admired of hosts of earnest and warm friends."[41]

In fairness to Irving Snyder's prediction, Spalding did not totally ignore the affairs of baseball or his business that had so preoccupied his earlier adult life. Although the 1905 edition of *The Book of Chicagoans* inaccurately listed him as living in New York and in charge of company affairs, as late as 1906 A.G. was still taking a personal hand in shaping the content of his baseball guide. Writing to Chadwick in January, he told him to delete a section on New York baseball from the upcoming edition because the guide "is national in character and if you talk about one city you have to talk about others." Always the businessman, he also instructed him to discontinue the use of American Association records as a model in a form letter Chadwick had planned to send to league secretaries soliciting baseball statistics because "this particular association has adopted other than the Spalding League Ball in the past. . . ."[42]

Nor did Spalding neglect his interest in promoting his beloved game around the world. Corresponding with European as well as with American baseball officials, he consistently urged international competition and the adoption of standard playing rules to facilitate it. Hopeful about the future, he told August Hermann, chairman of the National Baseball Commission in 1907, that "with a little encouragement, aid, and cooperation from those prominently connected with the game in the United States, I am confident that the time will come when Baseball will become the established and recognized field sport in the world."[43] One year later, Spalding expressed his devotion to baseball in a different style by participating in a charity game between old-time "Boston National League

World Beaters" and college players from Harvard, Dartmouth, and Yale who had last played in 1888. As a reporter for the Boston *Transcript* described it, A.G., dressed in clean white flannels, the "best known man in the Baseball world...the pitcher who made all the United States ring with Baseball enthusiasm in the days of the mighty Bostons and Chicagos," led his team to victory.[44]

Neither Spalding nor his San Diego neighbors would have disagreed with this assessment of his reputation. His nephew Albert Spalding, America's first internationally known violin virtuoso, would certainly have concurred when, on April 7, 1906, the *Sporting News* mistakenly identified him as "the son of A. G. Spalding, who became famous as a pitcher...and...owner of the Chicago Club of the National League." Indeed, the public's recognition of A.G.'s identity as a founding father of America's national game contributed to his standing among San Diego's elite and his role as the city's most famous promoter. Appropriately, both his status as a member of Southern California's gentry class and his prominence as "the best known man in the Baseball world" involved him in the most ambitious enterprise of his California years—his candidacy for the U.S. Senate.

A.G.'s reluctant bid for national office in 1910 represents a minor part of the story of California's sectional politics and the beginnings of the progressive movement in that state. On a more personal level, it served as a fitting climax for his own career and his belief in baseball's ability to prepare men for life. That a man with little formal education could convincingly campaign for the Senate by claiming that his attachment to and experience in baseball made him fit for the job suggests that many others shared such sentiments.

Spalding's opportunity arose directly from the successful efforts of dissident California Republicans to break the Southern Pacific Railroad Company's domination of state politics. Led by Hiram Johnson and George Rowell, they formed the Lincoln-Roosevelt League in 1907 and spearheaded efforts to reshape their party from one devoted to the interests of big business into one concerned with political, economic, and social reform.[45] One measure of their success was the passage of legislation in 1909 that abolished party nominating conventions, traditionally controlled by the railroad interests. Instead, candidates for state office would be selected by the electorate in primary elections. Less clear was the application of a similar scheme to the selection of hopefuls for the U.S. Senate. Because senators at this time were still chosen by state legislators rather than by direct, popular election, direct primaries for that office could not be legally binding. California's primary law reflected this situation. Under it, primary votes for senatorial candidates did not automatically commit state legislators to cast their ballots for a particular candidate. As the San Diego *Sun* reported, the state legislator had one of three choices. He could "lean back and...refuse to be bound by any kind of advisory vote," he could accept the advisory vote of his particular district and vote for the candidate his constituents favored, or he could ignore their preference and vote for the person who won the largest number of districts. Not mentioned was a fourth option. He could simply vote for the person who received a majority of the statewide, popular vote. Within this ambiguous and highly charged political setting, A.G.'s belated candidacy took shape.[46]

Although the Lincoln-Roosevelt insurgents utilized their growing popularity to handpick candidates for the 1910 primary elections, they experienced difficulty in deciding on a senatorial nominee. They finally selected John Works, a former state supreme court justice from Los Angeles. A reluctant "leaguer" at best, Works further jeopardized his credibility with California progressives by publicly opposing Theodore Roosevelt. Similar difficulties complicated the regular Republican organization's search for its candidate when Frank Flint, the incumbent senator, refused to run for reelection. Sensing the opportunity, San Diego's gentry proposed one of their own for the job.

Less than eight weeks before the primary election, G. A. Davidson, A.G.'s friend and former president of the city's chamber of commerce, chaired a committee of "prominent" businessmen who unanimously supported a Spalding candidacy. In a letter to A.G. of June 20, Davidson informed him of the news, emphasized the need to elect a Southern Californian, and urged him to allow his name to be placed on the primary ballot. Describing Spalding's attraction in ways that eventually defined his campaign strategy, Davidson noted that A.G. would be an "ideal candidate...free from entangling alliances with corporate interests of every kind," his "sympathies ever...with the masses." "No business man in America is more widely known or has a better reputation than you have," Davidson concluded; "your name, from Maine to California, is familiar as 'household words.' "[47]

Similar themes also marked a series of interviews with labor leaders, city officials, and local Republicans that was published two days later in the San Diego *Union* as evidence of Spalding's "senatorial boom." One supporter, who called A.G. "a man of business and a business man," opined that "it would be a great thing for San Diego if she could have one of the senators." Referring to him as a "model employer," the president of a local labor union, no doubt unfamiliar with his role in the Brotherhood War, argued that "laboring men would make no mistake in supporting a man who has shown by his deeds that he is their friend." Predicting a political landslide if Spalding only agreed to run, Austin Adams, a local Republican, pulled together metaphors from the arenas of sport, business, and politics in praise of his candidacy. "All through his nine innings of business life," Adams noted, "Spalding has 'played the game' squarely and with success. And my friends, the workingmen on the bleachers, know him as well as I do. They would not let the grandstand have the honor of doing...the most enthusiastic 'rooting' when Spalding goes to bat. He is a big, all-around American lover of Justice, absolutely unmortgaged by the 'interests' and he would 'play ball' on the floor of the senate with an eye single to the rules of the game." No less enthusiastic was the endorsement of the San Diego *Sun*, which praised Spalding's active role as the city's most prominent booster.[48]

News of the effort to push A.G. for the Senate spread quickly. Writing from New York on June 22, A. G. Mills informed Spalding of the New York *Herald*'s premature announcement of his candidacy. Mills addressed the letter to "My Dear Senator" and jokingly suggested that "Senator Spalding...congratulate Governor Tener," a reference to the former Chicago pitcher who was campaigning for the governorship in Pennsylvania. Aware of Spalding's desire for publicity, Mills also informed him that if he wanted "a few thousand copies" of the story, to be sure to purchase the *Herald*'s first edition.[49]

Although flattered by the attention, Spalding did not immediately accept the charge. Torn between the impulse to satisfy his long-standing love of attention and his desire to enjoy the relative repose and gentility offered by San Diego and Point Loma, A.G. equivocated. For over two weeks, despite successful county petition drives engineered in his behalf, talk that support for him was growing "like wildfire," and an editorial in the San Diego *Union* that labeled him as the ideal Southern Californian candidate—"a strong clear-headed Republican, affiliated with neither a party faction nor with special interests"—Spalding confused his promoters by both declining the nomination and expressing interest in it, often in the same breath.[50]

Typical was his response to Davidson's very first appeal that he accept the draft. In it, A.G. formally rejected the idea in a manner that could only have whetted the appetite of his supporters. Correctly identifying himself as a lifelong Republican from Republican Rockford, Spalding began by invoking his father's friendship with Abraham Lincoln and his role as one of the founders of the Republican party in Illinois. Distinguishing himself both from the Lincoln-Roosevelt and the Southern

Pacific factions, he emphasized that only if "national conditions demanded" and only if he could represent the "views of all the people of the state...unhampered by political commitments of any kind" would he be disposed to run.

Having established his pedigree and his politics, A.G. proceeded to outline four preconditions for the declaration of his candidacy. First, he wanted it understood that he would not "make any pre-election promises or...become committed to special interests." Second, befitting his gentry status, he also made it clear that he would make no personal canvass of the state to elicit support. Third, because of his concern about charges that he might use his fortune to "purchase" the election, Spalding demanded that the campaign be financed with only $7,500 of his own money, an amount equal to the annual salary of a U.S. senator, to be disbursed by a trustee whom he would appoint. Finally, he told Davidson that he could not consent to run unless his "committee of businessmen" could assure him that such a campaign could be conducted with a "reasonable chance of success." Certain that the committee would find his terms "impractible," A.G. closed the letter by declining to become a candidate.[51]

Despite Davidson's continual assurances that Spalding's terms were acceptable, A.G. waited until mid-July to announce his candidacy. Even then, he reiterated that he would stick to his four guidelines. For Spalding, adherence to them would allow him to keep his acquired gentility as well as to exercise personal control of the campaign.[52] Spalding's own involvement in his run for the Senate did indeed remain limited. His most aggressive contribution took place in the pages of newspapers owned by his millionaire friends. In a political atmosphere charged with anti corporate sentiments and progressive political rhetoric, at issue were Spalding's credentials as the people's candidate.

The controversy was joined on July 8 when the San Diego *Sun*, owned by Scripps, reprinted excerpts from a *Metropolitan Magazine* article entitled "The Capitalization of Amateur Athletics." Written by one James B. Connally, the article described A.G. as the kind of man that California's Lincoln-Roosevelt leaguers despised—an unscrupulous capitalist who used his power in an unethical, self-serving fashion. Specifically, Connally charged that Spalding controlled American amateur athletics by making the Amateur Athletic Union "an adjunct to the Athletic Goods Trust" that was A. G. Spalding and Brothers. Replete with a full-page picture of A.G. himself, captioned "A. G. Spalding, head of the Athletic Trust," Connally's story correctly noted that James Sullivan, president of the AAU, was also a key employee of the sporting-goods firm. In this dual capacity, Connally argued, Sullivan unfairly promoted Spalding products by requiring their use in officially sanctioned competition and by utilizing a variety of means to "educate the sporting public up to the idea that everything good in athletics had some sort of connection with their house." Connally even accused Spalding of dictating which athletes could represent the United States in the Olympic Games. Any athlete affiliated with the AAU, he concluded, inadvertently allowed himself to become "simply another advertising agent for the Athletic Goods Trust."[53]

Alongside this story, headlined "Spalding's Big Trust," was a brief column suggesting that A.G.'s reluctance to run stemmed from the difficulty he would have in refuting Connally's charges. It also noted that his initial decision not to become a candidate disappointed those who looked forward to enjoying the patronage his victory might bring. Spalding, the story concluded, "was busy on road work and...unavailable for comment."[54]

Spalding may have been unavailable to the *Sun*, but the next day's morning edition of the San Diego *Union* carried his angry response. Spalding dismissed the magazine article as "scurrilous, false and malicious" and denied that its publication had in any way affected his uncertainty in deciding whether to run for the Senate. Rather than attempting to refute charges that he was the head of a trust and a "corporate boss," A.G. instead accused Scripps of having a similar intent. Offering the *Union*'s readers a letter he received from him in early June, he asked them to judge whether Scripps's efforts to control his campaign and presumably his actions as senator were not reasons enough "to justify any self-respecting man in declining to enter the political arena as a candidate for any office."[55]

In fact, the letter offered as proof of Scripps's intentions appears to be a frank political assessment of the California scene, written by a man interested in supporting A.G.'s candidacy. Hopeful for Spalding's success, Scripps began by expressing his dislike for both the Lincoln-Roosevelt and the Southern-Pacific factions within the Republican party. Noting his personal belief that Spalding would be "a more interested and sympathetic servant of the common people" than Works, Scripps pointed out that his career as a sporting-goods entrepreneur and his reputation as a wealthy man would leave him open to charges that he was the candidate of "the corporate interests" and "opposed to the interests of the common people." In order to counter these claims, Scripps suggested, Spalding should accept a proposal made to him by Gifford Pinchot, the noted conservationist and friend of Theodore Roosevelt, that A.G. become "the local leader...of the 'conservation' movement." In so doing, Scripps argued, Spalding would establish his progressive

credentials and dispose of any suspicion that he was "a 'reactionary.' "
Only in closing did Scripps suggest anything that Spalding might con-
strue as an attempt to "boss" him. After expressing his "sincerest regard" for Spalding as a man, approval of his "style," and "confidence"
in his "ability," Scripps informed him that he would have to ask him
some straightforward questions about his wealth and his attitudes toward workers before he could announce to the "more than 100,000 voters
in California" who bought his papers that he was "just the right sort of
a man for them to choose for senator."[56]

Several more exchanges in the press between Spalding and Scripps
followed, but the *Sun* eventually supported A.G.'s candidacy. In the
July 18 editorial that announced its support, the paper urged San Diego
voters to do the same. His election, it concluded, "will mean great things
for San Diego, there can be no doubt about that."[57]

Ten days later the *Sun* presented other reasons for rallying behind
Spalding. Comparing the worlds of baseball and politics, the paper noted
that a ballplayer's career was controlled by "bosses" and that all ballplayers developed an intense dislike for "bossism" of any kind. Ignoring
the fact that A.G. was one of the game's premier "bosses," the *Sun*
assured its readers that the "ex-pitcher Spalding" would know how to
handle political "bosses" who tried to push him around. As to whether
a baseball player could be a competent senator, the *Sun* admitted that
while "ball players are not credited with knowing a heap about state-
craft... the U.S. Senate needs...a lot of fellows who know something
about patriotism....Ballplayers are for a square game, very likely to
stick to the popular views of things, and almost certain to wring the
noses of bosses....It really seems...a good thing to have some fearless,
kicking, boss-baiting ballplayers in that senate."[58]

Although A.G. offered no comment on the irony in the *Sun's* remarks,
he, too, saw a real advantage in emphasizing the positive role that
baseball had played in his life. In the midst of completing *America's
National Game*, which glorified baseball's ability to build character and
to prepare society's leaders, he based his campaign on advertisements
that portrayed him as a man whose career in baseball and business had
readied him for national office.

One such effort, put together by James Sullivan, who oversaw Spalding's campaign, was a full-page broadside that offered a brief history of
Spalding's decision to enter the race, complete with copies of the letters
that had passed between him and Davidson. Appropriately, it identified
A.G. as the "head of the great athletic goods establishment bearing his
name" and as "the old time champion pitcher." It also suggested that
Spalding's candidacy was "unique in the annals of American political

history" in that he chose to give up an ideal private existence in the face of "an irresistible demand from the people all over the state."[59]

Complementing this unsigned political advertisement was one carrying the signature of A. G. Mills, which Spalding had encouraged his friend to write. "Publicity and lots of it is my only chance," he told Mills, imploring him "for a word...with a little baseball twist."[60] Mills forwarded his effort to Sullivan on August 1. He noted that it included "a few points to offset" Connally's article, which, although a "mendacious...diatribe," still made "certain effective points that have not been met." Jokingly, Mills added, "I have managed to bring in Teddy—who is the whole thing in California. By the way, why don't you get him to issue an order for A.G.'s election? Then all A.G. would have to do would be to 'cough up' that $7,500 and buy his ticket for Washington!"[61]

In fact, Mills's broadside went well beyond the modest, though accurate, appraisal offered by its author. Against a narrative that briefly recounted A.G.'s career, Mills presented a paradigm of late-nineteenth-century values, personified by Spalding and nurtured by his career in baseball, that supported his qualifications to hold national office. Critical was the universal recognition that Spalding was the man chiefly responsible for "purifying" baseball, making it at once a "stable" business enterprise acceptable as a "safe and healthful...exercise" and an "attractive" entertainment. "If the millions of Americans interested in our National Game were called upon to select a representative," Mills argued, Spalding would be the one man to "whom all managers, players, amateurs, professionals, veterans, schoolboys, and spectators" would naturally turn.

For Mills, Spalding's success in establishing baseball as both a legitimate leisure-time pursuit and a profitable business enterprise depended upon his perseverance and foresight. Particularly important were his contributions to effective baseball and business organization. Moreover, one should not minimize, Mills continued, Spalding's role as a "mediator" in the many crises professional baseball encountered between 1876 and 1901—all resolved fairly "by the adoption of the just and impartial measures he...advocated."

Spalding was fair, hardworking, prescient, a firm believer in organization and efficient management, and his "ripe experience in the affairs of life" gave him all that he needed to be a U.S. senator. Mindful of his audience, Mills went on to compliment "the people of California" for being "a level-headed, practical folk, who know a good thing when they see it." Combining a bit of Horatio Alger, Teddy Roosevelt, progressive political rhetoric, and pure gall for good measure, Mills concluded that they saw in Spalding "not a practical politician...a captain of Industry nor a capitalist" but rather "a man in the prime of life, who, beginning as a country boy, has solely by square-dealing and honest effort, built up a business that extends the world over, and who therefore is just the man to further the trade interests of their State; who by his capable and unselfish service to the community in which he lives, has made that community—Republican or Democrat, capitalist and laborer—solid in support of his candidacy; whose freedom from entangling alliances, independence, integrity of character, personal popularity, and devotion to his State...make him...the ideal candidate."[62]

Mills's efforts in behalf of his friend's candidacy went beyond contributions of laudatory prose. In a letter to Spalding dated August 3, Mills suggested that the support of the Lincoln-Roosevelt league, formally committed to Works, was critical to A.G.'s success. In that regard Mills told Spalding that he had contacted "one of its leaders...an intimate friend of mine," Charles Bentley, who was active in the California Fruit Canners Association. "I have written him that, when you are elected, I intend to ask you to consult him about matters of interest to San Francisco and California. I thought it best to post you as to what I had done," he concluded, "in case you should get word from this man or some of his friends."[63]

Spalding never commented on the apparent contradiction between Mills's efforts and his announced position as a candidate free from all corporate or political entanglements. Nor could he precisely gauge the impact on his campaign of his promotional literature or letters such as the one in an August issue of the San Diego *Sun* that credited "our great game of baseball" with producing "a man like Spalding."[64] Certainly, as the New York *Times* reported on August 20, Spalding's occasional campaign speeches, full of aphorisms such as "[P]olitics can be played just as squarely as the game of baseball...in a manly, straightforward...honest, fearless and courageous...manner," underlined his belief that baseball had prepared him to serve the people.

At least for the New York *Times*, early election returns indicated that such appeals were not without results. Referring to A.G. as "the greatest of American pitchers of all time," it reported his early lead in the popular vote over John Works and suggested that "Baseball is likely to have a real representative in the United States Senate," much to the surprise of professional politicians who "had not counted on the baseball vote."[65]

The *Times*'s prediction proved premature. Complete returns for the August 16 primary showed Works with a slim margin in the popular vote over Spalding: 64,757 to 63,182. The breakdown of the vote by the state's 120 senatorial and assembly districts, however, gave Spalding majorities in 75.[66] Given the vagaries of the primary law, each man claimed the Republican nomination and assumed he would gain ultimate victory when the legislature met in January to make its choice.

Remarking on the outcome of the primary election to a reporter for the *Sporting News* in October, A.G. noted that he was "as anxious to win as I ever was to win a ballgame. The spirit is the same. I won the first game in the primaries 74 to 60, which sounds like an old time baseball score...." He compared his experiences in baseball with his recent excursion into politics and concluded that "a little integrity of baseball into politics would not hurt politics" at all.[67] His opinion was probably reinforced when the California legislature on January 9, 1911, voted overwhelmingly to make John Works one of its U.S. senators.[68]

Since the results of the primary election were both inconclusive and nonbinding and since Spalding disavowed all political connections, his defeat was not surprising. Lincoln-Roosevelt Republicans, exhilarated by the election of Hiram Johnson to the governorship and by their control of California's Republican party, used their leverage between August and January to swing legislative support behind their own candidate. Spalding, in keeping with his newfound gentility, offered no public comment on the outcome. Instead, he left it to his Point Loma neighbor and personal secretary, William Page, to publicize the injustice he no doubt felt.

In the pages of Spalding's 1911 baseball guide, Page detailed the history of A.G.'s campaign. Highlighted were the alleged political deals struck by the Lincoln-Roosevelt leaguers that had resulted in "the rape of the people's primary law" and in A.G.'s being "the victim of the outrage." Having chastised his friend's enemies, Page suggested that Spalding was fortunate to escape "a situation and a place that could have added but little to his honors and dignities." After all, Page concluded, "A. G. Spalding needs no greater fame than he has won for himself and the American people through the medium of the National Game and no greater monument than the grand old National League. As the case now stands, A. G. Spalding still belongs to the whole American people, instead of being claimed and monopolized by one state...only a speck on the vast map of the nation."[69] A.G. could not have agreed more. Win or lose, the campaign had provided one more opportunity for public attention and confirmed his gentry status. For him, the sense of his contributions to baseball, more than anything he might have accomplished as a senator, defined his bid for immortality.

8

The Father of Baseball

Confident of his place in history and comfortable with the role as civic booster and genteel aristocrat that his California life provided, Spalding had no difficulty in retiring once again to the relative anonymity of his roads, estate, and family, at Point Loma. As he told one visitor to Sunset Cliffs who was impressed with the beauty of the spot, "some artists work in paint, oil, and canvas, and others in marble, but I am devoting the evening of my life to carving in living stone and the earth, things of beauty."[1] One month later at Lomaland, in September, 1915, Spalding suffered a minor stroke, appeared on his way to recovery, and then succumbed suddenly on September 9 to a second one. As one newspaper reporter put it, "he was called out" at the age of sixty-five. "Baseball fans from coast to coast," the obituary continued, "and tens of thousands of small boys, who remind each other on the vacant lots to 'hold the bat with the Spalding up,' will feel a personal loss on the death of the 'father of baseball.'"[2]

More immediate was the grief of those who had been closest to A.G. during the last years of his life. Although Spalding was not a true believer in theosophy, his wife mounted an elaborate funeral service at the Temple of Aryans, officiated by the Purple Mother herself and attended only by members of the Universal Brotherhood. An array of distinguished theosophist friends offered tribute to Spalding, using as texts writings that Madame Tingley recognized to be consistent with the doctrine of reincarnation. Following a processional that weaved through the society's grounds, lined throughout by schoolchildren with hands raised in silent salute, the funeral cortege arrived at Greenwood Cemetery, where Spalding's body was cremated. There, after songs by the Raja Yoga girls' chorus and more remarks by members of the Women's and Men's International Theosophical Leagues, Tingley gave a final testimonial, in which she described Spalding's life as "an inspiration to those of us who live for the betterment of humanity. In the philosophy of my life, and that of all right thinking people, there is the knowledge of the eternal, and we know that the soul of the man we knew as Albert Spalding has risen to the higher life, and we feel all is well with him." According to one reporter for the San Diego *Union*, similar sentiments informed Elizabeth Spalding's demeanor throughout the service. "Although her emotions were perceptible at times," he observed, "there was none of the usual manifestations of grief, the spirit of the ceremonies being that the deceased had passed on to a happier life."[3]

Whatever the status of his soul, there is no question that Spalding would have been pleased with the public reaction to the meaning of his life. Baseball aficionados, old friends, and newspaper editors all hailed A.G. as one of America's best-known men, the man responsible for making all Americans "athletic," the father of America's national game, and its greatest figure.[4] The National League even issued formal resolutions acknowledging the "irreparable loss" that it and all "kindred organizations" suffered at the death of the game's "heroic figure," its "first and greatest missionary and propagandist ... the 'Father and Savior of Baseball,' " and "in many respects the greatest man the National Game has produced."[5]

Equal in praise and more precise about A.G.'s contributions were the extended remarks in the *Sporting News* a week after his death. In a story entitled "Spalding Enters Game's Valhalla," the paper gave the highlights of his career as ballplayer, manager, club and league official, missionary, and businessman. Spalding, the *News* pointed out, recognized and acted on the promise of personal fortune and social purpose inherent in the promotion of sport as an acceptable leisure-time activity. Noting that his efforts in behalf of baseball were inseparable from the advancement of himself and his business, the paper lauded A.G. for providing "entertainment for the masses" and for his "genius for organization," which had made professional baseball a stable, popular, and profitable sport.[6]

Accompanying this story was an editorial that went beyond a mere cataloguing of Spalding's accomplishments—it offered A.G. as the quintessence of American manhood:

> Mortals could ask no more of the gods than they granted Albert G. Spalding. His life was a full one; his death seems to have been the sort every sane man should wish for. ... Strong physically and mentally, sensing and grasping opportunity when it came to him, he builded [sic] for the world as much as for himself, took only his fair share of what his talents amassed and was satisfied and content to enjoy it, rather than strain and scramble

in blind greed for more. .... It was a joy to know Al Spalding. .... He was
an inspiration to the spirit and a fine example to the material man. He was
a jolly, grown-up boy to the end ... bubbling with merriment and rich
diversion, radiating happiness and contentment. His millions made not a
cent's worth of difference to him. .... Baseball is proud to claim such a man
as its own and points to him as an example of the real manhood that it
enlists and develops.[7]

Baseball had indeed served Spalding well. As a young, anxious boy,
he had received from it first self-confidence, then a career, and finally
a fortune. By the time of his death, as the *Sporting News* implied, he had
creatively shaped that sport into a vehicle that served not only his own
personal needs but also those of a whole generation looking for new
ways to deal with problems that accompanied the inception of "America's Century."

Spalding was not quite as flamboyant as P. T. Barnum, nineteenth-
century America's greatest showman, or nearly as articulate as Henry
Ward Beecher, one of its most popular Christian ministers, but he, too,
offered middle-class Americans, by example and by message, precisely
what they desired. In their own ways, all three men enjoyed successful
careers as businessmen. Creating and packaging products that ranged
from museums and circuses to athletic goods and sport and to romantic
Christianity, they satisfied the demands of their audience and also al-
layed its fears.

Although the careers of Barnum and Spalding overlapped for only a
brief time, both men made insatiable demands for public attention, and
they pitched their products in ways that appealed to their society's
fascination with extravagance and with bold claims to greatness. Selling
their wares and themselves at the same time, they significantly shaped
the leisure-time tastes of late-nineteenth century America.[8]

Beecher, too, died before Spalding rose to prominence as one of America's most recognizable men. Yet the brand of Christianity he offered
his middle-class audience was quite compatible with A.G.'s appeal to
them. Americans left anxious and uncertain by the industrial and urban
transformation of their society took heart from Beecher's message of
progress and his emphasis on self-reliance and self-control. Absolving
them from any guilt for their own excesses, Beecher persuaded his lis-
teners to balance their fixation on work and materialism with the pursuit
of leisure as a means of alleviating their fears about their physical and
moral decay and of simultaneously renewing their strength for life's
struggle.[9]

Spalding's ability to present sport as a secular means to such ends,
and the example of his own life as proof of the promise, helps explain

his significance for our understanding of the society in which he lived. Baseball's strong appeal in the late nineteenth century was surely related to its ability to offer a visual tie with a rural past to new urban audiences, to assure them that order prevailed even in "the turmoil of the modern city," and to demonstrate that traditional American values could be incorporated into the new demands of a complex society. Still, it took individuals like Spalding, capable of exploiting such connections and confident in their entrepreneurial and organizational skills, to realize the sport's potential.[10]

Spalding's contributions to the development of organized, professional baseball and to the acceptance of sport as a socially beneficial activity should not be minimized. However, that development was not dependent on one man. It clearly arose out of a particular social, economic, and psychological context, which demanded new institutions and new ways of organizing human activity that affected virtually every aspect of American life during the last quarter of the nineteenth and the first quarter of the twentieth centuries. As "the greatest organizing genius of the National Game," as an aggressive businessman who helped shape and dominate a new industry in sporting goods, as a participant in the organized-play movement, as a believer in baseball's ability to develop and control character, and even as a supporter of theosophy and a candidate for the U.S. Senate, Spalding reflected, in his preoccupation with organization and control, the manner in which many of his contemporaries confronted the demands of a changing society.[11] Moreover, like the attempts of many progresssive reformers and professionals in other areas of American life who sought to rationalize and control their part of a modernizing world, Spalding's efforts to consolidate and expand his sporting-goods business and his role in behalf of organized baseball were not always as benign as he made them out to be.

As A.G. strove to reform baseball and turn it into a stable, profitable, and respectable form of middle-class entertainment, the pursuit of self-serving interests muddied his vision, with painful consequences for anyone whom he viewed as an obstacle. Quite familiar with the ways of corporate capitalists who sought to drive out weaker competition by any means necessary to monopolize control over markets, A.G. adopted many of them in his constant battles to insure the hegemony of the National League in the competitive world of professional baseball. The disagreement and conflict that did occur were less over the goals of consolidation, control, efficient organization, or profit than over the qualifications and motives of the engineers in command. Anyone who questioned Spalding's authority, expertise, or ideas was simply unacceptable to him. Moreover, A.G. was not shy about letting such people know, by his words and actions, how he felt about them.

This double-edged nature of baseball reform was equally apparent in Spalding's attempts to manipulate and control labor to suit his own sense of the game's best interests. Although he had risen up from their ranks and praised the dignity of their profession, A.G. had no qualms about using whatever means were at his disposal to keep ballplayers in line, lest they upset the sensibilities of the middle-class audience he was trying to attract to the ballpark. If pushed too hard, he was capable of inflammatory rhetoric and ruthless aciton, as were capitalists in other industries who feared increasing conflict between labor and capital and who responded in a repressive and occasionally a violent fashion.

Although it was historically inaccurate for the Baseball Hall of Fame to celebrate baseball's centennial at Cooperstown, New York, in 1939, its posthumous admission of A. G. Spalding at that time was quite appropriate. An aggressive businessman with an eye on the main chance and a firm believer in American exceptionalism, A.G. had willed baseball to be an American invention as a means of insuring his fortune, validating his own life, and contributing to the continuation of American greatness. He would certainly have liked the inscription on his Hall of Fame plaque— "the organizational genius of Baseball's pioneer days" and the "Organizer of Baseball's First Round the World Tour." Spalding was all this and more. He was an empire builder, and his imperial vision, like many others of his time, stretched to the corners of the globe. Baseball surely was not American in origin, but it was packaged and promoted as such by a man whose life illuminated the major tendencies of a whole generation of middle-class Americans and who was an essential figure in filling their leisure-time needs. Baseball's persistence as our national pastime and the development of sport as a significant institution of American life owe much to Albert Goodwill Spalding, a man with a nose for business and a knack for promoting himself and his game.

Notes

The following abbreviations have been used in the notes:

AGS	Albert Goodwill Spalding
CBC	Chicago Baseball Club, Chicago Historical Society
Chadwick Scrapbook	Chadwick Scrapbooks, Spalding Collection, New York Public Library
Guide	*Spalding's Official Base Ball Guide* (New York, 1877–1916)
Kuhn Scrapbook	R. C. Kuhn Scrapbooks, Chicago Historical Society
Mills Papers	A. G. Mills Papers, Baseball Hall of Fame Library, Cooperstown, N.Y.
Spalding Papers	Spalding Papers, Baseball Hall of Fame Library, Cooperstown, N.Y.
Spalding Scrapbook	Spalding Scrapbooks, Spalding Collection, New York Public Library
Wright Corresp.	Harry Wright Correspondence, Spalding Collection, New York Public Library

Introduction

1. Neil Harris, *Humbug: The Art of P. T. Barnum* (Boston, 1973), is a provocative analysis of Barnum, which I found very useful. Arthur Bartlett, *Baseball and Mr. Spalding: The History and Romance of Baseball* (New York, 1951), is a lightly written, unfootnoted account of Spalding's life that relies heavily on Spalding's own autobiographical account of baseball, *America's National Game*, published in 1911. One Spalding employee told me that Bartlett's

book was offered as a present to company employees in 1951 to mark the firm's seventy-fifth anniversary.

2. This overview draws on an extensive reading of primary and secondary sources. Throughout the text, I acknowledge authors whose work has influenced my thinking.

1. Rising in the World

1. *Reminiscences of Harriet I. Spalding* (East Orange, N.J., 1910), provides information on Spalding's family. The quotations are on pp. 46, 60.
2. Ibid., 46–81. The quotation is on p. 49.
3. Charles W. Spalding, *The Spalding Memorial: A Genealogical History of Edward Spalding . . . and His Descendants* (Chicago, 1897), 899.
4. *Reminiscences of Harriet I. Spalding*, 59, 81.
5. Ibid., 70–72.
6. See, e.g., Rockford *Gazette*, Dec. 26, 1867, May 28, June 6, Aug. 6, 1868, from which all the quotations are taken.
7. Ibid., Aug. 6, 1868.
8. Ibid., June 11, 1868.
9. AGS, *America's National Game* (New York, 1911), 510.
10. See, e.g., William Mathews, *Getting On in the World* (Chicago, 1874), 19–33. Daniel T. Rodgers, *The Work Ethic in Industrial America, 1850–1920* (Chicago, 1978), discusses the elements contained in such tales and the advice offered Americans about how to succeed in life. The quotations are from AGS, *America's National Game*, 510.
11. AGS, *America's National Game*, 511.
12. AGS, "Baseball," unnamed magazine (1890), 604–5, in Spalding Papers; AGS, *America's National Game*, 117–18.
13. AGS, *America's National Game*, 605.
14. For useful treatments of this transformation, see David Voigt, *American Baseball: From Gentleman's Sport to the Commissioner System* (Norman, Okla., 1966), 3–34; Harold Seymour, *Baseball: The Early Years* (New York, 1960), 35–59. Also see Stephen Friedman, "The Baseball Fad in Chicago, 1865–1870: An Exploration of Sport in the Nineteenth-Century City," *Journal of Sport History*, 5 (Summer 1978), 42–64; Steven A. Riess, *Touching Base; Professional Baseball and American Culture in the Progressive Era* (Westport, Conn., 1980).
15. AGS, *America's National Game*, 118–26. Biographical information on club members comes from Newton Bateman and Paul Selby, *Historical Encyclopedia of Illinois and History of Winnebago County*, vols. 1 and 2 (Chicago, 1916).
16. *Reminiscences of Harriet I. Spalding*, 82.
17. AGS, *America's National Game*, 106–7.
18. Ibid., 107.
19. *Guide*, 1907, p. 49. Spalding's guides began appearing on a yearly basis in 1877. Published first in Chicago and then in New York, they are an important source for the early history of professional baseball and for insights into Spalding and his affairs. For descriptions of rules, pitching, and fields

see Seymour, *Baseball*, 38–39, 133–39; AGS, *America's National Game*, 481–82.

20. Rockford *Register*, Aug. 1, 17, 1867.
21. AGS, *America's National Game*, 109.
22. Ibid., 119, 122, 512.
23. Ibid., 119–22, contains the preceding account and all the quotations.
24. Ibid., 513; *Reminiscences of Harriet I. Spalding*, 83.
25. Rockford *Register*, July 11, Dec. 26, 1867, contains specific references to Vanderbilt and the quotations. For other examples see ibid., May 28, 1868, March 24, 1870.
26. Rockford *Gazette*, Dec. 12, 1866.
27. Voigt, *American Baseball*, 23–34.
28. Unnamed paper, March 29, 1868, in Spalding Scrapbook #3. The New York Public Library houses the Spalding Collection, donated to it in 1922 by Spalding's widow. Aside from many of the sporting publications published by Spalding's company, it also contains three series of scrapbooks maintained by Henry Chadwick, Harry Wright (includes correspondence books), and Spalding. The unpaginated scrapbooks of Chadwick and Spalding, composed primarily of newspaper clippings, are badly deteriorated. The Wright correspondence deals primarily with his years as manager of the Boston Red Stockings.
29. Rockford *Register*, July 9, 1868; AGS, *America's National Game*, 123–26. According to the *Register*, the Forest City's also tied the Red Stockings in a game played before 2,000 people in Rockford in early July 1870. See Rockford *Register*, July 14, 1870.
30. Cited in Voigt, *American Baseball*, 95, as having been first published in the New York *Star* and reprinted in the Rockford *Register*, June 4, 1870. To be sure, Spalding was not always treated so kindly. After he lost to the Excelsiors by a 28–14 score in June 1870, the Chicago *Times*, June 17, 1870, compared Spalding's performance on the mound to that of a "Greek slave."
31. Boston *Herald*, Nov. 14, 1870, in Spalding Scrapbook #3. The story was entitled "Baseball as a Pastime and as a Business."

2. Boston's Hero

1. Rockford *Register*, Jan. 1, 1871.
2. David Voigt, *America through Baseball* (Chicago, 1976), 47–64; idem, *American Baseball: From Gentleman's Sport to the Commissioner System* (Norman, Okla., 1966), 35–37; idem, "The Boston Red Stockings: The Birth of Major League Baseball," *New England Quarterly*, 42 (Dec. 1970), 531–49.
3. New York *Clipper*, July 25, 1874; *Guide*, 1892, p. 118, 1907, p. 47.
4. AGS, *America's National Game* (New York, 1911), 141–43.
5. *Reminiscences of Harriet I. Spalding* (East Orange, N.J., 1910), 84.
6. AGS, *America's National Game*, 141–43.
7. Voigt, *American Baseball*, 35–37.
8. Arthur Bartlett, *Baseball and Mr. Spalding: The History and Romance of Baseball* (New York, 1951), 40–47, and baseball source books provide this information. The quotation is from Chicago *Times*, July 23, 1876.

9. Boston *Journal*, March 3, 1871, in Chadwick Scrapbook #19.

10. Boston *Globe*, July 14–16, 1873.

11. Harold Seymour, *Baeball: The Early Years* (New York, 1960), 61–63.

12. Boston *Globe*, July 5, 1873.

13. AGS, *America's National Game*, 163–67.

14. *Beadle's Dime Baseball Player*, 1876, p. 67; Bartlett, *Baseball and Mr. Spalding*, 46.

15. Voigt, "Boston Red Stockings," 546–47.

16. Ibid., 544; Harry Wright to James Ferguson, Jan. 1, 1874, Wright Corresp. #1.

17. AGS, *America's National Game*, 175–86, contains his account of the 1874 tour. All of his quotations and his version of the tour, unless otherwise noted, come from this source. Also see Bartlett, *Baseball and Mr. Spalding*, 56–71.

18. Harry Wright to James Ferguson, Jan. 1, 1874, Wright Corresp. #1. Other letters in this volume also indicate Spalding's role.

19. Harry Wright to Harry E. Sharpe, April 22, 1874, Wright Corresp. #1.

20. Harry Wright to James Ferguson, March 13, 1874, Wright Corresp. #1; Harry Wright to C. W. Alcock, May 31, 1874, Wright Corresp. #2.

21. For accounts of the cricket matches see London *Times*, Aug. 4, 1874; Manchester *Guardian*, Aug. 5, 1874; St. Louis *Post Dispatch*, Aug. 6, 7, 13, 1874. I want to thank Ray Smith, who provided me with clippings from British and American newspapers that he has collected concerning the tour. Voigt, *American Baseball*, 48, notes that the British offered the unequal sides as a friendly gesture to the Americans.

22. London *Standard*, July 31, 1874, reported in New York *Times*, Aug. 13, 1874.

23. London *Telegraph*, July 21, 1874, reported in New York *Times*, Aug. 3, 1874. Also see Manchester *Guardian*, July 31, 1874, and London *Observer*, Aug. 9, 1874.

24. Adrian C. Anson, *A Ball Player's Career* (Chicago, 1900), 78; Voigt, *American Baseball*, 49.

25. *Beadle's Dime Baseball Player*, 1875, pp. 57–58. Wright's comments are quoted in Voigt, "Boston Red Stockings," 549.

26. Rockford *Register*, Sept. 5, 1874.

27. Towanda *Reporter*, Nov. 19, 21, 1874, in Spalding Scrapbook #1.

28. *Sporting News*, June 13, 1891; *Guide*, 1892, p. 118.

29. Rockford *Register*, Nov. 28, 1874.

3. Spalding's Chicago White Stockings

1. Worcester (Mass.) *Spy*, July 24, 1875, in Spalding Scrapbook #1.

2. *Sporting News*, April 18, 1891.

3. Stephen Friedman, "The Baseball Fad in Chicago, 1865–1870," *Journal of Sport History*, 5 (Summer 1978), 42–64, describes the connection between the ball team and the city.

4. AGS, *America's National Game* (New York, 1911), 201–3.

5. Chicago White Stockings, Stockholders' Report, July 3, 1875, CBC.

6. Ibid., July 16, 1875.

7. AGS, *America's National Game*, 203.

8. Boston *Globe*, July 28, Aug. 2, 1875. Also see New York *Clipper*, July 31, 1875.

were released by Spalding for "bad habits" displayed on the 1889 world tour. See Chapter 6 for a full discussion of that event.

77. Chicago *Times*, July 10, 1886.
78. Chicago *Evening Journal*, April 30, 1887; Riess, *Touching Base*, 122–23.
79. AGS to A. G. Mills, Jan. 5, 1884, Mills Papers.
80. Spalding, *America's National Game*, 527–28.
81. Chicago *News*, June 26, 1889, Sept. 9, 1887.
82. *Sporting News*, June 28, 1886.
83. The list is in Box 5, CBC. Also see AGS to Mr. White, April 22, 1884, CBC.
84. A survey of the *Proceedings of the Chicago City Council* (*PCCC*) for the 1880s found brief references concerning the ball club involving permission to rent the grounds to circuses (*PCCC*, 1883–84, pp. 13, 135), and the condition of alleys near the ballpark (*PCCC*, 1884–85, pp. 489, 493, 527; 1885–86, p. 525).
85. AGS to John Lake, Sept. 16, 1884, CBC. Also see AGS to D. W. Ruggles, June 16, 1882, CBC.
86. The description and quotation are from a newspaper clipping from *American Sports* (Chicago), April 28, 1883, in Chadwick Scrapbook #19.
87. New York *Clipper*, March 29, May 31, July 5, 1884. Also see AGS to W. Irving Culver, May 28, 1884, CBC.
88. Chicago *Tribune*, May 3, 1885; New York *Clipper*, April 25, May 3, June 6, 1885.
89. *Sporting News*, April 23, 1893; Riess, *Touching Base*, 86.
90. AGS to A. G. Mills, June 30, 1883, CBC.
91. Unnamed Chicago newspaper clipping, ca. Nov.–Dec. 1886, in Kuhn Scrapbook.
92. John Brown to C. H. Morton, April 11, 1884, CBC.
93. *Sporting Life*, Sept. 21, 1887; Anson, *Ball Player's Career*, 148, 150, 221. Anson's references were specifically aimed at Clarence Duval, Chicago's black mascot. See Chapter 6 for a discussion of Duval.
94. The best account of the integration of major league baseball is Jules Tygiel, *Baseball's Great Experiment: Jackie Robinson and His Legacy* (New York, 1983). For good accounts of the Negro leagues, see Harold Peterson, *Only the Ball Was White* (Englewood Cliffs, 1970); Donn Rogosin, *Invisible Men: Life in Baseball's Negro Leagues* (New York, 1983).
95. *Sporting News*, Oct. 17, 1896.
96. Anson, *Ball Player's Career*, 304–5, presents his view of the affair. *Sporting News*, Feb. 29, 1898, contains Spalding's statement. For other information on the controversy, see New York *Clipper*, Dec. 25, 1897, Feb. 19, April 9, 1898; *Sporting News*, July 31, Oct. 9, Nov. 20, 27, 1897, Feb. 12, 1898.

4. The Brains of the National League

1. New York *Times*, Jan. 25, 1891.
2. *Sporting News*, April 18, 1891.
3. Ibid., April 18, 25, 1891. The person who labeled A.G. "the brains" was John Montgomery Ward, a New York Giant shortstop and Spalding's chief adversary in the Brotherhood War. Spalding Scrapbook, unnumbered (world tour material), contains the quotation from *Spirit of the Times*, Nov. 10, 1888.

9. Boston *Globe*, July 27, 1875.
10. Ibid., July 28, 1875.
11. New York *Clipper*, Aug. 8, Oct. 30, 1875. The headline in the Oct. 30 issue read "Chicago. '76 vs. Boston '76."
12. Arthur Bartlett, *Baseball and Mr. Spalding: The History and Romance of Baseball* (New York, 1951), 79.
13. AGS, *America's National Game*, 209.
14. David Voigt, *American Baseball: From Gentleman's Sport to the Commissioner System* (Norman, Okla., 1966), 64–65.
15. AGS to Mr. Joyce, Jan. 28, 1876, CBC.
16. New York *Clipper*, Feb. 12, 1876.
17. AGS to Henry Chadwick, Feb. 27, 1876, reprinted in *Guide*, 1908, pp. 19–20.
18. AGS, *America's National Game*, 208; *Sporting News*, April 13, 1895; AGS, *America's National Game*, 309.
19. For stimulating discussions of Barnum and Beecher that are compatible with this argument, see Neil Harris, *Humbug: The Art of P. T. Barnum* (Boston, 1973), and Clifford E. Clark, Jr., *Henry Ward Beecher: Spokesman for a Middle-Class America* (Urbana, 1978).
20. William Mathews, *Getting On in the World* (Chicago, 1874), 187.
21. My analysis of Spalding and his connection to the larger culture relies in part on Burton J. Bledstein, *The Culture of Professionalism: The Middle Class and the Development of Higher Education in America* (New York, 1976). The reference to the professional as magician appears on pp. 92–93. Bledstein also discusses the development of professional baseball as part of the culture of professionalism on pp. 81–85.
22. Most influential on my thinking were Paul Boyer, *Urban Masses and Moral Order in America, 1820–1920* (Cambridge, 1978); George M. Fredrickson, *The Inner Civil War: Northern Intellectuals and the Crisis of the Union* (New York, 1965); Samuel P. Hays, *The Response to Industrialism, 1885–1914* (Chicago, 1973); Gabriel Kolko, *The Triumph of Conservatism: A Reinterpretation of American History, 1900–1916* (Chicago, 1963); Donald J. Mrozek, *Sport and American Mentality, 1880–1910* (Knoxville, 1983); Steven A. Riess, *Touching Base: Professional Baseball and American Culture in the Progressive Era* (Westport, Conn., 1980); Robert Wiebe, *The Search for Order, 1877–1920* (Chicago, 1963).
23. Diehl, 1915, p. 5. Chadwick's remarks appear in AGS, *America's National Game*, 471–72. Also see 425–31, for a description of the tasks of the baseball magnate as Spalding understood them.
24. AGS to Riverside Baseball Club, Dec. 28, 1875, CBC. The letterbooks of the Chicago Baseball Club for the 1880s offer abundant examples of Spalding's correspondence concerning his roles as manager, captain, and owner of the club. They are a key source for this chapter.
25. AGS to James Kelly, June 5, 1877, CBC. Other examples, selected from numerous letters, are AGS to E. A. Holbrook, March 20, 1876, and AGS to William P. Rogers, March 15, 1876.
26. New York *Clipper*, Dec. 2, 1876; Chicago *Tribune*, July 14, 1876.
27. Chicago *Evening Journal*, Sept. 9, 1876; Chicago *Tribune*, Oct. 1, 1876. The Kuhn Scrapbooks contain clippings on the White Stockings from Chicago newspapers for the 1880s. These books supplemented my own reading of

the Chicago *Tribune* and the Chicago *Times*. I have cited the scrapbooks directly only when the newspaper source is not clear.

28. New York *Clipper*, June 30, Oct. 13, Nov. 17, 1877.

29. Chicago *Tribune*, April 11–13, 16, May 6, 1882; New York *Clipper*, April 15, May 6, 1882; AGS to W. J. Culver, June 15, 1882, CBC. Hulbert's health problems left Spalding in charge during much of the 1881 season as well.

30. Statistics on club and player records throughout are from *The Baseball Encyclopedia* (Toronto, 1969). Chicago *Tribune*, May 6, July 7, 1880. Of the twenty-two victories, only twenty were against National League opponents. Chicago also posted winning percentages of .777 in 1885 and .726 in 1886.

31. Adrian C. Anson, *A Ball Player's Career* (Chicago, 1900), 128, 113.

32. Lee Allen, *The National League Story: The Official History* (New York, 1965), 44–46.

33. AGS, *America's National Game*, 184.

34. Anson, *Ball Player's Career*, 133.

35. AGS, *America's National Game*, 440–41.

36. Chicago *Tribune*, Sept. 3, 1882.

37. Ibid., Sept. 13–15, 1882; AGS to Adrian Anson, May 23, 1883, CBC.

38. Chicago *Tribune*, July 4, 5, Sept. 30, Oct. 1, 2, 4, 1885.

39. For a description of Von der Ahe, see Douglass Wallop, *Baseball: An Informal History* (New York, 1969), 65.

40. Chicago *Tribune*, Oct. 15, 1885.

41. Ibid., Oct. 15, 16, 1885.

42. Ibid., Oct. 25, 26, 1885. Also see New York *Clipper*, Nov. 14, 1885; *Guide*, 1887, pp. 21–22.

43. *Sporting News*, Oct. 18, 1886.

44. St. Louis *Republican*, Oct. 1886, in Kuhn Scrapbook.

45. *St. Louis Republican*, Oct. 1886, *The Morning News*, Oct. 1886, in Kuhn Scrapbook.

46. Chicago *Tribune*, Oct. 24, 1886. Also see New York *Clipper*, Oct. 19, 23, 30, 1886, and *Sporting News*, Oct. 4, 11, 1886, for accounts of the series.

47. Chicago dropped two of three games in St. Louis on its way home from spring training. See Chicago *Tribune* April 3, 8–10, 1887.

48. Sporting columns in newspapers consistently used these terms in the late 1880s. For example see Chicago *Herald*, Aug. 30, 1889; *Sporting Life*, May 9, June 27, 1888; New York *Clipper*, Oct. 13, 1888.

49. Ledger Book of Chicago Baseball Club; William Hulbert to H. D. McKnight, Nov. 30, 1881, CBC.

50. AGS to Allen J. Chase, Dec. 10, 1883, CBC.

51. Jonathan Brown to Nick Young, July 1, Aug. 4, 25, 1884, Ledger Book of Chicago Baseball Club, 1878–1879; William Hulbert to H. D. McKnight, Nov. 30, 1881, CBC; *Sporting News*, Aug. 30, 1886; New York *Clipper*, Oct. 29, 1887; San Francisco *Examiner*, Nov. 10, 1888 (in Spalding Scrapbook, no number, that focused on the 1888–89 World Tour); *Sporting News*, Aug. 31, 1889.

52. New York *Times*, Dec. 18, 1892.

53. Spalding, *America's National Game*, 423.

54. Ibid., 192–93.

55. AGS to Adrian Anson, Sept. 12, 1883, Feb. 29, March 7, July 23, 1884, CBC; Chicago *Tribune*, Feb. 1887, in Kuhn Collection; Chicago *Mail*, May 1, 1888; Chicago *Tribune*, Nov. 20, 1886; *Sporting Life*, July 27, 1887, Jan. 18, 1888; New York *Clipper*, April 28, 1888.

56. *Sporting News*, Sept. 13, 1886; undated, unnamed newspaper clipping entitled "Spalding's Charges," in Chadwick Scrapbook #2.

57. Chicago *News*, June 26, 1889.

58. Club correspondence in CBC offers page after page of evidence. On hiring mascots, also see New York *Clipper*, June 16, 1888; *Sporting News*, April 13, 1887.

59. AGS to A. C. Goldsmith, April 29, 1884, AGS to Barnum, Bailey, and Hutchinson, Aug. 4, 1884, CBC.

60. Spalding, *America's National Game*, 193.

61. G. W. Thompson to William Hulbert, Oct. 30, 1875, CBC; Anson, *Ball Player's Career*, 93.

62. AGS to Cap Anson, Jan. 8, 1876, CBC.

63. *Sporting Life*, April 27, May 11, 1887. Van Haltren pitched in twenty gam[es] for Chicago in 1887, compiling an 11–7 record. The following year he a[p-] peared in thirty games, registering a 13–13 mark.

64. *Sporting News*, April 16, 1887; New York *Clipper*, Oct. 27, 1887. For ot[her] examples of Spalding's ability to obtain ballplayers, see *Sporting News*, A[pril] 30, 1886, April 23, 1887, April 27, May 18, June 9, July 27, 1889; *Spor[ting] Life*, Nov. 16, 1887; AGS to J. P. McLoughlin, Nov. 6, 1883, AGS to Jo[nathan] Brown, Aug. 4, 1884, AGS to George W. Howe, July 29, 1884, CBC.

65. *Sporting News*, Nov. 26, 1887.

66. Ibid., Feb. 2, 1888; *Sporting Life*, Feb. 8, 1888.

67. Spalding, *America's National Game*, 195.

68. Unnamed newspaper clipping, Dec. 1886, in Kuhn Scrapbook; *S[porting] News*, Jan. 22, 1887.

69. Spalding, *America's National Game*, 515–518; *Sporting News*, Jan. 15, 1887; Chicago *Times*, Feb. 11, 1887.

70. *Sporting News*, March 5, 1887.

71. AGS to Henry Graham, Dec. 26, 1883, CBC.

72. AGS to Frank Flint, Nov. 15, 1883, and to Charles Jeffreys, Nov[.] CBC. Spalding was particularly bothered by ballplayers who advances on their salaries during the winter months. Spaldin[g] them interest on the loans, which he always accompanied with ments about proper behavior. See, e.g., AGS to Fred Pfeffer, N[ov.] to Cap Anson, Feb. 14, 1884, to Thomas Burns, to George Gore, J[ ] to Frank Flint, March 6, 1884, and to Ed Williamson, Jan. 18, 1[884].

73. AGS to George Gore, to Frank Flint, and to Cap Anson, M[ ] CBC.

74. Chicago *Daily Baseball Gazette*, April 22, 1887, in Chadwick S[ ] *Sporting News*, Jan. 22, 1887.

75. *Sporting News*, March 17, 1886.

76. Ibid., Jan. 22, 1887. For 1888 club policy see New York *Cl[ipper]* 1888. New York *Times*, April 25, 1889, reported that four (

4. David Voigt, *American Baseball: From Gentleman's Sport to the Commissioner System* (Norman, Okla., 1966), 69–73; AGS, *America's National Game* (New York, 1911), 233.

5. AGS to H. D. McKnight, Feb. 1, 10, 1877, AGS to Mr. Clark, March 23, 1877, CBC.

6. Lee Lowenfish and Tony Lupien, *The Imperfect Diamond: The Story of Baseball's Reserve System and the Men Who Fought to Change It* (New York, 1980), 18.

7. Voigt, *American Baseball*, 121–25.

8. William Hulbert to H. D. McKnight, Nov. 8, 18, 1881, CBC.

9. Voigt, *American Baseball*, 123–24.

10. Gabriel Kolko, *The Triumph of Conservatism: A Reinterpretation of American History, 1900–1916* (Chicago, 1963).

11. AGS, *America's National Game*, 244–47, contains a copy of the National Agreement.

12. Ibid., 242; Voigt, *American Baseball*, 129–30.

13. Some examples of these activities include AGS to O. P. Caylor, Feb. 20, 1884, to Arthur Soden, Jan. 1, 1885, to John Day, Feb. 15, 1884, to Harry Wright, Feb. 21, 1884, and to James Wilson, Feb. 25, 1884, CBC; *Sporting News*, June 28, 1886, April 2, 1887, Nov. 5, 1887, Nov. 24, 1888; *Sporting Life*, Nov. 16, 1887; New York *Clipper*, March 18, Oct. 7, 1882, Dec. 1, 1883, Nov. 29, 1884, Oct. 24, 1885; *Guide*, 1879, pp. 96–97, 1883, pp. 31–32, 97–101.

14. *Guide*, 1882, p.26. Also see *Guide*, 1880, p. 85; AGS, "Baseball," unnamed magazine (1890), 607, in Spalding Papers. For a discussion of the liquor stand, see A. G. Mills to AGS, May 18, June 7, 1883, Mills Papers.

15. *Guide*, 1884, pp. 42–44.

16. AGS to A. G. Mills, Oct. 23, 1883, CBC; AGS to A. G. Mills, Oct. 3, 1883, Mills Papers.

17. Excerpt from Providence *Evening Bulletin*, Oct. 1, 1883, in Spalding Scrapbook #4.

18. In the CBC are many letters by Clarke concerning scheduling, e.g., E. D. Clarke to Mr. Leffler, Secretary of Bloomington (Indiana) Baseball Club, April 17, 1884. On the championship see AGS to A. G. Mills, March 11, 1884, CBC.

19. AGS to John Brown, May 9, 1884, to E. D. Clarke, June 3, 1884, to G. O. Craig, June 26, 1884, to E. D. Clarke, June 9, 24, 27, July 5, 1884, to D. R. Jenks, July 16, 23, 25, 1884, and to George Howe, July 20, 1884, CBC. Spalding figured his losses on the "reserve scheme" at $2,000.

20. AGS to (illegible), Dec. 26, 1883, CBC.

21. New York *Clipper*, Dec. 15, 1883.

22. AGS to A. G. Mills, Dec. 10, 1883, to Nick Young, Dec. 7, 10, 1883, CBC.

23. AGS to A. G. Mills, Dec. 10, 12, 1883, to Larry Corcoran, Dec. 10, 1883, CBC; A. G. Mills to AGS, Dec. 10, 14, 17, 22, 26, 31, 1883, Jan. 7, 9, 12, March 13, 1884, Mills Papers. New York *Clipper*, Dec. 22, 1883. The Mills correspondence reveals the league president's close monitoring of the affair and his concern that Spalding abide by league rules. In that spirit, one week after Spalding warned Corcoran, he notified the secretary of the Union Association of the situation. See AGS to Warren White, Dec. 18, 1883, CBC.

24. AGS to Cap Anson, Dec. 19, 29, 1883, Jan. 4, 1884, CBC.
25. AGS to A. G. Mills, Jan. 5, 1884, A. G. Mills to AGS, Jan. 5, 19, 1884, Mills Papers.
26. AGS to A. G. Mills, Jan. 5, 21, 28, March 11, June 30, Sept. 10, 1884, CBC; *Guide*, 1885, p. 9; A. G. Mills to AGS, Feb. 9, March 18, 1884, Mills Papers.
27. AGS to A. G. Mills, Sept. 24, 1884, CBC. On one occasion, Mills cautioned Spalding against starting rumors that the National League would give George Lucas a St. Louis franchise if he abandoned the Union Association. Ironically, such a condition was part of the settlement that saw the Association's defeat. See A. G. Mills to AGS, June 28, July 8, 1884, Mills Papers.
28. Chicago *Tribune*, Nov. 22, 1888. Statistics on franchises were drawn from *The Baseball Encyclopedia* (Toronto, 1969).
29. *Sporting Life*, June 8, 1887; A. G. Mills to AGS, Nov. 27, 1886, Mills Papers. Mills voiced his approval of consolidation, suggesting that the timing was inopportune, and denied having any interest in the post.
30. Ibid., July 13, Aug. 24, Sept. 21, 1887; *Sporting News*, Sept. 27, 1886.
31. AGS to Charlie Byrne, Nov. 21, 1887, in *Sporting News*, Dec. 3, 1887. On Dec. 10, 1883, the *News* reported acceptance of the plan.
32. New York *Clipper*, July 20, 1889, carries the letter.
33. Ibid.; Chicago *Herald*, Nov. 12, 1889.
34. New York *Times*, July 14, 1889.
35. *Sporting Life*, Nov. 30, 1887. Also see Ibid., Sept. 28, 1887; *Sporting News*, Nov. 19, 1887; Voigt, *American Baseball*, 158–59.
36. Harold Seymour, *Baseball: The Early Years*, (New York, 1960), 129.
37. Chicago *Tribune*, Sept. 21, 22, 27, 1889.
38. Ibid, Sept. 23, 1889; *Sporting News*, Sept. 21, Nov. 2, 1889.
39. AGS TO A. G. Mills, Aug. 1, Sept. 25, 1889, Mills Papers. Mills's response was mixed. While assuring Spalding that he did not plan to join the Brotherhood, he blamed the National League for the problems that had resulted in player unrest. He also told Spalding that although he would like to become involved in league business, his personal situation prevented it. See A. G. Mills to AGS, Oct.2, 1889, and also July 30, 1889, Mills Papers.
40. Chicago *Inter-Ocean*, Sept. 25, 1889; *Sporting News*, Sept. 28, 1889.
41. AGS, *America's National Game*, 272–73, presents the manifesto.
42. For useful accounts of the Brotherhood War, see Voigt, *American Baseball*, 154–69; Lowenfish and Lupien, *Imperfect Diamond*, 36; Seymour, *Baseball*, 221–39.
43. *Baseball Encyclopedia*; Chicago *Times*, May 8, 1890.
44. New York *Clipper*, Nov. 23, 1889; *Sporting Life*, Nov. 20, 1889.
45. AGS, *America's National Game*, 285.
46. *Guide*, 1890, pp. 28–31; Chicago *Times*, Nov. 22, 1898; A. G. Mills to AGS, Nov. 23, 1889, Mills Papers.
47. Chicago *Herald*, May 11, 1890.
48. Chicago *Evening Post*, May 28, 1890.
49. Chicago *Times*, May 11, 1890.
50. Chicago *Tribune*, May 18, 1890. The Chicago Players' figures were based on five home games and the White Stockings' on nine.
51. *Sporting News*, Oct. 26, 1889, March 29, 1890; Voigt, *American Baseball*, 165.

52. New York *Clipper*, Aug. 16, 1890.
53. AGS, *America's National Game*, 287–88.
54. Chicago *Herald*, May 11, 1890; Chicago *Evening Post*, May 28, 1890.
55. *Guide*, 1890, pp. 11–26.
56. Lowenfish and Lupien, *Imperfect Diamond*, 45, cites one estimate of 913,000 for the Players League and 853,000 for the National League in 1890. Also see *Sporting News*, May 10, 1890.
57. New York *Clipper*, July 19, 1890; *Sporting News*, July 19, 26, 1890; New York *Clipper*, Feb. 16, 1895.
58. AGS, *America's National Game*, 295–97.
59. Chicago *Herald*, Oct. 23, 1890.
60. New York *Clipper*, Oct. 18, 1890; *Sporting News*, Oct. 8, 11, Nov. 1, 1890; Chicago *Herald*, Oct. 8, 1890, Nov. 14, 1890; Chicago *Tribune*, Nov. 18, 1890; New York *Times*, Oct. 23, 1890.
61. AGS, *America's National Game*, 288.
62. *Sporting News*, Nov. 15, 22, Dec. 27, 1890; New York *Clipper*, Nov. 26, Dec. 6, 20, 1890; Chicago *Herald*, Nov. 20, 1890; Chicago *Tribune*, Nov. 21, 1890.
63. New York *Clipper*, Jan. 10, 1891; Chicago *Times*, Dec. 28, 1890; Chicago *Herald*, Oct. 28, 29, Nov. 1, 2, 11, 12, 13, 14, 15, 23, 1890; Chicago *Tribune*, Nov. 14, 16, 21, 1890.
64. Chicago *Times*, Dec. 28, 1890; New York *Clipper*, Dec. 6, 1890, carried the *Ledger* story.
65. Chicago *Herald*, Nov. 23, 1890.
66. Chicago *Tribune*, Dec. 19, 1890; Chicago *Herald*, Dec. 20, 1890.
67. Seymour, *Baseball*, 249; *Guide*, 1891, pp. 52–63; *Sporting News*, Aug. 22, 1891.
68. Chicago *Herald*, Feb. 14, 1891; A. G. Mills to AGS, Jan. 22, 26, Feb. 12, 1891, Mills Papers.
69. AGS to A. G. Mills, Jan. 24, 1891, Mills Papers.
70. Chapters 5 and 6 deal with these aspects of Spalding's life.
71. Arthur Bartlett, *Baseball and Mr. Spalding: The History and Romance of Baseball* (New York, 1951), 233, contains the quotation.
72. New York *Clipper*, Dec. 1, 1894; *Sporting News*, Dec. 12, 1894. Other instances of A.G.'s opinions are in New York *Clipper*, Jan. 1, Feb. 24, 1894, Feb. 16, 26, 1898; *Sporting News*, Feb. 2, April 2, 1892, Nov. 24, Dec. 1, 12, 23, 1894, March 16, Dec. 7, 1895, Oct. 23, 1897, Feb. 11, Dec. 23, 1899.
73. *Sporting News*, Feb. 10, 1894.
74. Ibid., Feb. 2, 1895, March 18, 25, 1899; AGS, *America's National Game*, 302.
75. AGS, *America's National Game*, 301–3.
76. Ibid., 308–14. A typescript copy of the speech is in Mills Papers.
77. Undated clipping, in Chadwick Scrapbook #4.
78. AGS, *America's National Game*, 306.
79. Voigt, *American Baseball*, 312–14; Seymour, *Baseball*, 307–18.
80. AGS, *America's National Game*, 310. Similar sentiments about professional baseball's becoming too much of a business appeared in New York *Times*, Sept. 23, 1900, in an editorial entitled "Decline of Baseball."
81. AGS, *America's National Game*, 307.

82. New York *Times*, Dec. 14, 1901; undated, unnamed newspaper clipping, in Chadwick Scrapbook #4.
83. *Sporting News*, Dec. 21, 1901.
84. Undated, unnamed newspaper clipping, in Chadwick Scrapbook #4. Also see New York *Times*, Dec. 14, 1901.
85. New York *Clipper*, Dec. 21, 1901.
86. Undated clipping, in Chadwick Scrapbook #4; AGS, *America's National Game*, 320.
87. *Sporting News*, March 29, April 5, 1902; Lowenfish and Lupien, *Imperfect Diamond*, 68; Voigt, *American Baseball*, 305.
88. *Sporting News*, Dec. 2, 1902.
89. Ibid., April 18, 1891.
90. *Guide*, 1915, p. 5.

5. A. G. Spalding and Brothers: The Business of Sport

1. Chicago *Inter-Ocean*, *Chicago's First Half Century, 1833–1883* (Chicago, 1883), 31–32.
2. George Orear, *Commercial and Architectural Chicago* (Chicago, 1887), 221.
3. Chicago *Times*, March 5, 1876; Arthur Bartlett, *Baseball and Mr. Spalding: The History and Romance of Baseball* (New York, 1951), 98–99.
4. Charles W. Spalding, *The Spalding Memorial: A Genealogical History of Edward Spalding . . . and His Descendants* (Chicago, 1897), 904; *Spalding Store News*, Sept. 9, 1915, p. 7.
5. New York *Clipper*, April 24, June 19, 1875.
6. Ibid., February 2, 1878. Also see the April 8, 1882, issue for general comments on the profitability of the sporting-goods business.
7. Ibid., Nov. 4, April 15, 1882. Also see Detroit *Telegram*, July 29, 1883, in Spalding Scrapbook #4.
8. *Spalding Store News*, Sept. 9, 1915, contains a copy of the partnership agreement.
9. Mrs. C. F. Robbins to Peter Levine, Feb. 14, 1980. Robbins is the daughter of Mary Brown, A.G.'s sister. Also see *Reminiscences of Harriet I. Spalding* (East Orange, N.Y., 1910), 96–97; Chicago *Tribune*, Feb. 13, March 12, April 23, 1876.
10. *Reminiscences of Harriet I. Spalding*, 97.
11. Dun and Bradstreet, Inc., Cook County, Illinois, vol. 16, p. 122; *Reminiscences of Harriet I. Spalding*, 96–98; *Spalding Store News*, May 11, 1916.
12. Bessie L. Pierce, *A History of Chicago*, vol. 3, *The Rise of a Modern City, 1871–1893* (New York, 1957), 20–63; Homer Hoyt, *One Hundred Years of Land Values in Chicago* (Chicago, 1933), 128–29, 142.
13. Chicago *Times*, March 5, 1876, in Spalding Scrapbook #2.
14. Chicago *Tribune*, March 30, 1873, quoted in Pierce, *History of Chicago*, 63.
15. Gunther Barth, *City People: The Rise of Modern City Culture in Nineteenth-Century America* (New York, 1980), 148–91, discusses the rise of professional baseball as part of a new urban culture that satisfied these needs. Also see Allen Guttmann, *From Ritual to Record: The Nature of Modern Sport* (New

9. Boston *Globe*, July 27, 1875.

10. Ibid., July 28, 1875.

11. New York *Clipper*, Aug. 8, Oct. 30, 1875. The headline in the Oct. 30 issue read "Chicago. '76 vs. Boston '76."

12. Arthur Bartlett, *Baseball and Mr. Spalding: The History and Romance of Baseball* (New York, 1951), 79.

13. AGS, *America's National Game*, 209.

14. David Voigt, *American Baseball: From Gentleman's Sport to the Commissioner System* (Norman, Okla., 1966), 64–65.

15. AGS to Mr. Joyce, Jan. 28, 1876, CBC.

16. New York *Clipper*, Feb. 12, 1876.

17. AGS to Henry Chadwick, Feb. 27, 1876, reprinted in *Guide*, 1908, pp. 19–20.

18. AGS, *America's National Game*, 208; *Sporting News*, April 13, 1895; AGS, *America's National Game*, 309.

19. For stimulating discussions of Barnum and Beecher that are compatible with this argument, see Neil Harris, *Humbug: The Art of P. T. Barnum* (Boston, 1973), and Clifford E. Clark, Jr., *Henry Ward Beecher: Spokesman for a Middle-Class America* (Urbana, 1978).

20. William Mathews, *Getting On in the World* (Chicago, 1874), 187.

21. My analysis of Spalding and his connection to the larger culture relies in part on Burton J. Bledstein, *The Culture of Professionalism: The Middle Class and the Development of Higher Education in America* (New York, 1976). The reference to the professional as magician appears on pp. 92–93. Bledstein also discusses the development of professional baseball as part of the culture of professionalism on pp. 81–85.

22. Most influential on my thinking were Paul Boyer, *Urban Masses and Moral Order in America, 1820–1920* (Cambridge, 1978); George M. Fredrickson, *The Inner Civil War: Northern Intellectuals and the Crisis of the Union* (New York, 1965); Samuel P. Hays, *The Response to Industrialism, 1885–1914* (Chicago, 1973); Gabriel Kolko, *The Triumph of Conservatism: A Reinterpretation of American History, 1900–1916* (Chicago, 1963); Donald J. Mrozek, *Sport and American Mentality, 1880–1910* (Knoxville, 1983); Steven A. Riess, *Touching Base: Professional Baseball and American Culture in the Progresive Era* (Westport, Conn., 1980); Robert Wiebe, *The Search for Order, 1877–1920* (Chicago, 1963).

23. *Guide*, 1915, p. 5. Chadwick's remarks appear in AGS, *America's National Game*, 471–72. Also see 425–31, for a description of the tasks of the baseball magnate as Spalding understood them.

24. AGS to Riverside Baseball Club, Dec. 28, 1875, CBC. The letterbooks of the Chicago Baseball Club for the 1880s offer abundant examples of Spalding's correspondence concerning his roles as manager, captain, and owner of the club. They are a key source for this chapter.

25. AGS to James Kelly, June 5, 1877, CBC. Other examples, selected from numerous letters, are AGS to E. A. Holbrook, March 20, 1876, and AGS to William P. Rogers, March 15, 1876.

26. New York *Clipper*, Dec. 2, 1876; Chicago *Tribune*, July 14, 1876.

27. Chicago *Evening Journal*, Sept. 9, 1876; Chicago *Tribune*, Oct. 1, 1876. The Kuhn Scrapbooks contain clippings on the White Stockings from Chicago newspapers for the 1880s. These books supplemented my own reading of

the Chicago *Tribune* and the Chicago *Times*. I have cited the scrapbooks directly only when the newspaper source is not clear.

28. New York *Clipper*, June 30, Oct. 13, Nov. 17, 1877.
29. Chicago *Tribune*, April 11–13, 16, May 6, 1882; New York *Clipper*, April 15, May 6, 1882; AGS to W. J. Culver, June 15, 1882, CBC. Hulbert's health problems left Spalding in charge during much of the 1881 season as well.
30. Statistics on club and player records throughout are from *The Baseball Encyclopedia* (Toronto, 1969). Chicago *Tribune*, May 6, July 7, 1880. Of the twenty-two victories, only twenty were against National League opponents. Chicago also posted winning percentages of .777 in 1885 and .726 in 1886.
31. Adrian C. Anson, *A Ball Player's Career* (Chicago, 1900), 128, 113.
32. Lee Allen, *The National League Story: The Official History* (New York, 1965), 44–46.
33. AGS, *America's National Game*, 184.
34. Anson, *Ball Player's Career*, 133.
35. AGS, *America's National Game*, 440–41.
36. Chicago *Tribune*, Sept. 3, 1882.
37. Ibid., Sept. 13–15, 1882; AGS to Adrian Anson, May 23, 1883, CBC.
38. Chicago *Tribune*, July 4, 5, Sept. 30, Oct. 1, 2, 4, 1885.
39. For a description of Von der Ahe, see Douglass Wallop, *Baseball: An Informal History* (New York, 1969), 65.
40. Chicago *Tribune*, Oct. 15, 1885.
41. Ibid., Oct. 15, 16, 1885.
42. Ibid., Oct. 25, 26, 1885. Also see New York *Clipper*, Nov. 14, 1885; *Guide*, 1887, pp. 21–22.
43. *Sporting News*, Oct. 18, 1886.
44. St. Louis *Republican*, Oct. 1886, in Kuhn Scrapbook.
45. *St. Louis Republican*, Oct. 1886, *The Morning News*, Oct. 1886, in Kuhn Scrapbook.
46. Chicago *Tribune*, Oct. 24, 1886. Also see New York *Clipper*, Oct. 19, 23, 30, 1886, and *Sporting News*, Oct. 4, 11, 1886, for accounts of the series.
47. Chicago dropped two of three games in St. Louis on its way home from spring training. See Chicago *Tribune* April 3, 8–10, 1887.
48. Sporting columns in newspapers consistently used these terms in the late 1880s. For example see Chicago *Herald*, Aug. 30, 1889; *Sporting Life*, May 9, June 27, 1888; New York *Clipper*, Oct. 13, 1888.
49. Ledger Book of Chicago Baseball Club; William Hulbert to H. D. McKnight, Nov. 30, 1881, CBC.
50. AGS to Allen J. Chase, Dec. 10, 1883, CBC.
51. Jonathan Brown to Nick Young, July 1, Aug. 4, 25, 1884, Ledger Book of Chicago Baseball Club, 1878–1879; William Hulbert to H. D. McKnight, Nov. 30, 1881, CBC; *Sporting News*, Aug. 30, 1886; New York *Clipper*, Oct. 29, 1887; San Francisco *Examiner*, Nov. 10, 1888 (in Spalding Scrapbook, no number, that focused on the 1888–89 World Tour); *Sporting News*, Aug. 31, 1889.
52. New York *Times*, Dec. 18, 1892.
53. Spalding, *America's National Game*, 423.

54. Ibid., 192–93.
55. AGS to Adrian Anson, Sept. 12, 1883, Feb. 29, March 7, July 23, 1884, CBC; Chicago *Tribune*, Feb. 1887, in Kuhn Collection; Chicago *Mail*, May 1, 1888; Chicago *Tribune*, Nov. 20, 1886; *Sporting Life*, July 27, 1887, Jan. 18, 1888; New York *Clipper*, April 28, 1888.
56. *Sporting News*, Sept. 13, 1886; undated, unnamed newspaper clipping entitled "Spalding's Charges," in Chadwick Scrapbook #2.
57. Chicago *News*, June 26, 1889.
58. Club correspondence in CBC offers page after page of evidence. On hiring mascots, also see New York *Clipper*, June 16, 1888; *Sporting News*, April 13, 1887.
59. AGS to A. C. Goldsmith, April 29, 1884, AGS to Barnum, Bailey, and Hutchinson, Aug. 4, 1884, CBC.
60. Spalding, *America's National Game*, 193.
61. G. W. Thompson to William Hulbert, Oct. 30, 1875, CBC; Anson, *Ball Player's Career*, 93.
62. AGS to Cap Anson, Jan. 8, 1876, CBC.
63. *Sporting Life*, April 27, May 11, 1887. Van Haltren pitched in twenty games for Chicago in 1887, compiling an 11–7 record. The following year he appeared in thirty games, registering a 13–13 mark.
64. *Sporting News*, April 16, 1887; New York *Clipper*, Oct. 27, 1887. For other examples of Spalding's ability to obtain ballplayers, see *Sporting News*, Aug. 30, 1886, April 23, 1887, April 27, May 18, June 9, July 27, 1889; *Sporting Life*, Nov. 16, 1887; AGS to J. P. McLoughlin, Nov. 6, 1883, AGS to Joseph Brown, Aug. 4, 1884, AGS to George W. Howe, July 29, 1884, CBC.
65. *Sporting News*, Nov. 26, 1887.
66. Ibid., Feb. 2, 1888; *Sporting Life*, Feb. 8, 1888.
67. Spalding, *America's National Game*, 195.
68. Unnamed newspaper clipping, Dec. 1886, in Kuhn Scrapbook; *Sporting News*, Jan. 22, 1887.
69. Spalding, *America's National Game*, 515–518; *Sporting News*, Jan. 15, Feb. 12, 1887; Chicago *Times*, Feb. 11, 1887.
70. *Sporting News*, March 5, 1887.
71. AGS to Henry Graham, Dec. 26, 1883, CBC.
72. AGS to Frank Flint, Nov. 15, 1883, and to Charles Jeffreys, Nov. 5, 1883, CBC. Spalding was particularly bothered by ballplayers who asked for advances on their salaries during the winter months. Spalding charged them interest on the loans, which he always accompanied with admonishments about proper behavior. See, e.g., AGS to Fred Pfeffer, Nov. 10, 1883, to Cap Anson, Feb. 14, 1884, to Thomas Burns, to George Gore, Jan. 15, 1884, to Frank Flint, March 6, 1884, and to Ed Williamson, Jan. 18, 1884, CBC.
73. AGS to George Gore, to Frank Flint, and to Cap Anson, May 20, 1884, CBC.
74. Chicago *Daily Baseball Gazette*, April 22, 1887, in Chadwick Scrapbook #2; *Sporting News*, Jan. 22, 1887.
75. *Sporting News*, March 17, 1886.
76. Ibid., Jan. 22, 1887. For 1888 club policy see New York *Clipper*, April 28, 1888. New York *Times*, April 25, 1889, reported that four Chicago players

were released by Spalding for "bad habits" displayed on the 1889 world tour. See Chapter 6 for a full discussion of that event.

77. Chicago *Times*, July 10, 1886.
78. Chicago *Evening Journal*, April 30, 1887; Riess, *Touching Base*, 122–23.
79. AGS to A. G. Mills, Jan. 5, 1884, Mills Papers.
80. Spalding, *America's National Game*, 527–28.
81. Chicago *News*, June 26, 1889, Sept. 9, 1887.
82. *Sporting News*, June 28, 1886.
83. The list is in Box 5, CBC. Also see AGS to Mr. White, April 22, 1884, CBC.
84. A survey of the *Proceedings of the Chicago City Council* (*PCCC*) for the 1880s found brief references concerning the ball club involving permission to rent the grounds to circuses (*PCCC*, 1883–84, pp. 13, 135), and the condition of alleys near the ballpark (*PCCC*, 1884–85, pp. 489, 493, 527; 1885–86, p. 525).
85. AGS to John Lake, Sept. 16, 1884, CBC. Also see AGS to D. W. Ruggles, June 16, 1882, CBC.
86. The description and quotation are from a newspaper clipping from *American Sports* (Chicago), April 28, 1883, in Chadwick Scrapbook #19.
87. New York *Clipper*, March 29, May 31, July 5, 1884. Also see AGS to W. Irving Culver, May 28, 1884, CBC.
88. Chicago *Tribune*, May 3, 1885; New York *Clipper*, April 25, May 3, June 6, 1885.
89. *Sporting News*, April 23, 1893; Riess, *Touching Base*, 86.
90. AGS to A. G. Mills, June 30, 1883, CBC.
91. Unnamed Chicago newspaper clipping, ca. Nov.–Dec. 1886, in Kuhn Scrapbook.
92. John Brown to C. H. Morton, April 11, 1884, CBC.
93. *Sporting Life*, Sept. 21, 1887; Anson, *Ball Player's Career*, 148, 150, 221. Anson's references were specifically aimed at Clarence Duval, Chicago's black mascot. See Chapter 6 for a discussion of Duval.
94. The best account of the integration of major league baseball is Jules Tygiel, *Baseball's Great Experiment: Jackie Robinson and His Legacy* (New York, 1983). For good accounts of the Negro leagues, see Harold Peterson, *Only the Ball Was White* (Englewood Cliffs, 1970); Donn Rogosin, *Invisible Men: Life in Baseball's Negro Leagues* (New York, 1983).
95. *Sporting News*, Oct. 17, 1896.
96. Anson, *Ball Player's Career*, 304–5, presents his view of the affair. *Sporting News*, Feb. 29, 1898, contains Spalding's statement. For other information on the controversy, see New York *Clipper*, Dec. 25, 1897, Feb. 19, April 9, 1898; *Sporting News*, July 31, Oct. 9, Nov. 20, 27, 1897, Feb. 12, 1898.

4. The Brains of the National League

1. New York *Times*, Jan. 25, 1891.
2. *Sporting News*, April 18, 1891.
3. Ibid., April 18, 25, 1891. The person who labeled A.G. "the brains" was John Montgomery Ward, a New York Giant shortstop and Spalding's chief adversary in the Brotherhood War. Spalding Scrapbook, unnumbered (world tour material), contains the quotation from *Spirit of the Times*, Nov. 10, 1888.

4. David Voigt, *American Baseball: From Gentleman's Sport to the Commissioner System* (Norman, Okla., 1966), 69–73; AGS, *America's National Game* (New York, 1911), 233.

5. AGS to H. D. McKnight, Feb. 1, 10, 1877, AGS to Mr. Clark, March 23, 1877, CBC.

6. Lee Lowenfish and Tony Lupien, *The Imperfect Diamond: The Story of Baseball's Reserve System and the Men Who Fought to Change It* (New York, 1980), 18.

7. Voigt, *American Baseball*, 121–25.

8. William Hulbert to H. D. McKnight, Nov. 8, 18, 1881, CBC.

9. Voigt, *American Baseball*, 123–24.

10. Gabriel Kolko, *The Triumph of Conservatism: A Reinterpretation of American History, 1900–1916* (Chicago, 1963).

11. AGS, *America's National Game*, 244–47, contains a copy of the National Agreement.

12. Ibid., 242; Voigt, *American Baseball*, 129–30.

13. Some examples of these activities include AGS to O. P. Caylor, Feb. 20, 1884, to Arthur Soden, Jan. 1, 1885, to John Day, Feb. 15, 1884, to Harry Wright, Feb. 21, 1884, and to James Wilson, Feb. 25, 1884, CBC; *Sporting News*, June 28, 1886, April 2, 1887, Nov. 5, 1887, Nov. 24, 1888; *Sporting Life*, Nov. 16, 1887; New York *Clipper*, March 18, Oct. 7, 1882, Dec. 1, 1883, Nov. 29, 1884, Oct. 24, 1885; *Guide*, 1879, pp. 96–97, 1883, pp. 31–32, 97–101.

14. *Guide*, 1882, p.26. Also see *Guide*, 1880, p. 85; AGS, "Baseball," unnamed magazine (1890), 607, in Spalding Papers. For a discussion of the liquor stand, see A. G. Mills to AGS, May 18, June 7, 1883, Mills Papers.

15. *Guide*, 1884, pp. 42–44.

16. AGS to A. G. Mills, Oct. 23, 1883, CBC; AGS to A. G. Mills, Oct. 3, 1883, Mills Papers.

17. Excerpt from Providence *Evening Bulletin*, Oct. 1, 1883, in Spalding Scrapbook #4.

18. In the CBC are many letters by Clarke concerning scheduling, e.g., E. D. Clarke to Mr. Leffler, Secretary of Bloomington (Indiana) Baseball Club, April 17, 1884. On the championship see AGS to A. G. Mills, March 11, 1884, CBC.

19. AGS to John Brown, May 9, 1884, to E. D. Clarke, June 3, 1884, to G. O. Craig, June 26, 1884, to E. D. Clarke, June 9, 24, 27, July 5, 1884, to D. R. Jenks, July 16, 23, 25, 1884, and to George Howe, July 20, 1884, CBC. Spalding figured his losses on the "reserve scheme" at $2,000.

20. AGS to (illegible), Dec. 26, 1883, CBC.

21. New York *Clipper*, Dec. 15, 1883.

22. AGS to A. G. Mills, Dec. 10, 1883, to Nick Young, Dec. 7, 10, 1883, CBC.

23. AGS to A. G. Mills, Dec. 10, 12, 1883, to Larry Corcoran, Dec. 10, 1883, CBC; A. G. Mills to AGS, Dec. 10, 14, 17, 22, 26, 31, 1883, Jan. 7, 9, 12, March 13, 1884, Mills Papers. New York *Clipper*, Dec. 22, 1883. The Mills correspondence reveals the league president's close monitoring of the affair and his concern that Spalding abide by league rules. In that spirit, one week after Spalding warned Corcoran, he notified the secretary of the Union Association of the situation. See AGS to Warren White, Dec. 18, 1883, CBC.

24. AGS to Cap Anson, Dec. 19, 29, 1883, Jan. 4, 1884, CBC.
25. AGS to A. G. Mills, Jan. 5, 1884, A. G. Mills to AGS, Jan. 5, 19, 1884, Mills Papers.
26. AGS to A. G. Mills, Jan. 5, 21, 28, March 11, June 30, Sept. 10, 1884, CBC; *Guide*, 1885, p. 9; A. G. Mills to AGS, Feb. 9, March 18, 1884, Mills Papers.
27. AGS to A. G. Mills, Sept. 24, 1884, CBC. On one occasion, Mills cautioned Spalding against starting rumors that the National League would give George Lucas a St. Louis franchise if he abandoned the Union Association. Ironically, such a condition was part of the settlement that saw the Association's defeat. See A. G. Mills to AGS, June 28, July 8, 1884, Mills Papers.
28. Chicago *Tribune*, Nov. 22, 1888. Statistics on franchises were drawn from *The Baseball Encyclopedia* (Toronto, 1969).
29. *Sporting Life*, June 8, 1887; A. G. Mills to AGS, Nov. 27, 1886, Mills Papers. Mills voiced his approval of consolidation, suggesting that the timing was inopportune, and denied having any interest in the post.
30. Ibid., July 13, Aug. 24, Sept. 21, 1887; *Sporting News*, Sept. 27, 1886.
31. AGS to Charlie Byrne, Nov. 21, 1887, in *Sporting News*, Dec. 3, 1887. On Dec. 10, 1883, the *News* reported acceptance of the plan.
32. New York *Clipper*, July 20, 1889, carries the letter.
33. Ibid.; Chicago *Herald*, Nov. 12, 1889.
34. New York *Times*, July 14, 1889.
35. *Sporting Life*, Nov. 30, 1887. Also see Ibid., Sept. 28, 1887; *Sporting News*, Nov. 19, 1887; Voigt, *American Baseball*, 158–59.
36. Harold Seymour, *Baseball: The Early Years*, (New York, 1960), 129.
37. Chicago *Tribune*, Sept. 21, 22, 27, 1889.
38. Ibid, Sept. 23, 1889; *Sporting News*, Sept. 21, Nov. 2, 1889.
39. AGS TO A. G. Mills, Aug. 1, Sept. 25, 1889, Mills Papers. Mills's response was mixed. While assuring Spalding that he did not plan to join the Brotherhood, he blamed the National League for the problems that had resulted in player unrest. He also told Spalding that although he would like to become involved in league business, his personal situation prevented it. See A. G. Mills to AGS, Oct.2, 1889, and also July 30, 1889, Mills Papers.
40. Chicago *Inter-Ocean*, Sept. 25, 1889; *Sporting News*, Sept. 28, 1889.
41. AGS, *America's National Game*, 272–73, presents the manifesto.
42. For useful accounts of the Brotherhood War, see Voigt, *American Baseball*, 154–69; Lowenfish and Lupien, *Imperfect Diamond*, 36; Seymour, *Baseball*, 221–39.
43. *Baseball Encyclopedia*; Chicago *Times*, May 8, 1890.
44. New York *Clipper*, Nov. 23, 1889; *Sporting Life*, Nov. 20, 1889.
45. AGS, *America's National Game*, 285.
46. *Guide*, 1890, pp. 28–31; Chicago *Times*, Nov. 22, 1898; A. G. Mills to AGS, Nov. 23, 1889, Mills Papers.
47. Chicago *Herald*, May 11, 1890.
48. Chicago *Evening Post*, May 28, 1890.
49. Chicago *Times*, May 11, 1890.
50. Chicago *Tribune*, May 18, 1890. The Chicago Players' figures were based on five home games and the White Stockings' on nine.
51. *Sporting News*, Oct. 26, 1889, March 29, 1890; Voigt, *American Baseball*, 165.

52. New York *Clipper*, Aug. 16, 1890.

53. AGS, *America's National Game*, 287–88.

54. Chicago *Herald*, May 11, 1890; Chicago *Evening Post*, May 28, 1890.

55. *Guide*, 1890, pp. 11–26.

56. Lowenfish and Lupien, *Imperfect Diamond*, 45, cites one estimate of 913,000 for the Players League and 853,000 for the National League in 1890. Also see *Sporting News*, May 10, 1890.

57. New York *Clipper*, July 19, 1890; *Sporting News*, July 19, 26, 1890; New York *Clipper*, Feb. 16, 1895.

58. AGS, *America's National Game*, 295–97.

59. Chicago *Herald*, Oct. 23, 1890.

60. New York *Clipper*, Oct. 18, 1890; *Sporting News*, Oct. 8, 11, Nov. 1, 1890; Chicago *Herald*, Oct. 8, 1890, Nov. 14, 1890; Chicago *Tribune*, Nov. 18, 1890; New York *Times*, Oct. 23, 1890.

61. AGS, *America's National Game*, 288.

62. *Sporting News*, Nov. 15, 22, Dec. 27, 1890; New York *Clipper*, Nov. 26, Dec. 6, 20, 1890; Chicago *Herald*, Nov. 20, 1890, Chicago *Tribune*, Nov. 21, 1890.

63. New York *Clipper*, Jan. 10, 1891; Chicago *Times*, Dec. 28, 1890; Chicago *Herald*, Oct. 28, 29, Nov. 1, 2, 11, 12, 13, 14, 15, 23, 1890; Chicago *Tribune*, Nov. 14, 16, 21, 1890.

64. Chicago *Times*, Dec. 28, 1890; New York *Clipper*, Dec. 6, 1890, carried the *Ledger* story.

65. Chicago *Herald*, Nov. 23, 1890.

66. Chicago *Tribune*, Dec. 19, 1890; Chicago *Herald*, Dec. 20, 1890.

67. Seymour, *Baseball*, 249; *Guide*, 1891, pp. 52–63; *Sporting News*, Aug. 22, 1891.

68. Chicago *Herald*, Feb. 14, 1891; A. G. Mills to AGS, Jan. 22, 26, Feb. 12, 1891, Mills Papers.

69. AGS to A. G. Mills, Jan. 24, 1891, Mills Papers.

70. Chapters 5 and 6 deal with these aspects of Spalding's life.

71. Arthur Bartlett, *Baseball and Mr. Spalding: The History and Romance of Baseball* (New York, 1951), 233, contains the quotation.

72. New York *Clipper*, Dec. 1, 1894; *Sporting News*, Dec. 12, 1894. Other instances of A.G.'s opinions are in New York *Clipper*, Jan. 1, Feb. 24, 1894, Feb. 16, 26, 1898; *Sporting News*, Feb. 2, April 2, 1892, Nov. 24, Dec. 1, 12, 23, 1894, March 16, Dec. 7, 1895, Oct. 23, 1897, Feb. 11, Dec. 23, 1899.

73. *Sporting News*, Feb. 10, 1894.

74. Ibid., Feb. 2, 1895, March 18, 25, 1899; AGS, *America's National Game*, 302.

75. AGS, *America's National Game*, 301–3.

76. Ibid., 308–14. A typescript copy of the speech is in Mills Papers.

77. Undated clipping, in Chadwick Scrapbook #4.

78. AGS, *America's National Game*, 306.

79. Voigt, *American Baseball*, 312–14; Seymour, *Baseball*, 307–18.

80. AGS, *America's National Game*, 310. Similar sentiments about professional baseball's becoming too much of a business appeared in New York *Times*, Sept. 23, 1900, in an editorial entitled "Decline of Baseball."

81. AGS, *America's National Game*, 307.

82. New York *Times*, Dec. 14, 1901; undated, unnamed newspaper clipping, in Chadwick Scrapbook #4.

83. *Sporting News*, Dec. 21, 1901.

84. Undated, unnamed newspaper clipping, in Chadwick Scrapbook #4. Also see New York *Times*, Dec. 14, 1901.

85. New York *Clipper*, Dec. 21, 1901.

86. Undated clipping, in Chadwick Scrapbook #4; AGS, *America's National Game*, 320.

87. *Sporting News*, March 29, April 5, 1902; Lowenfish and Lupien, *Imperfect Diamond*, 68; Voigt, *American Baseball*, 305.

88. *Sporting News*, Dec. 2, 1902.

89. Ibid., April 18, 1891.

90. *Guide*, 1915, p. 5.

5. A. G. Spalding and Brothers: The Business of Sport

1. Chicago *Inter-Ocean, Chicago's First Half Century, 1833–1883* (Chicago, 1883), 31–32.

2. George Orear, *Commercial and Architectural Chicago* (Chicago, 1887), 221.

3. Chicago *Times*, March 5, 1876; Arthur Bartlett, *Baseball and Mr. Spalding: The History and Romance of Baseball* (New York, 1951), 98–99.

4. Charles W. Spalding, *The Spalding Memorial: A Genealogical History of Edward Spalding . . . and His Descendants* (Chicago, 1897), 904; *Spalding Store News*, Sept. 9, 1915, p. 7.

5. New York *Clipper*, April 24, June 19, 1875.

6. Ibid., February 2, 1878. Also see the April 8, 1882, issue for general comments on the profitability of the sporting-goods business.

7. Ibid., Nov. 4, April 15, 1882. Also see Detroit *Telegram*, July 29, 1883, in Spalding Scrapbook #4.

8. *Spalding Store News*, Sept. 9, 1915, contains a copy of the partnership agreement.

9. Mrs. C. F. Robbins to Peter Levine, Feb. 14, 1980. Robbins is the daughter of Mary Brown, A.G.'s sister. Also see *Reminiscences of Harriet I. Spalding* (East Orange, N.Y., 1910), 96–97; Chicago *Tribune*, Feb. 13, March 12, April 23, 1876.

10. *Reminiscences of Harriet I. Spalding*, 97.

11. Dun and Bradstreet, Inc., Cook County, Illinois, vol. 16, p. 122; *Reminiscences of Harriet I. Spalding*, 96–98; *Spalding Store News*, May 11, 1916.

12. Bessie L. Pierce, *A History of Chicago*, vol. 3, *The Rise of a Modern City, 1871–1893* (New York, 1957), 20–63; Homer Hoyt, *One Hundred Years of Land Values in Chicago* (Chicago, 1933), 128–29, 142.

13. Chicago *Times*, March 5, 1876, in Spalding Scrapbook #2.

14. Chicago *Tribune*, March 30, 1873, quoted in Pierce, *History of Chicago*, 63.

15. Gunther Barth, *City People: The Rise of Modern City Culture in Nineteenth-Century America* (New York, 1980), 148–91, discusses the rise of professional baseball as part of a new urban culture that satisfied these needs. Also see Allen Guttmann, *From Ritual to Record: The Nature of Modern Sport* (New

York, 1978). The Twain quotation is in Paul Fatout, ed., *Mark Twain Speaking, 1835–1910* (Iowa City, 1976), 244–47. Barth's analysis is provocative and useful for explaining urban, native middle-class Americans. But other people lived in cities as well. Barth plays down a good deal of the real ethnic and class conflict that figured so strongly in the urban growth he describes and that worked against the homogeneous cultural development he implies took place.

16. A full discussion of the ways in which Spalding promoted sport appears in Chapter 6.
17. *Guide*, 1879, p. 111, 1883, p. 105.
18. *Guide*, 1877, pp. 50–56; David Voigt, *American Baseball: From Gentleman's Sport to the Commissioner System* (Norman, Okla., 1966), 69.
19. For an example of the picture and the statement, see *Guide*, 1880. A. G. Mills to AGS, April 10, 14, 21, 28, May 11, 1883, April 1, 1884, Mills Papers.
20. Harry Wright to Charles Fowle, Feb. 13, 1877, Wright Corresp. #2.
21. New York *Clipper*, March 29, 1884; AGS to Proprietors of Barnum Hotel, Baltimore, Jan. 29, 1884, AGS to Managers of Clifton House Hotel, Chicago, Feb. 14, 1884, CBC.
22. AGS to O. P. Caylor, Feb. 15, 1884, CBC.
23. AGS to A. G. Mills, Feb. 14, 24, 1884, AGS to Nick Young, Jan. 24, Feb. 4, 1884, CBC.
24. *Guide*, 1879, pp. 2, 96.
25. Ibid., 1880, p. 113. Mills demanded in 1883 that Spalding cease making the claim. See A. G. Mills to AGS, April 10, 1883, Mills Papers.
26. *Guide*, 1884, advertisement, 1890, p. 36.
27. *Guide*, 1882, advertisement. Also see Harry Wright to A. G. Spalding and Brothers, March 17, 1882, Harry Wright to Joe Stuart, March 9, 1882, Harry Wright to John Ward, March 10, 1882, Wright Corresp. #4. Also see Voigt, *American Baseball*, 68.
28. *Guide*, 1882, advertisement.
29. *Sporting Store News*, Oct. 7, 1915, p. 4; *History of Allegan and Barry Counties, Michigan* (Philadelphia, 1880), 373.
30. *History of Allegan and Barry Counties*, 373; *Guide*, 1880, advertisement.
31. *Sporting News*, April 2, 1887.
32. Hastings (Michigan) *Banner*, Dec. 14, 1967, reports on the fire. *Sporting News*, Dec. 3, 1887. An advertisement for 100,000 bat tongues appeared in the same paper on Feb. 25, 1888.
33. *Sporting News*, March 21, 1896. Also see New York *Times*, March 3, 1896. On Oct. 18, 1908, the Barnard firm was renamed the A. G. Spalding and Brothers Manufacturing Company. See *Corporations of New Jersey: List of Certificates to December 31, 1911* (Trenton, 1914).
34. *Guide*, 1894, advertisement; New York *Times*, March 5, 1894; New York *Clipper*, Sept. 7, 1889; Voigt, *American Baseball*, 216–18; *Sporting News*, April 18, 1891, March 2, 1901; *Sporting Goods Gazette*, March 1889.
35. *Sporting News*, March 30, 1895.
36. *Sporting Goods Gazette*, March 1892, p. 6; New York *Times*, Feb. 5, 1892; *Corporations of New Jersey: List*. In 1913 the company was recapitalized at $6 million. See New York *Times*, Dec. 30, 1913.

37. *Sporting News*, Dec. 11, 1886.
38. Advertisements in newspapers and Spalding publications provide the information on the array of products offered by the company. For examples, see *Guide*, 1915, advertisements; New York *Clipper*, June 17, 1882; *Sporting News*, Sept. 29, 1894. Henry Chadwick inadvertently documented the firm's reputation for innovation when he encouraged the Spaldings to invent a leg guard for pitchers. See undated handwritten note, in Chadwick Scrapbook #6.
39. New York *Clipper*, April 8, May 6, 1876, March 22, 29, 1884; *Sporting Goods Gazette*, May 1889; *Sporting News*, June 3, 1893; *Sporting Life*, March 28, 1888.
40. New York *Clipper*, Feb. 13, 1886; *Guide*, 1889, advertisement.
41. *Guide*, 1885, advertisement.
42. Form letter, Jan. 1, 1884, CBC.
43. *Official Guide of the National Association of Professional Baseball Leagues* (New York, 1909), itself a Spalding publication, contains a seven-page (unpaginated) history of the origins and scope of the American Sports Library and includes this quotation.
44. *Guide*, 1916, advertisement. Spalding also brought out the official publications of organizations such as the YMCA, the Public School Athletic League, the National Association of Amateur Oarsmen as well as annual baseball books listing the records of all amateur and professional baseball teams in particular cities, e.g., *Spalding's Official Chicago Baseball Book*, 1910. Guides for every sport imaginable also were turned out, along with specialized publications like James A. Moss, *Military Cycling in the Rocky Mountains* (New York, 1897).
45. New York *Clipper*, April 4, 1885, April 12, Nov. 1, 22, 1884. Commenting on the retail branch in April 4, 1885, the *Clipper* noted that "no expense had been spared to render the establishment a credit to the metropolis and worthy of patronage and support."
46. *Guide*, 1889, pp. 4–5. Also see *Guide*, 1886, last page, 1887, last page, 1888, pp. 3–4; *Sporting News*, Aug. 19, 1905; *Official Guide of the National Association of Professional Baseball Leagues*, 1909.
47. *Sporting Goods Gazette*, April 1899, advertisement.
48. *Offical Guide of the National Association of Professional Baseball Leagues*, 1908, two-page advertisement.
49. *Sporting News*, July 1, 1899. Also see *Sporting Goods Gazette*, July 1899; *Sporting News*, April 15, 1899.
50. *Sporting News*, May 4, 1895, June 1, 1895, juxtaposes advertisements for Barnum and Spalding. *Sporting News*, July 2, 1904.
51. *Guide*, 1882, advertisement.
52. Ibid., 1895, advertisement, back cover.
53. *Official Guide of the National Association of Professional Baseball Leagues*, 1908, advertisement.
54. *Guide*, 1884, advertisement.
55. *Sporting Goods Gazette*, April 1899, p. 23.
56. *Guide*, 1886, 1887, advertisements. Chadwick Scrapbook #2 contains an undated newspaper column headed "Bogus Sporting Goods Agencies," which discusses the problem.

57. *Guide*, 1896, p. 165. A letter in the 1915 *Guide*, signed by A. G. Spalding and Brothers, warned youngsters to avoid "just as good" dealers who put an inferior ball in a Spalding box and then "try to palm it off on the boy as a genuine Spalding article."

58. *Sporting News*, June 3, 1893. The June 10, 1893, issue carried an advertisement for a baseball duffel bag under the heading "DROPPED SOMETHING?"

59. Ibid., April 3, 1897.

60. *Spalding's Official Cycle Guide*, 1900, advertisements.

61. *Guide*, 1886, advertisement.

62. New York *Clipper*, April 24, 1886.

63. *Sporting Goods Gazette*, May 1888, p. 20. Also see *Guide*, 1896, advertisement.

64. Spalding's world tour of professional baseball players, undertaken in 1888–89, and his involvement in the organized-play movement also provided ample opportunity for similar promotions. Because these ventures also demonstrated Spalding's views on the social role of sport, I discuss them in some detail in Chapter 6.

65. *Sporting News*, March 28, April 18, May 30, 1896.

66. *Sporting Goods Gazette*, May 1900.

67. New York *Clipper*, June 23, 30, July 28, 1900; New York *Times*, July 16, 1900; *Sporting News*, Nov. 10, 1900.

68. New York *Times*, Dec. 22, 1901.

69. *Spalding's Official Guide of the National Association of Professional Baseball Leagues* (New York, 1905), advertisement.

70. *Guide*, 1893, pp. 96–97; *Sporting News*, Nov. 16, 1895, Oct. 2, 1897; *Spalding Store News*, Nov. 25, 1915.

71. *Guide*, 1893, pp. 131–32.

72. *Guide*, 1908, p. 21.

73. Reprinted in *Guide*, 1909, p. 139.

74. *Sporting News*, Feb. 13, 1897.

75. *National Cyclopedia of American Biography*, vol. 33 (New York, 1930), 384–86.

76. *Sporting Goods Gazette*, May 1888, p. 13.

77. *Spalding Store News*, April 8, 1915, "The Merit System."

78. Boston newspaper article, Aug. 12, 1890, in Chadwick Scrapbook #8, p. 59. Robert A. Smith, *A Social History of the Bicycle: Its Early Life and Times in America* (New York, 1973), provides a general history.

79. *Sporting News*, June 23, 1894.

80. *Guide*, 1894, advertisement, notes Spalding's presidency.

81. *Sporting News*, Dec. 29, 1894, Jan. 5, March 9, 1895; *Sporting Goods Gazette*, April 1895.

82. See, e.g., *Spalding's Official Cycle Guide*, 1896.

83. Ibid., 1898, p. 63.

84. New York *Times*, Jan. 25, 1895. Also see New York *Times*, Jan. 21, 23, 24, 26, July 20, 1896, Feb. 7, 1897, Jan. 22, 1899.

85. Ibid., March 31, May 28, 1895.

86. *Sporting News*, May 15, Nov. 6, 1897. Also see *Sporting Goods Gazette*, April 1895, p. 41.

87. *Sporting News*, Jan. 26, Feb. 9, May 11, 1895; *Spalding's Official Cycle Guide*, 1896, pp. 15, 47, 62–63, 1897, advertisement.
88. *Sporting News*, Sept. 7, 1895.
89. For coverage of the affair, which also involved a third rider, who was not a member of the Spalding Team, see *Sporting News*, Dec. 7, 1895, Jan. 11, 25, Feb. 15, Aug. 22, 1896. Also see Smith, *Social History of the Bicycle*, 158–59.
90. *Sporting News*, Feb. 2, 16, 1895.
91. New York *Times*, Jan. 27, 1895.
92. Ibid., Jan. 22, 1896; *Sporting News*, April 13, May 18, July 14, 1895, Jan. 25, Feb. 1, 1896.
93. *Sporting News*, Feb. 16, 1895.
94. Arthur S. Dewing, *Corporate Promotion and Reorganizations* (Cambridge, 1924), 252. A variety of conflicting figures about the number of companies and the size of ABC's capitalization exist. The *Sporting Goods Gazette*, May 1899, originally reported the capitalization at $30 million. *Spalding's Official Cycle Guide*, 1900, p. 87, reported twenty-eight factories involved. New York *Times*, July 19, 1899, reported forty-five companies and $40 million.
95. *Report of the Industrial Commission Trusts and Industrial Combinations*, vol. 13 (Washington, D.C.), 689; *Spalding's Official Cycle Guide*, 1900, p. 75; *Sporting Goods Gazette*, May 1900.
96. New York *Times*, Sept. 13, 1900.
97. Dewing, *Corporate Promotion and Reorganizations*, 249–68, details the rise and fall of ABC. Also see New York *Times*, June 16, Sept. 3, 4, 18, Dec. 22, 1902, March 6, 29, May 2, 1903.
98. *Spalding Store News*, Aug. 8, 1915.

6. Touching Bases around the World: The Social Promise of Sport

1. Undated, unnamed newspaper clipping, in Chadwick Scrapbook #3. The content suggests the date to be around 1900.
2. Particularly useful here are Burton J. Bledstein, *The Culture of Professionalism: The Middle Class and the Development of Higher Education in America* (New York, 1976); Lawrence A. Finfer, "Leisure as Social Work in the Urban Community: The Progressive Recreation Movement, 1890–1920" (Ph.D. diss., Dept. of History, Michigan State Univ., 1974); T. J. Jackson Lears, *No Place of Grace: Antimodernism and the Transformation of American Culture, 1880–1920* (New York, 1982); Benjamin Rader, *American Sports: From the Age of Folk Games to the Age of Spectators* (Englewood Cliffs, 1983), 145–70; Steven A. Riess, *Touching Base: Professional Baseball and American Culture in the Progressive Era* (Westport, Conn., 1980); Gerald Roberts, "The Strenuous Life: The Cult of Manliness in the Era of Theodore Roosevelt" (Ph.D. diss., Dept. of History, Michigan State Univ., 1970); Daniel T. Rodgers, *The Work Ethic in Industrial America, 1850–1920* (Chicago, 1978); and Roy Rosenzweig, "Middle-Class Parks and Working-Class Play: The Struggle over Recreational Space in Worcester, Massachusetts, 1870–1910," *Radical History Review*, 21 (Fall 1979), 31–46. Special note should be made of Donald J. Mrozek's

Sport and American Mentality, 1880–1910 (Knoxville, 1983), whose analysis of the emergence of modern sport dovetails with my own analysis of baseball and Spalding. I also had the opportunity to read Mrozek's work in manuscript form under the title of "Sport and Americans' Experience."

3. Mrozek, "Sport and Americans' Experience," 6.

4. *Sporting News*, Jan. 30, 1892; Price Collier, "Sports' Place in the National Well-Being," *Outing Magazine*, July 1898, p. 384, quoted in Roberts, "Strenuous Life," 82. America's version of Tom Brown was Gilbert Patten's Frank Merriwell.

5. Gustav Kobbe, "The Country Club and Its Influence upon American Social Life," *Outlook*, June 1, 1901, pp. 255, 266, quoted in Roberts, "Strenuous Life," 118.

6. Lears, *No Place of Grace*, 52–60, 108; Rodgers, *Work Ethic in Industrial America*, 103–9.

7. Mrozek, *Sport and American Mentality*, Rodgers, *Work Ethic in Industrial America*, and particularly Lears, *No Place of Grace*, focus on this subject.

8. Frank R. Rossiter, *Charles Ives and His America* (New York, 1975), 31–32.

9. H. Addington Bruce, "Baseball and the National Life," *Outlook*, May 1913, p. 107; AGS, *America's National Game* (New York, 1911), 4.

10. Harry Palmer, *Athletic Sports in America, England and Australia* (Philadelphia, 1889), 6.

11. *Guide*, 1889, p. 97.

12. *Sporting Life*, March 28, April 11, 1888. AGS kept several scrapbooks of newspaper clippings on the world tour. Most of the references to newspaper articles on the tour in my discussion of it come from them. They, too, are part of the Spalding Collection in the New York Public Library. A. G. Mills assured Spalding of the business possibilities and offered him letters of introduction to "influential" Australian businessmen. See A. G. Mills to AGS, April 9, 1889, Mills Papers.

13. *Sporting Life*, March 28, 1888.

14. *Chicago Tribune*, Nov. 25, 1888, Jan. 6, 1889; New York *Clipper*, April 28, May 5, 1888; *Outing*, Nov. 1888, p. 166.

15. *Sporting Life*, July 11, 1888.

16. *Sporting News*, Sept. 22, 29, 1888.

17. New York *Herald*, Oct. 10, 1888; AGS, *America's National Game*, 252.

18. *Sporting Life*, Oct. 17, 24, 1888.

19. *Chicago Times*, Oct. 21, 1888.

20. AGS, *America's National Game*, 252–53; Palmer, *Athletic Sports*, 157–59.

21. *Chicago Times*, Oct. 26, 1888; Palmer, *Athletic Sports*, 160, 168; New York *Herald*, March 10, 1889; *Cincinnati Enquirer*, March 17, 1889.

22. *Chicago Tribune*, Nov. 25, 1888; *Outing*, Nov. 1888, p. 166.

23. *Chicago Times*, Nov. 3, 6, 1888.

24. *Sporting News*, Nov. 7, 24, 1888. Throughout its coverage of the tour, the *News* referred to Spalding as the fakir.

25. *Chicago Times*, Nov. 25, 1888; *Chicago Tribune*, Nov. 25, 1888; menu card, in Spalding Scrapbook #8.

26. *Chicago Tribune*, Dec. 30, 1888.

27. Melbourne *Herald*, Dec. 17, 1883; Chicago *Tribune*, Jan. 6, 1889; Chicago *Times*, Dec. 13, 16, 1888.

28. Unnamed Australian newspaper, Dec. 10, 1888, Melbourne *Age*, Dec. 24, 1888, Melbourne *Punch*, Dec. 20, 1888, all in Spalding Scrapbook #11.

29. Chicago *Tribune*, Dec. 25, 1888.

30. *Spalding's Official Baseball Guide*, Australian ed. (Chicago, 1889).

31. New York *Times*, Dec. 30, 1888; Palmer, *Athletic Sports*, 252; Chicago *Tribune*, Dec. 29, 1888; Chicago *Times*, Nov. 22, 1888.

32. Unnamed, undated column titled "Mr. Spalding's Genius"; Chicago *Times*, Jan. 2, 1889, in Kuhn Scrapbook #5, p. 243.

33. *Sporting News*, Feb. 2, 1889.

34. Chicago *Inter-Ocean*, March 10, 1889.

35. New York *Clipper*, Feb. 16, 1889; Chicago *Tribune*, Feb. 10, 1889; Spalding, *America's National Game*, 258.

36. New York *Herald*, March 10, 1889; Palmer, *Athletic Sports*, 315. For other racial incidents involving Duval, see Cincinnati *Inquirer*, March 17, 1889; Chicago *Tribune*, Jan. 27, 1889; Palmer, *Athletic Sports*, 285–86.

37. Chicago *Times*, Feb. 13, 18, 24, 1889; D. J. O'Connell, Rector, American Colleges, Rome, to AGS, Feb. 22, 1889, in Spalding Scrapbook #10.

38. Chicago *Times*, March 13, 1889; New York *Times*, March 14, 1889; Henry White to AGS, n.d., in Spalding Scrapbook #10.

39. Palmer, *Athletic Sports*, 432.

40. *House Colonial Mail*, March 22, 1889; Lancashire *Evening Post*, March 14, 1889.

41. AGS, *America's National Game*, 261–63, contains A.G.'s accounts and all quotations.

42. *Sporting News*, Feb. 9, 1889; *Sporting Life*, Feb. 13, 1889. Crowd estimates were compiled from figures given by game in Palmer, *Athletic Sports*, 708–11.

43. Chicago *Times*, April 7, 1889. For a discussion of homecoming plans for New York, see Chicago *Times*, Jan. 25, April 9, 1889; New York *Clipper*, Jan. 12, 1889; New York *Times*, March 24, April 7, April 20, 1889; A. G. Mills to ——— (form letter requesting participation), March 1, 1889, A. G. Mills to Walter Stanton, March 11, 1889, Mills Papers.

44. Chicago *Inter-Ocean*, April 7, 1889.

45. New York *Clipper*, April 13, 1889. The Mills Papers contain extensive correspondence about Mills's role in organizing the banquet, including making suggestions to Mark Twain about what he might say—suggestions that Twain incorporated into his remarks. See A. G. Mills to Samuel Clemens, March 22, 1889, Mills Papers.

46. Donald Roden, "Baseball and the Quest for National Dignity in Meiji Japan," *American Historical Review*, 85 (June 1980), 517, offers a useful discussion of the world tour in this context.

47. New York *Clipper*, April 13, 1889; Palmer, *Athletic Sports*, 444–45; Chicago *Times*, April 9, 1889.

48. Paul Fatout, ed., *Mark Twain Speaking, 1835–1910* (Iowa City, 1976), 244–47. Also in Palmer, *Athletic Sports*, 447.

49. Palmer, *Athletic Sports*, 455; Philadelphia *Inquirer*, April 12, 1889. For brief accounts of stops at Boston, Cleveland, Indianapolis, Baltimore, and Phil-

adelphia, see New York *Clipper*, April 20, 1889; Chicago *Herald*, Feb. 24, 1889; Chicago *Tribune*, April 18, 1889; Chicago *Times*, April 11, 13, 14, 1889.

50. Chicago *Tribune*, March 17, 1889; *Sporting News*, April 13, 1889; Charles W. Spalding, *The Spalding Memorial: A Genealogical History of Edward Spalding . . . and His Descendants* (Chicago, 1897), 903.

51. Chicago *Herald*, March 14, 1889; Chicago *Times*, April 14, 19, 1889; *Sporting News*, April 20, 1889; Chicago *Tribune*, April 20, 1889.

52. Chicago *Inter-Ocean*, April 20, 1889; Chicago *Times*, April 14, 20, 1889.

53. Chicago *Inter-Ocean*, April 20, 1889. Turner's speech was entitled "The National Value of Athletics."

54. Chicago *Times*, April 17, 20, 1889.

55. *Sporting News*, Feb. 2, 1889.

56. Chicago *Times*, April 21, 1889; Adrian C. Anson, *A Ball Player's Career* (Chicago, 1900), 204–5. For other comments on finances, see Chicago *Times*, March 24, 1889; *Guide*, 1890, p. 117. Anson, in *A Ball Player's Career*, 282, claimed he lost $1,500 of his own money invested in the tour.

57. *Guide*, 1890, p. 117.

58. My understanding of the organized-play movement was enhanced by Dominick Cavallo, *Muscles and Morals: Organized Playgrounds and Urban Reform, 1880–1920* (Philadelphia, 1981); Finfer, "Leisure as Social Work"; Cary Goodman, *Choosing Sides: Playground and Street Life on the Lower East Side* (New York, 1979); Rosenzweig, "Middle-Class Parks and Working-Class Play"; Joel Spring, "Mass Culture and School Sports," *History of Education Quarterly*, 14 (Winter 1974), 483–98.

59. Michael P. McCarthy, "Politics and Parks: Chicago Businessmen and the Recreation Movement," *Journal of the Illinois State Historical Society*, 65 (Summer 1972), 158–71, discusses the organized-play movement in Chicago. Spalding was not actively involved.

60. Rader, *American Sports*, 158.

61. Ethel Dorgan, *Luther Halsey Gulick, 1865–1918* (New York, 1934); Cavallo, *Muscles and Morals*, 33–38; Rader, *American Sports*, 157.

62. *Spalding's Chicago Guide* (New York, 1911), advertisement; *Guide*, 1915, p. 337.

63. *Official Handbook of the P.S.A.L.* (New York, 1906), 29–33; *Guide*, 1909, p. 353. Similar comments also filled Spalding's speech before the Springfield, Massachusetts, YMCA in 1904 when he referred to "baseball" as "a sentiment" whose spirit had "permeated into every part of our strenuous life." See *Sporting News*, Jan. 14, 1905; *Guide*, 1906, pp. 15–21.

64. *Guide*, 1910, pp. 321–25.

65. Goodman's *Choosing Sides*, for example, grossly misunderstands the degree of resistance that immigrants offered to attempts at acculturation. See a review of his book by Peter Levine and Kenneth Waltzer, *Journal of Ethnic History*, 8 (Summer 1980), 115–17. Also see Finfer, "Leisure as Social Work"; Rosenzweig, "Middle-Class Parks and Working-Class Play."

66. *Spalding Store News*, May 20, 1915, p. 2.

67. *Guide*, 1878, p. 5.

68. *Guide*, 1905, pp. 15–19.

69. Ibid., 9–13.

70. Ibid., 29.

71. *Sporting News*, Dec. 2, 1905. For a nice account of this dispute, see Robert Henderson, *Ball, Bat and Bishop: The Origin of Ball Games* (New York, 1947).
72. "Extract from argument of Albert G. Spalding," July 28, 1907, "Extract from Graves' letter," Nov. 17, 1905, Mills Papers.
73. Henderson, *Ball, Bat and Bishop*, 178.
74. Ibid., 179; A. G. Mills to Col. Edward Fowler, Dec. 20, 1907, "Typescript on Origins of Baseball," Mills Papers.
75. A. G. Mills to James E. Sullivan, Dec. 30, 1907, Mills Papers.
76. Henderson, *Ball, Bat and Bishop*, 180–81; *Guide*, 1908, pp. 35–49.
77. Henry Chadwick to A. G. Mills, March 20, 1908, Mills Papers.
78. David Voigt, *American Baseball: From Gentleman's Sport to the Commissioner System* (Norman, Okla., 1966), 5, first used the term *immaculate conception* in this context. The Hall of Fame was established in 1936 but did not open its facility in Cooperstown until 1939.
79. Al Michaels, announcing the 1982 All-Star game for NBC television from Montreal, did say, however, that Abner Doubleday would never have believed that the game he "invented" would be played on Canadian soil.
80. AGS to Henry Chadwick, Nov. 25, 1905, in Chadwick Scrapbook #26.
81. Arthur Bartlett, *Baseball and Mr. Spalding: The History and Romance of Baseball* (New York, 1951), 224; AGS to Henry Chadwick, Nov. 28, 1905, Chadwick Scrapbook #26.
82. AGS to Henry Chadwick, Nov. 28, 1905, in Chadwick Scrapbook #26.
83. In the acknowledgment, Spalding notes the help of his longtime friend William Page in writing the book. Spalding, *America's National Game*, x–xi.
84. Ibid., 159.
85. Ibid., 194, 273.
86. Ibid., 503; *Sporting News*, Dec. 1, 1894.
87. AGS, *America's National Game*, 3.
88. Ibid., 6.
89. Ibid., 5.
90. Ibid., 7, 362.
91. Ibid., 248.
92. Ibid., 533–42.
93. These reminiscences are interspersed throughout the book. I made use of some of this material, with appropriate footnotes, in earlier chapters.
94. Guide, *1912*, review of the book by John Foster.
95. The New York *American* reference appears in a scrapbook of clippings and letters of acknowledgment about the publication of the book, kept by Spalding and located in the Spalding Collection, New York Public Library. The Los Angeles *Times* reference is in Spalding Scrapbook #7.
96. Ibid.
97. Form letter dated Nov. 16, 1911, in Spalding Scrapbook #7.
98. G. E. Reynolds to American Sports Publishing Company, Nov. 2, 1911, in Spalding Scrapbook #7.
99. Form letter, Spalding Acknowledgment Book. Spalding Collection, New York Public Library.
100. James Sullivan to Managers of A. G. Spalding and Brothers Stores, Nov.

6, 1911, James Sullivan to Dear Sir, Oct. 3, 1911, in Spalding Scrapbook #7.

101. Francis Richter to AGS, Dec. 26, 1911, in Spalding Scrapbook #7.

7. Retirement to California: Theosophy and the U.S. Senate

1. Undated, unnamed newspaper column entitled "Spalding's Retirement Doubted by Friends," in Chadwick Scrapbook #7.
2. Arthur Bartlett, *Baseball and Mr. Spalding: The History and Romance of Baseball* (New York, 1951), 287.
3. Carey McWilliams, *Southern California Country* (New York, 1946), 8, contains this quotation from one L. P. Jacks.
4. Charles D. Warner, *Our Italy* (New York, 1891), 89. Useful in understanding Southern California as America's Mediterranean is Kevin Starr, *Americans and the California Dream* (New York, 1973), 365–414.
5. Richard Pourade, *Gold in the Sun* (San Diego, 1965), 4; Starr, *Americans and the California Dream*, 402.
6. Information on Spalding's place in Chicago society comes from a variety of sources, including city directories, records of Chicago's various clubs, newspapers, and biographical dictionaries. The collection of such materials in the Newberry Library was very helpful here. Spalding, for instance, belonged to the Union League Club, the Chicago Athletic Association, and the Chicago Club. His name and address appear in the city's 1894 and 1895 social registers as well as in the 1884 Elite Directory and Club list of Chicago. Clearly, however, A.G. was not an active member, either as officer, money-raiser, or organizer, in the various civic and philanthropic enterprises of the city's business community. The only major exception was his term as president of the Chicago Athletic Association in 1893, an organization he had helped form. In that post, he helped organize three days of Amateur Athletic Union track-and-field competition held in conjunction with the 1893 Chicago World's Fair. The competition was held at the Chicago Brotherhood baseball grounds, which he owned, in Sept. 1893. See New York *Times*, Jan. 15, 17, 25, Feb. 7, 19, 23, March 6, Sept. 15, 17, 1893; Chicago *Tribune*, Sept. 15, 17, 1893; A. G. Mills to AGS, June 16, July 23, Aug. 4, 10, Sept. 17, Nov. 22, 1892, Jan. 16, 1893, Mills Papers. Compared with that of other Chicago businessmen who were involved in the fair, Spalding's role was minimal.

   Recent literature on cultural philanthropy in Chicago underlines this point. See Kathleen D. McCarthy, *Noblesse Oblige: Charity and Cultural Philanthropy in Chicago, 1849–1929* (Chicago, 1982); Helen Horowitz, *Culture and the City: Cultural Philanthropy in Chicago from the 1880s to 1917* (Lexington, 1976); Rodney Badger, "The World's Columbian Exposition: Patterns of Change and Control in the 1890s" (Ph.D. diss., Syracuse Univ. 1975); Jane Allen Shikoh, "The 'Higher Life' in the American City of the 1890s: A Study of Its Leaders and Their Activities in New York, Chicago, Philadelphia, St. Louis, Boston, and Buffalo" (Ph.D. diss., Dept. of History, New York Univ., 1972); Sidney Roberts, "Businessmen in Revolt: Chicago, 1874–1900" (Ph.D.

diss., Dept. of History, Northwestern Univ., 1960); and Frederic Cople Jaher, *The Urban Establishment: Upper Strata in Boston, New York, Charleston, Chicago, and Los Angeles* (Urbana, 1983). Information on Spalding's home and neighborhood is in Jean F. Block, *Hyde Park Houses: An Informal History, 1856–1910* (Chicago, 1978). The Chadwick quotation is in Bartlett, *Baseball and Mr. Spalding*, 256. The quotation concerning A.G.'s rise "from the ranks" is in a MS copy of an article on Spalding written by Henry Chadwick, ca. 1888, in Chadwick Scrapbook #15.

7. *Sporting News*, July 15, 1899.
8. Mrs. Suzanne Winston to Peter Levine, April 10, 1980, informs me of the connection between Mayer and Spalding and the arrangements regarding their son. Further evidence concerning the adoption and name change is in AGS, Last Will and Testament, Record of Wills, Superior Court, San Diego County, vol. 9, 1917, pp. 342–45.
9. The best treatment of Point Loma and theosophy, on which I relied greatly, is Emmett A. Greenwalt, *The Point Loma Community in California, 1897–1942: A Theosophical Experiment* (Berkeley, 1955). Also useful are Paul Kagan, *New World Utopias: A Photographic History of the Search for Community* (New York, 1975), 48–64; and Robert V. Hine, *California's Utopian Colonies* (New Haven, 1966). For specific citations on Mayer see Ruth V. Held, *Beach Town: Early Days in Ocean Beach* (San Diego, 1975), 60; Greenwalt, *Point Loma Community*, 41–48, 101; *Theosophical Path*, 32 (Jan. 1927), 96.
10. This summary comes from my reading of Greenwalt as well as issues of the community's journal, the *Theosophical Path*. Also helpful was Ray Stannard Baker, "An Extraordinary Experiment in Brotherhood: The Theosophical Institution at Point Loma, California," *American Magazine*, 63 (Jan. 1907), 227–40.
11. Greenwalt, *Point Loma Community*, 18.
12. Baker, "Extraordinary Experiment," 227, 228. Also see McWilliams, *Southern California Country*, 252; Greenwalt, *Point Loma Community*, 48.
13. McWilliams, *Southern California Country*, 252.
14. Greenwalt, *Point Loma Community*, 99–102.
15. Ibid., 47. In New York *Herald*, Dec. 8, 1902, A.G. claimed he was not a practitioner. He was, however, listed as a cabinet member of the Universal Brotherhood.
16. Elizabeth Spalding to Katherine Tingley, Jan. 8, 1901, Theosophical Society Archives, Pasadena, Calif., describes plans for the house, which cost $10,000. Also see Greenwalt, *Point Loma Community*, 47–50. Photos are from Theosophical Society Archives and Kagan, *New World Utopias*, 48–64. Also see Baker, "Extraordinary Experiment," 232.
17. Greenwalt, *Point Loma Community*, 57–58; New York *Times*, Nov. 2, 1902. Unless noted otherwise, my general account of this episode comes from Greenwalt, *Point Loma Community*, 57–66.
18. *Searchlight*, Nov. 1902, pp. 1–36, contains an account of this entire episode and includes correspondence and newspaper articles relating to it. This letter appears on pp. 1–3 and was published in the San Diego *Union*, Nov. 11, 1902. *Searchlight* was a magazine published at Point Loma by Tingley's Cabinet of the Universal Brotherhood.

19. Ibid., 6, from San Diego *Union*, Nov. 4, 1902; New York *Times*, Nov. 8, 1902.
20. New York *Times*, Nov. 6, 1902.
21. Ibid., Nov. 8, 1902; *Searchlight*, 1 (Nov. 1902), 8, 10–11.
22. *Searchlight*, 1 (Nov. 1902) 10–11.
23. Ibid., 10–36. Also see New York *Times*, Nov. 4, 18, 28, 30, Dec. 5, 7, 1902.
24. New York *Herald*, Dec. 8, 1902; New York *Times*, Dec. 7, 1902.
25. New York *Herald*, Dec. 8, 1902; New York *Tribune*, Dec. 8, 1902; New York *Sun*, Dec. 8, 1902; New York *Times*, Dec. 8, 1902.
26. In May 1909, for example, a former Cuban student at the Raja Yoga school, one Antonio, tried to con A.G. into bringing him into the business and recommending him to Cuban baseball officials. In denying both requests, A.G. noted that "from personal observation" he considered the Raja Yoga school as one of the best in the world. See Antonio to AGS, April 20, 1909, AGS, Jr., to AGS, n.d., AGS to Antonio, May 6, 1909, Theosophical Society Archives, Pasadena, Calif.
27. Pourade, *Gold in the Sun*, 8.
28. New York *Clipper*, Feb. 11, 1899.
29. Pourade, *Gold in the Sun*, 8, 15; McWilliams, *Southern California Country*, 156. Also see H. Austin Adams, *The Man John D. Spreckels* (San Diego, 1924).
30. San Diego *Union*, June 9, July 14, Nov. 12, 1909. The April 25, 1976, issue of the paper carried a retrospective essay on Spalding by Joe Stone, which also contained some useful information. Also see Raymond C. Chaney, Jr., "Racetrack to Highway: San Diego's Early Automobile Days," *Journal of San Diego History*, 17 (Spring 1971), 28–40.
31. Chaney, Jr., "Racetrack to Highway," 30–31; San Diego *Union*, July 14, 1909; Pourade, *Gold in the Sun*, 133; *Memoirs of Ed Fletcher* (San Diego, 1952), 277–79.
32. San Diego *Union*, April 25, 1976; Pourade, *Gold in the Sun*, 137–38.
33. Starr, *Americans and the California Dream*, 402–6; Pourade, *Gold in the Sun*, 127; Held, *Beach Town*, 61; San Diego *Evening Tribune*, Jan. 18, 22, 1912.
34. *A. G. Spalding Land Association Plat Book* (Chicago, n.d.), 1–6; Harvey Land Association, *The Town of Harvey, Illinois* (1892), 9–10, 14, 20; *Sporting News*, Feb. 7, 1891.
35. San Diego *Evening Tribune*, Jan. 18, 22, 1912; Certificate of Creation, San Diego Securities Company, June 14, 1913.
36. San Diego *Evening Tribune*, Jan. 18, 25, 1912; San Diego *Union*, April 8, 1912. A month after his death the *Union* reported on Spalding's plans to develop part of the land held by a company into a base for the U.S. Navy (Oct. 15, 1915).
37. San Diego *Union*, March 5, 1912.
38. Ibid., May 22, 1912. For discussions of the IWW in San Diego, see Pourade, *Gold in the Sun*, 150–58; McWilliams, *Southern California Country*, 287–89; William C. Mills, "Comes the Revolution! San Diego: 1912," *San Diego Magazine*, Oct. 1959, Nov. 1959; Hyman Weintraub, "The I.W.W. in California: 1905–1931" (M.A. thesis, Dept. of History, Univ. of California, Los Angeles, 1947).

39. San Diego *Union*, June 14, 1912.
40. New York *Times*, April 28, 1915. Also see Gerald S. Henig, "He Did Not Have a Fair Trial: California Progressives React to the Leo Frank Case," *California History* 58 (Summer 1979), 166–78.
41. *Sporting News*, Jan. 21, 1905.
42. *The Book of Chicagoans* (Chicago, 1905), 540; AGS to Henry Chadwick, Jan. 2, 1906, Chadwick Scrapbook #26.
43. AGS to August Hermann, April 29, 1907, Spalding Papers. In this letter Spalding notes that he is writing a similar letter to Ban Johnson. In the same collection also see Spalding's letters to British baseball officials; AGS to Nelson P. Cook, April 22, 1907, and Nelson P. Cook to AGS, Feb. 23, 1907.
44. Boston *Globe*, Sept. 20, 1908; quotation about Spalding in the Boston *Transcript* reprinted in AGS, *America's National Game*, 354, and *Guide*, 1909, p. 139.
45. George Mowry, *The California Progressives* (Chicago, 1963), 68–81. Also see Spencer C. Colin, Jr., *California's Prodigal Sons: Hiram Johnson and the Progressives, 1911–1917* (Berkeley, 1968).
46. Mowry, *California Progressives*, 81–82; Colin, Jr., *California's Prodigal Sons*, 195; Franklin Hichborn, *The Story of the Session of the California Legislature of 1911* (San Francisco, 1911), 50–70; San Diego *Sun*, July 26, 1910.
47. G. A. Davidson to AGS, June 20, 1910, in "Spalding Campaign Broadside," Mills Papers.
48. San Diego *Union*, June 22, 1910; San Diego *Sun*, June 22, 1910.
49. A. G. Mills to AGS, June 22, 1910, Mills Papers.
50. AGS to A. G. Mills, June 28, 1910, Mills Papers; San Diego *Sun*, July 11, 1912; San Diego *Union*, July 2, 1910.
51. AGS to G. A. Davidson, June 23, 1910, in "Spalding Campaign Broadside," Mills Papers. Also see San Diego *Union*, June 25, 1910.
52. AGS to G. A. Davidson, July 6, 1910, in "Spalding Campaign Broadside," Mills Papers.
53. James Connally, "The Capitalization of Amateur Athletics," *Metropolitan Magazine*, July 1910, 443–54.
54. San Diego *Sun*, July 8, 1910.
55. San Diego *Union*, July 9, 1910.
56. Ibid.
57. San Diego *Sun*, July 18, 1910.
58. Ibid., July 27, 1910.
59. "Spalding Campaign Broadside," Mills Papers.
60. AGS to A. G. Mills, July 19, 1910, Mills Papers.
61. A. G. Mills to James Sullivan, Aug. 1, 1910, Mills Papers.
62. A. G. Mills, "A. G. Spalding for United States Senator," Mills Papers.
63. A. G. Mills to AGS, Aug. 3, 1910, A. G. Mills to James Sullivan, Aug. 1, 1910, Mills Papers.
64. San Diego *Sun*, Aug. 13, 1910. The same issue carried an endorsement from the cartoonist Homer Davenport, who referred to baseball's role in making Spalding "one of the highest types of an American."
65. New York *Times*, Aug. 20, 1910.

66. Hichborn, *California Legislature of 1911*, 61.
67. *Sporting News*, Oct. 27, 1910. Spalding's claim of 74 districts and his total of 134 districts were inaccurate, although there were other discrepancies reported at the time about the vote, e.g., in New York *Times*, Sept. 6, 1910.
68. Hichborn, *California Legislature of 1911*, 68–70.
69. *Guide*, 1911, pp. 344–47.

8. The Father of Baseball

1. Unnamed newspaper clipping, Sept. 26, 1915, Theosophical Society Archives, Pasadena, Calif.
2. Obituary, San Diego unnamed, undated newspaper clipping, Spalding Papers.
3. San Diego *Union*, Sept. 12, 1915. Although Spalding's funeral was peaceful, the settlement of his estate was not. In his will, Spalding left each of his three sons and stepsons $100,000, less advances given to them while he was alive. The rest of his estate, includling $1.4 million subject to California inheritance tax, went to his wife. Keith Spalding contested the will, claiming, among other things, that his father had not been in his right mind for several years and had fallen under the influence of his wife and Madame Tingley, who stood to benefit from his will. A separate contest was also entered by A.G.'s brother, J. Walter, on behalf of A. G. Spalding, Jr., after the young man's death in World War II. In the end, both contests were voluntarily withdrawn; according to one newspaper account, an out-of-court settlement awarded $700,000 to one son and $500,000 to the other's estate. Tingley, much to her chagrin, received nothing, even after the death of Elizabeth Spalding in 1926. See New York *Times*, Oct. 6, 1915; San Diego *Union*, April 25, 1976; *Spalding Store News*, Aug. 10, 1916; Emmett A. Greenwalt, *The Point Loma Community in California, 1897–1942: A Theosophical Experiment* (Berkeley, 1955), 179–80; Iverson Harris, "Reminiscences of Lomaland: Madame Tingley and the Theosophical Institute in San Diego," *Journal of San Diego History*, 20 (Summer 1974), 24; *Record of Wills*, Superior Court, San Diego Court, vol. 9, pp. 342–45; *Probate Orders and Decrees*, Superior Court, San Diego County, vol. 64, pp. 171–72, 206–7, vol. 65, pp. 7–11, 230, 260–62, vol. 66, pp. 222–23, 224–56, vol. 67, pp. 112–13, 129, 132, 199, 239, 263, 281–82, vol. 68, pp. 182–83, 318–26, 389–93, San Diego Historical Society.
4. *Sporting News*, Sept. 16, 1915; *Guide*, 1916, "Tribute," *Spalding Store News*, Sept. 9, 1916, pp. 4–17; New York *Times*, Sept. 11, 1915.
5. *Guide*, 1916, printed the National League resolutions, which were adopted on Dec. 14, 1915.
6. *Sporting News*, Sept. 16, 1915.
7. Ibid.
8. Barnum died in 1891. See Neil Harris, *Humbug: The Art of P. T. Barnum* (Boston, 1973), for an illuminating discussion of Barnum.
9. Clifford E. Clark, Jr., *Henry Ward Beecher; Spokesman for a Middle-Class America* (Urbana, 1978), is useful for its definition of Beecher's appeal. Aside

from a vast and interesting literature on Beecher, see T. J. Jackson Lears, *No Place of Grace: Antimodernism and the Transformation of American Culture, 1880–1920* (New York, 1982), 23–26, and Daniel T. Rodgers, *The Work Ethic in Industrial America, 1850–1920* (Chicago, 1978), 94–124, for useful discussions of Beecher's appeal.

10. Gunther Barth, *City People: The Rise of Modern City Culture in Nineteenth-Century America* (New York, 1980), Steven A. Riess, *Touching Base: Professional Baseball and American Culture in the Progressive Era* (Westport, Conn., 1980), Allen Guttmann, *From Ritual to Record: The Nature of Modern Sport* (New York, 1978), and David Voigt, *American Baseball: From Gentleman's Sport to the Commissioner System* (Norman, Okla., 1966), all discuss baseball's appeal in these ways.

11. Obituary by John Foster, *Guide*, 1916.

Bibliographic Note

My intention is not to provide a complete listing of all materials consulted, nor to repeat discussions already undertaken in chapter notes; it is, rather, to pull together those primary and secondary sources most relevant and interesting for understanding particular parts of the story I have told.

For a very public man, Spalding was not especially revealing about his private life. *Reminiscences of Harriet I. Spalding* (East Orange, N.J., 1910) and A.G.'s *America's National Game* (New York, 1911) provide occasional glimpses into his childhood and early years. Also useful are his scrapbooks, located in the Spalding Collection at the New York Public Library, and both the Rockford *Gazette* and the Rockford *Register*.

Spalding's career in baseball is less difficult to follow. Rich material, located in newspapers like the New York *Clipper*, the New York *Times*, the Chicago *Tribune*, the Chicago *Times*, the *Sporting News*, and *Sporting Life*, all of which I read thoroughly for the 1880s and the 1890s, complemented newspaper clippings located in the Spalding Scrapbooks and the Chadwick Scrapbooks, also part of the Spalding Collection, and in the R. C. Kuhn Scrapbooks at the Chicago Historical Society. A complete run of Spalding's official baseball guides offered abundant information as well as editorial comments, with A.G.'s slant. Also useful for Spalding's Boston years were Harry Wright's correspondence, in the Spalding Collection, and the A. G. Mills Papers and a smaller file on Spalding housed at the Baseball Library at Cooperstown, New York. The records of the Chicago Baseball Club at the Chicago Historical Society proved an invaluable source for Spalding's years as manager and owner of the Chicago White Stockings. The *Baseball Encyclopedia* (Toronto, 1969) contained much of the information necessary for reconstructing the cast of characters that made up Spalding's world of professional baseball.

An impressive secondary literature on baseball helped locate Spalding's place in the development of the professional game. Harold Seymour, *Baseball: The Early Years* (New York, 1960), and David Voigt, *American Baseball: From Gentleman's Sport to the Commissioner System* (Norman, Okla., 1966), provide excellent overviews, complete with discussions of key events and personalities. Steven A. Riess, *Touching Base: Professional Baseball and American Culture in the Progresssive Era* (Westport, Conn., 1980), complements their work in more analytical fashion by putting America's fascination with baseball in the context of values associated with the idea of progressivism—a theme that I found important for understanding some of the impulses that motivated Spalding. Stephen Friedman, "The Baseball Fad in Chicago, 1865–1870: An Exploration of Sport in the Nineteenth-Century City," *Journal of Sport History*, 5 (Summer 1978), 42–64, nicely depicts the baseball world that Spalding entered as a young professional, while Lee Lowenfish and Tony Lupien, *The Imperfect Diamond: The Story of Baseball's Reserve System and the Men Who Fought to Change It* (New York, 1980), provides the historical backdrop for Spalding's later involvement in National League affairs, most particularly in the Brotherhood War. Finally, in ways with which I am not in full agreement, Gunther Barth's discussion of popular interest in baseball in his *City People: The Rise of Modern City Culture in Nineteenth-Century America* (New York, 1980) and Allen Guttmann's analysis of the same issue in *From Ritual to Record: The Nature of Modern Sport* (New York, 1978) offer provocative ideas that helped me think through my own sense of baseball's importance to Victorian middle-class culture.

The story of Spalding's sporting-goods business rests on primary and secondary sources less neatly packaged than those on baseball. No company records exist, and Spalding rarely spoke about personal or business matters in his available correspondence. Newspaper accounts, including those found in an interesting trade publication, the *Sporting Goods Gazette*, supplemented material garnered from the many Spalding publications—from baseball guides to cycling magazines—conveniently housed in the New York Public Library annex. The company's in-house magazine, the *Spalding Store News*, was helpful for understanding the scope of the business during Spalding's later years. Although hardly the most recent effort to detail Chicago's history, Bessie L. Pierce, *A History of Chicago*, vol. 3, *The Rise of a Modern City, 1871–1893* (New York, 1957), remains the best treatment of the economic and social setting that propelled Spalding's business endeavors.

The 1888–89 world tour is a key event for comprehending Spalding's ability to offer baseball as an incubator of American values and as an acceptable leisure-time activity in ways compatible with his own desires for self-promotion and material advancement. Spalding's own treatment of it in *America's National Game*, the scrapbooks he compiled about the tour in the Spalding Collection, Harry Palmer's description of the tour in his *Athletic Sports in America, England and Australia* (Philadelphia, 1889), and Cap Anson's account in his *A Ball Player's Career* (Chicago, 1900) were also helpful in uncovering the story.

Robert Henderson's *Ball, Bat and Bishop: The Origin of Ball Games* (New York, 1947) provided a nice backdrop for Spalding's involvement in mythologizing Abner Doubleday, while material in the A. G. Mills Papers offered the primary sources necessary for the discussion of baseball's immaculate conception. A.G.'s interest in the organized-play movement emerges best from his published statements and speeches on the role of sport that appeared in his baseball guides and in the press. Important general studies on leisure and organized play are Lawrence A. Finfer, "Leisure as Social Work in the Urban Community: The

Progressive Recreation Movement, 1880–1920" (Ph.D. diss., Dept. of History, Michigan State Univ., 1974), and Roy Rosenzweig, "Middle-Class Parks and Working-Class Play: The Struggle over Recreational Space in Worcester, Massachusetts, 1870–1910," *Radical History Review*, 21 (Fall 1979), 31–46. Although problematic in its interpretation, Cary Goodman, *Choosing Sides: Playground and Street Life on the Lower East Side* (New York, 1979), usefully describes the official rhetoric of organizations like the Playground Association of America and the Public Schools Athletic League. The best presentation of Spalding's views on the importance of baseball as well as his most important piece of self-promotion is his *America's National Game*.

Spalding's California years offered a nice change of pace, both in terms of the story told and the material utilized. Charles D. Warner, *Our Italy* (New York, 1891), provided a lyrical account of the beauties of Southern California that lured so many midwesterners there at the turn of the century. Nicely supplementing it were Carey McWilliams, *Southern California Country* (New York, 1946), Richard Pourade, *Gold in the Sun* (San Diego, 1965), and Kevin Starr, *Americans and the California Dream* (New York, 1973). Emmett A. Greenwalt's recently reissued *The Point Loma Community in California, 1897–1942: A Theosophical Experiment* (Berkeley, 1955) was invaluable for understanding the Point Loma community and theosophy. Also interesting was Ray Stannard Baker's contemporary account, "An Extraordinary Experiment in Brotherhood: The Theosophical Institution at Point Loma, California," *American Magazine*, 63 (Jan. 1907), 227–240. The Theosophical Society's publications, especially *Searchlight*, proved an important primary source, as did stories on Katherine Tingley and her world that appeared in the San Diego *Union* and the San Diego *Sun*. These two newspapers also offered information on Spalding's place in San Diego and his campaign for the U.S. Senate. George Mowry, *The California Progressives* (Chicago, 1963), Spencer C. Colin, Jr., *California's Prodigal Sons: Hiram Johnson and the Progressives, 1911–1917* (Berkeley, 1968), and material located in the A. G. Mills Papers were also helpful.

My view of Spalding's connection to the larger culture and my understanding of him both as a product and as a representative figure of late-Victorian America depended upon a wide reading in a rich and diverse literature on nineteenth-century America. Although I hardly agreed with all that I read, the works listed here were, in one way or another, important in shaping my knowledge of that world and of Spalding's place in it.

Neil Harris, *Humbug: The Art of P. T. Barnum* (Boston, 1973), Clifford E. Clark, Jr., *Henry Ward Beecher: Spokesman for a Middle-Class America* (Urbana, 1978), and Frank Rossiter, *Charles Ives and His America* (New York, 1975), offered portraits of men whose careers overlapped Spalding's in more ways than simply chronologically. Daniel T. Rodgers, *The Work Ethic in Industrial America, 1850–1920* (Chicago, 1978), and Gerald Roberts, "The Strenuous Life: The Cult of Manliness in the Era of Theodore Roosevelt" (Ph.D. diss., Dept. of History, Michigan State Univ., 1970), set out the concerns late-nineteenth-century Americans had with leisure and work that were essential for Spalding's ability to promote sport as a profitable commercial venture and as an acceptable social activity. Burton J. Bledstein, *The Culture of Professionalism: The Middle Class and the Development of Higher Education in America* (New York, 1976), T. J. Jackson Lears, *No Place of*

Grace: Antimodernism and the Transformation of American Culture, 1880–1920 (New York, 1982), and Donald Mrozek, *Sport and American Mentality, 1880–1920* (Knoxville, 1983), books that complement each other's understanding of late-nineteenth-century middle-class Americans and their responses to feelings of anxiety and concern about their society's future, were extremely important in helping me understand Spalding's success and his own awareness of what was possible. Less recent, but no less important for comprehending Spalding's world were George M. Fredrickson, *The Inner Civil War: Northern Intellectuals and the Crisis of the Union* (New York, 1965), Samuel P. Hays, *The Response to Industrialism, 1885–1914* (Chicago, 1973), Gabriel Kolko, *The Triumph of Conservatism: A Reinterpretation of American History, 1900–1916* (Chicago, 1963), and Robert Wiebe, *The Search for Order, 1877–1920* (Chicago, 1963).

Index